Reise an kein Ende der Welt

Journey to No End of the World

REISE AN KEIN ENDE DER WELT

JOURNEY TO NO END OF THE WORLD

Judaica aus der Gross Family Collection, Tel Aviv

Judaica of the Gross Family Collection, Tel Aviv

Herausgegeben von/ Edited by

FELICITAS HEIMANN-JELINEK

im Auftrag des Jüdischen Museums Wien/on behalf of the Jewish Museum Vienna

Der Katalog erscheint anlässlich der Ausstellung

REISE AN KEIN ENDE DER WELT

Judaica aus der Gross Family Collection, Tel Aviv

Sommer 2001, im Jüdischen Museum der Stadt Wien

This Catalogue has appeared on the occasion of the exhibition

JOURNEY TO NO END OF THE WORLD

Judaica of the Gross Family Collection, Tel Aviv

Summer 2001, in the Jewish Museum of the City of Vienna

Ausstellung/Exhibition

Ausstellungskonzept und Kuratorenschaft/Exhibition concept and curatorship

Felicitas Heimann-Jelinek

Assistenz/Assistence

Nina Krick

Objektrecherche/Object research

William L. Gross

Ausstellungsgestaltung/Exhibition design

Martin Kohlbauer

Ausstellungsgrafik/Graphic Design

Maria-Anna Friedl

Restauratorische Betreuung/Conservator

Bettina Dräxler

Ausstellungsaufbau/Exhibition installation

BJS/die Ausstellungswerkstatt

Katalog/Catalogue

Herausgegeben von/Edited by

Felicitas Heimann-Jelinek im Auftrag des Jüdischen Museums Wien/on behalf of the Jewish Museum Vienna

© Jüdisches Museum Wien, 2001, Alle Rechte vorbehalten/all Rights reserved

Lektorat/Proof readers

Bettina Englmann, Nina Krick

Übersetzung/Translations

Lilian Dombrowski, Quality Translations International

Sarah Gilboa Karni

Objektfotos/Object photography

David Peters

Druck/Print

Holzhausen Wien

ISBN 3-901398-20-1

Vorwort

Meine persönlichen Beziehungen zum Jüdischen Museum gehen zurück auf die Zeit vor seiner offiziellen Eröffnung. Mein Wiener Freund Jenö Eisenberger, ebenfalls ein Kunstsammler, brachte Dr. Karl Albrecht-Weinberger, den jetzigen Direktor des Museums, gegen Ende der achtziger Jahre in mein Haus nach Israel. Bei meinem nächsten Besuch in Wien zeigte mir Herr Albrecht-Weinberger freundlicherweise die Sammlung Berger, die damals im Historischen Museum der Stadt Wien untergebracht war und später zu einem Hauptbestandteil des neuen Jüdischen Museums wurde. Seitdem besteht meine „Wiener Connection" und es ist eine Ehre für mich, mit den Mitarbeitern des Museums zusammenzuarbeiten, und während des letzten Jahrzehnts mit meiner Sammlung an mehreren sehr gut gemachten Ausstellungen in den Räumen dieser Einrichtung beteiligt gewesen zu sein.

Die gegenwärtige Ausstellung REISE AN KEIN ENDE DER WELT nimmt jedoch einen ganz besonderen Platz in meinem Herzen ein. Es ist an sich schon eine außerordentliche Ehre, an einer größeren Ausstellung teilzunehmen, die aus Objekten der Sammlung der Familie Gross aufgebaut ist. Noch mehr jedoch ist es die Ausstellung als Verkörperung einer von Respekt und Freundschaft getragenen, ganz besonderen Beziehung zur Kuratorin, Frau Dr. Felicitas Heimann-Jelinek, und zum Architekten, Martin Kohlbauer, sowie ihren Familien, die meiner Frau Lisa und mir am meisten Freude bereitet.

Es ist das von Frau Heimann-Jelinek entwickelte und eindringlich formulierte Motiv des Reisens, welches diese Ausstellung in gewissem Sinne zu einer materiellen Umsetzung des Leitmotivs meiner sammlerischen Bemühungen

werden läßt. Seit über 35 Jahren bin ich ein Sammler von Judaica. Im Laufe dieser Zeit habe ich mich zum Vertreter einer Theorie entwickelt, die ich leicht ironisch als die „Judaica-Fenstertheorie nach William Gross" bezeichne. Hiermit soll zum Ausdruck gebracht werden, dass jedes Objekt einen Ausblick auf eine bestimmte Zeit und einen bestimmten Ort gewährt und ein Verständnis des Kontextes dieses Ortes ermöglicht, des künstlerischen, kulturellen, religiösen, sozialen und ökonomischen Umfeldes, in welchem das spezielle Objekt geschaffen wurde. Eines der primären Kriterien bildet hierbei die kulturelle Geographie. Ich versuche, eine Vielfalt jüdischer Objekte von zahlreichen Stätten jüdischer Niederlassung zu finden, sie nebeneinander zu stellen und zu erforschen, um auf diese Weise etwas über jüdisches Leben zu lernen.

Durch die ganze Zeit des Sammelns hindurch war ich immer ein leidenschaftlicher und aktiver Reisender, häufig ohne meine Bibliothek je zu verlassen. Mit diesen Objekten bin ich durch die Welt gezogen. Frau Dr. Heimann-Jelinek verstand es, zusammen mit den brillianten architektonischen Ideen von Martin Kohlbauer, eine Ausstellung zu konzipieren und zu produzieren, die sowohl durch ihre Gegenstände wie auch durch ihre physische Darbietung meine persönlichen Beziehungen zu dieser Sammlung zum Ausdruck bringt.

Es erfüllt mich mit tiefster Befriedigung zu wissen, dass nunmehr ein breiteres Publikum in der Lage ist, an dieser Reise von Ort zu Ort teilzunehmen und meine Entdeckerfreude zu teilen, ohne das Gebäude des Jüdischen Museums Wien zu verlassen.

William L. Gross

Preface

My connection with the Juedisches Museum Wien precedes the official opening of the Museum. In the late 1980's my Viennese friend and fellow collector Jenö Eisenberger brought Dr. Karl Albrecht-Weinberger, the current Director of the Museum, to my home in Israel. When I subsequently visited Vienna, Dr. Albrecht-Weinberger graciously showed to me the Berger collection that was then deposited in the Historisches Museum Wien and which later became one of the main exhibits in the new Juedisches Museum. My „Viennese connection" has never ceased and I have been privileged to work with the staff of the Museum and to participate over the last decade, through my collection, in several of the fine exhibitions presented in the rooms of this institution.

But the present exhibition, JOURNEY TO NO END OF THE WORLD, holds a very special place in my heart. Of course, it is a great privilege to be a part of a major exhibition that is built from the objects in the Gross Family Collection. But it is the exhibition as the embodiment of the very special relationship of respect and friendship that I have with the curator, Dr. Felicitas Heimann-Jelinek, and the architect, Martin Kohlbauer, and their families that brings the most pleasure to my wife, Lisa, and to me.

Through the incisive concept of travel, which Heimann-Jelinek developed, it is as if she designed an exhibition that is a material realization of the leitmotif of my collecting efforts. I have been collecting Judaica for more than 35 years. Over that time I have espoused what I call, tongue in cheek, the „William Gross Window Theory of Judaica".

That is to say that every object provides an opening through which it is possible to view a time and place and to understand the context of that place – artistic, cultural, religious, social and economic – in which this particular object was created. The primary criterion is one of cultural geography. I try to find a variety of Jewish objects from the many locations of Jewish settlement and through the juxtaposition of these items to do research and to learn about Jewish life. Through this period of collecting, I have always been a passionate and active traveler, often without moving from my library. Through these objects I have wandered the world. Dr. Heimann-Jelinek has been able to conceive and produce, with the brilliant architectural ideas of Martin Kohlbauer, an exhibition that expresses, both through the objects themselves and the very means of physical presentation, my most personal relationship with the collection. Knowing that a wider audience will be able to join in this travel from place to place, without ever leaving the building of the Juedisches Museum Wien, and will be able to experience with me the absolute delight of discovery, brings great satisfaction.

William L. Gross

FELICITAS HEIMANN-JELINEK

Reise an kein Ende der Welt

Judaica aus der Gross Family Collection, Tel Aviv

Das jüdische Exil begann im Jahr 733/32 v.d.Z., als der Assyrerkönig Tiglat-Pileser III. in Galiläa einmarschierte, das Nordreich Israel eroberte und 13.520 Menschen aus diesem Gebiet nach Assyrien – hauptsächlich nach Medien – zwangsumsiedeln ließ. In dieser Zeit gingen zehn der zwölf Stämme Israels verloren. Die Verlorenen Stämme sollten in der Zukunft die Phantasie etlicher Reisender und den Forschergeist vieler Wissenschaftler beschäftigen.[1] Nach der Zerstörung des Ersten Tempels durch Nebukadnezars Heer im Jahr 586 wurde wieder eine erhebliche Anzahl der Oberschicht aus Erez Israel – diesmal aus Judäa – nach Babylonien deportiert, die zum Teil dort blieb, auch nachdem Cyrus ihr 538 v.d.Z. die Rückkehr in die Heimat und den Wiederaufbau des Zentralheiligtums erlaubt hatte. Als Gründe für die freiwillige Annahme des Exils kann man sicher ökonomische vermuten, aber wohl auch Zweifel an der tatsächlichen Erfüllung der messianischen Verheißung. Weitere jüdische Gemeinden in Kleinasien, Griechenland, Italien, Ägypten und der Cyrenaica entstanden im Laufe der Zeit nicht nur auf der Basis von Kriegshandlungen und Sklaverei, sondern auch auf Grund von Handelsbeziehungen, diplomatischen Vertretungsaufgaben und kulturellem Austausch. Nach dem verlorenen jüdischen Krieg bekam das Exil dann eine völlig andere, nämlich negative Qualität. Denn mit der Zerstörung des Zweiten Tempels im Jahre 70 d.Z. durch die Römer, der Einnahme Massadas vier Jahre später, respektive mit der Zerschlagung des Bar-Kochba-Aufstandes 135 wurde Jerusalem und ein weites Umland den Juden verboten. Ein jüdisches Siedlungsgebiet in der nunmehr „Syria Palästina" genannten Provinz war mehr oder weniger auf Galiläa beschränkt. Damit wurde die Diaspora für fast zwei Jahrtausende die zwingende Existenzform für die Judenheit.

Schon früh fragte man sich, wo denn überall Juden lebten, und ob die eine Diaspora anders ausschauen würde als die andere. So machten sich ab dem frühen Mittelalter Reisende auf den Weg zu den entlegensten Orten, ans „Ende der Welt", um nach jüdischen Enklaven zu fahnden und der Welt von ihrer erstaunlichen Existenz zu berichten. Was sie trieb, mag man Neugier nennen,

Abenteuerlust, Forscherdrang oder auch Sehnsucht, wie Max Grunwald es formulierte: „die Sehnsucht, die schon Mose beseelte, hinauszugehen, um zu sehen, wie es den jüdischen Brüdern ergehe. Eine Sehnsucht, die durch abenteuerliche Botschaften über Reste der zehn Stämme Israels und andere jüdische Reiche im fernen Osten genährt wurde."[2] Für viele dieser Reisenden waren ihre Fahrten „Reisen ans Ende der Welt", wobei des Einen Weltende Isfahan sein konnte, das des Anderen vielleicht Wien. Das „Hier" des Einen ist immer das „Dort" des Anderen, und weder „Hier" noch „Dort" sind absolut. So war die Sichtweise der Reisenden abhängig von ihrer Herkunft. Sie fanden jedoch, gleich wohin sie reisten, immer eine jüdische Welt vor, die zwar auf vielen Ebenen der eigenen fremd sein konnte, aber im Prinzip immer auch die eigene Welt war. Was sie fanden, war das Eigene im Fremden und damit auch das Fremde im Eigenen. Ihre jeweilige Reise wurde damit keine „Reise ans Ende der Welt", sondern eine „Reise an kein Ende der Welt". In einem jüdisch-messianischen Kontext kann es überdies ein absehbares „Ende der Welt" nicht geben. Wohl überlegt schrieb Menasse ben Israel im Amsterdam des 17. Jahrhunderts: „Erst wenn die jüdische Diaspora wirklich von einem Ende der Welt bis zum anderen reicht, können die Juden von dort in das Land der Verheißung zurückgeführt werden."[3] Dabei geht diese messianische Idee über die jüdische Zukunft hinaus in die Zukunft der gesamten Menschheit: Denn solange der heilsgeschichtliche Auftrag des Judentums nicht erfüllt ist, solange wird es an allen „Weltenden" Juden geben und geben müssen. Dass man also aus jüdischer Sicht nur eine „Reise an kein Ende der Welt" unternehmen kann, thematisiert die Ausstellung dieses Titels mit Judaica-Objekten aus der Gross Family Collection.

Als Judaica werden allgemein jüdische Kultgeräte bezeichnet. Entsprechend ihres heiligen Charakters wird auf die Ausstattung, die Gewandung und Schmückung der Torarolle mit Torakronen, -aufsätzen und -schildern besonderer Wert gelegt. Auch wenn wir keine dreidimensionalen materiellen Zeugnisse jüdischen Kultgerätes aus der Zeit vor 1500 kennen, so ist deren frühere Existenz jedoch allein aus Illustrationen hebräischer Handschriften belegbar. Überdies ist im Talmud die Auffassung verankert, daß zur Verehrung Gottes adäquat wertvolle rituelle Gerätschaften gehören. So heißt es beispielsweise in einem talmudischen Kommentar zu Exodus 15,2: „Er ist mein Gott, ich will ihn verherrlichen": „Es wird nämlich gelehrt: ‚Er ist mein Gott, ich will ihn verherrlichen‘, verherrliche ihn bei der Ausführung der Gebote, Ihm [zu Ehren] errichte dir eine schöne Festhütte, [schaffe dir] einen schönen Feststrauß an, eine schöne Posaune, schöne Zizit, eine schöne Tararolle, schreibe sie auf seinem Namen mit schöner Tinte, mit schöner Feder, durch einen geübten Schreiber und hülle sie in schöne Seidengewänder."[4] Die hebräische Version spricht von „nae" für „schön" und was als „geübter Schreiber" übersetzt wird, heißt im Original „Künstler", „uman". Denn der hebräische „uman" ist – wie im griechischen Sinne auch – jener, dessen Kunst von Können kommt, er kann der „professionelle Architekt" ebenso sein wie der „geübte Baumeister", der „Geschickte" als Kunsthandwerker sowie als Künstler. Und das hebräische „nae" heißt „schön" im Sinne nicht nur von „hübsch, gutaussehend, gefällig", sondern insbesondere als Nomen bedeutet es auch tatsächlich „Schönheit" im Sinne eines inneren Wertes, wie auch Platon und Aristoteles den Begriff definiert haben. Die Schönheit der Ausstattung für alles, was mit dem Gottesdienst zu tun hat, soll also auf den inneren Wert nicht nur der Tora, sondern auch des Aktes ihrer Verehrung hinweisen.

In welchem Maße Kultgerät religiöses Selbstverständnis ausdrückt, widerspiegelt sich aber auch schon in den Fußbodenmosaiken spätantiker Synagogen, wie sie beispielsweise aus den Ausgrabungen von Chammat Tiberias, Bet Alfa oder Isfiya bekannt sind. Auf diesen Mosaiken sieht man nicht nur den Toraschrein dargestellt, sondern auch den Toravorhang, die Menora, Etrog, Lulaw, Schofar und Ewiges Licht. Schließlich sei noch – als ältestes Zeugnis für die Herstellung und Verwendung von Kultgerät – auf die Bibel selbst verwiesen, die insbesondere im Buch Exodus sehr genau auf die Schaffung und Verwendung von Ritualobjekten für die Einrichtung des Stiftszeltes bzw. des späteren Tempels und des darin abgehaltenen Gottesdienstes eingeht. Herstellung und Gebrauch von Kultgerät läßt sich also von biblischer bis in die moderne Zeit nachvollziehen.

Die Judaica der Gross Family Collection decken den Zeitraum von der frühen Neuzeit bis ins 20. Jahrhundert ab. In der Sammlung finden sich einige Stücke, die zu den ältesten bekannten Judaica zählen. Was nun ist diese Sammlung? Eine Sammlung ganz allgemein kann die Akkumulation von Objekten sein, die in irgendeiner Beziehung zueinander stehen, z.B.: Die gesammelten Objekte sind gleicher Herkunft, sie bezeugen eine bestimmte Zeit, sie hatten ähnliche Funktionen, das eine Objekt komplettiert eine Gruppe anderer u.s.w. Man kann nach vielen Kriterien sammeln, und wahrscheinlich haben alle Kriterien eine gewisse Berechtigung. Sammlungskriterium für die Objekte der Sammlung Gross ist die Definition als Judaica-Objekt. Sie sind untereinander dadurch verbunden, daß sie aus einem jüdisch-religiösen Kontext stammen. Eine Judaica-Sammlung besteht also aus Gegenständen, die nicht irgendeinen praktisch-prosaischen Gebrauchswert hatten, sondern die für einen ganz konkreten kultischen Gebrauch angefertigt wurden. Da sie im Augenblick der Überführung in eine Sammlung ihrer ursprünglich religiösen Funktion beraubt werden, müssen sie für die Sammlung bzw. den Sammler eine andere Bedeutung haben. Diese Bedeutung kann dann einerseits im historischen oder auch soziologischen Ursprungs-Kontext der Objekte liegen, andererseits aber auch in der Beziehung zwischen Sammler und Gesammeltem. Wenn „wir sind, was wir sammeln",[5] dann ist ein Judaica-Sammler ein „homo judaicus", einer, der sich – das muß nicht ausschließlich sein – über seine Sammlung als Jude definiert und sich mittels seiner Sammlung in die Kette jüdischer Geschichte einklinkt, einer, der durch den Erwerb eines physischen Teiles von ihr auch auf der nichtmateriellen Ebene anteilig an ihr wird. Die Sammlung Gross ist eine aus Leidenschaft zusammengetragene Sammlung, Leidenschaft für das Judentum, für die Geschichte des Judentums, für die zu erhaltende Erinnerung des Judentums. Der Judaica-Sammler William Gross hat sich bei der Auswahl des zu Sammelnden wohl unbewußt an ein Plädoyer für Unterschiede gehalten wie Isaiah Berlin es ausdrückte: „Wir erblicken in der Vielfalt nicht etwas, das unsere grundlegende Einheit bedroht, im Gegenteil …".[6] In diesem Sinne war Gross beim Aufbau seiner Sammlung bemüht, diese als eine global-jüdische anzulegen, um die prinzipielle Einheit jüdischer Religion und Tradition gerade durch die Vielfalt zu demonstrieren.

Insofern handelte es sich bei der Gross Family Collection um eine idealtypische Sammlung für die Ausstellung „Reise an kein Ende der Welt", die 33 – je nach Standort – nahe und ferne Orte jüdischen Lebens zeigt, Orte von Frankfurt bis nach Cochin, von Wien bis nach Aleppo und von Wilna bis nach Djerba. Die Orte werden repräsentiert durch jeweils einige Judaica-Objekte und hebräische Handschriften, die wohl typisch für den kulturellen Kontext ihrer Entstehungsumgebung, doch immer auch typisch für ihren traditionell jüdischen Kontext sind. So steht mit den Objekten keinesfalls der ethnographische Aspekt, sondern die Schnittstelle zwischen jüdischer Kultur und Umgebungskultur im Vordergrund.
Jedem Ort ist ein einschlägiges literarhistorisches Reisezeugnis beigegeben. Es verweist auf die jüdische Geschichte des Ortes, so wie sie sich dem Reisenden dargestellt hat. Diese Zeugnisse reichen vom Mittelalter bis in das 20. Jahrhundert, denn so ortsungebunden jüdische Tradition ist, so unabhängig ist sie auch von der Zeit. Viele, zu viele der besuchten Orte verbindet ein ähnliches Schicksal: das des Aufbaus, der Blütezeit und der Vernichtung. Viele der besuchten Orte verbindet aber auch ihre Bedeutung als Zentren jüdischer Gelehrsamkeit, säkularer Wissenschaft und wirtschaftlicher Größe. Einige der besuchten Orte verbindet die Hoffnung auf eine neue Zukunft. So ist die Reise durch den Raum an kein Ende der Welt auch eine Reise durch die Zeit an kein Ende der Welt.

Damit die REISE AN KEIN ENDE DER WELT nicht in der geschichtlichen Vergangenheit erstarrt, bildet die Basis jeden Ortes ein gegenwärtiges Foto jüdischen Lebens an dem besuchten Ort. Damit wird eine Brücke geschlagen zwischen Vergangenheit und Gegenwart, zwischen Nicht-mehr-Vorhandenem und Noch- oder Wieder-Vorhandenem. Ein nostalgischer Rückblick auf eine verklärte Vergangenheit ist damit ausgeschlossen. Weiters soll durch diesen Brückenschlag verdeutlicht werden, dass die Judaica-Objekte nicht Relikte eines vergangenen jüdisch-religiösen Kultes sind, sondern selbstverständliche Bestandteile auch heutigen jüdischen Lebens. Und einen weiteren Verweis mag dieses zeitgenössische Foto geben: Die Menschen, die an diesem Ort leben, sollten eigentlich das Recht auf „ihre" Objekte haben und behalten, auf die Gegenstände, die in ihrem Umfeld, nach ihrem Selbstverständnis, an diesem Ort und an keinem anderen ihren „Sitz im Leben" haben. Denn wirklich authentisch ist das Objekt nur an seinem Ort. Diese Anmerkung widerspricht natürlich jedem Sammlungskonzept jedes kulturhistorischen Museums, überhaupt jedes institutionellen und jedes privaten Sammelns.

Die Ausstellung REISE AN KEIN ENDE DER WELT beschäftigt sich mit jüdischen Traditionen in unterschiedlichen kulturellen, sozialen, politischen und historischen Kontexten. Sichtbar gemacht werden die Kontexte durch Objekte. Die Objekte sind die Spuren der Geschichte, unsere Garanten für die Geschichte. Inwieweit die Garanten tatsächlich absolute sind, sei dahingestellt. Hinterfragen aber kann man schon, ob sie Zeugnis ablegen von der Vergangenheit, der Gegenwart oder der Zukunft. Denn sie bezeugen Vergangenheit, da sie von bestimmten Menschen unter bestimmten Bedingungen für einen bestimmten Zweck geschaffen wurden. Die Menschen, die Bedingungen und der Zweck, in deren Kontext sie anzusiedeln sind, gibt es nicht mehr. Daher sind sie in gewisser Weise ihres Kontextes verlustig gegangen und nurmehr Träger von etwas Vergangenem. Doch sie bezeugen auch Gegenwart, damit nämlich, daß sie gegenwärtig ihrer Herkunft entfremdet sind, „woanders" sind, in einer anderen Gegenwart, in der sie einen völlig neuen Platz haben, neu kontextuiert sind, an einem Ort, der mit ihrem ursprünglichen nichts mehr gemein hat. Und sie bezeugen Zukunft. Eine Zukunft, die wir nicht voraussagen können, über die wir aber phantasieren können. Eine Zukunft, in der sie vielleicht in eine andere Sammlung überführt werden, in der sie aber auch rekontextualisiert werden könnten, in der sie auf jeden Fall eine gewisse Rolle spielen werden. Und das ist Zukunft: daß wir nicht wissen, was sein wird, in der Hoffnung es möge so oder ähnlich sein, wie wir es uns wünschen. Paul Ricœur spricht von der „Triade der Vergangenheit-Gegenwart-Zukunft" als verknüpfbar mit der „Triade des Eigenen, des Nahen und des Fernen",[7] worin die Parallelen zur Bedeutung des Objekts gut sichtbar werden, ist es doch das, was ein Objekt in der Auseinandersetzung mit dem Betrachter kennzeichnet: die Frage nach der zeitlichen Dimension des Objekts und die Frage nach der Stellung des Objektes zu einem selbst, nach der Relation, in die man zu ihm treten kann bzw. in die es zu einem tritt. Und auch das will die Präsentation dieses Aus-

schnitts einer Sammlung zeigen, daß etwas war, das jetzt etwas anderes ist und in Zukunft noch etwas anderes sein wird, und daß wir als Betrachter dazu Stellung nehmen müssen, obwohl wir die Dinge in ihrer Gesamtheit, in allen ihnen inneliegenden Dimensionen wohl nie erfassen können.

So weist uns die Sammlung Gross, die für die „Reise an kein Ende der Welt" die Basis schuf, auch darauf hin, daß die Objekte relativ sind, daß aber auch wir als die Sammlungs-Betrachter nur einen relativen Platz einnehmen angesichts des letztlich unerfahrbaren Inhalts jedes einzelnen Stücks dieser Sammlung: „Das Eine – gesucht, gefunden, entdeckt – ist des Erstaunens wohl wert. Solch Eines ist gegenüber dem Keinen Alles. Ein Viel-Eines ist gegenüber dem Einen schon staunend-erfassend-erfahrend ein Überwältigendes. Ein Viel-Eines, worin das ‚Eine' gar ein Vieles ist, vermag den Atem zu rauben. Es ist, als stünde die innere Zeit still – angesichts der Erfahrung einer Zeitlichkeit, in der der eigene Horizont zum nichtigen Weg wird."[8]

1 Vgl z.B. Sarah Harel-Hoschen/Yossi Avner (ed.), Beyond the Sambatyon. The Myth of the Ten Lost Tribes, Tel Aviv 1991.
2 Max Grunwald, Anteil der Juden an den geographischen Entdeckungen, in: Menorah, IV. Jg., Nr.8, 1926, S. 427–442, S. 427.
3 Ich danke Johannes Reiss für den Hinweis auf diese Formulierung Menasse ben Israels.
4 Babylonischer Talmud, Schabbat 133b.
5 Boris Groys, Logik der Sammlung. Am Ende des musealen Zeitalters, München/Wien 1997, S. 48.
6 Isaiah Berlin, Das krumme Holz der Humanität, Frankfurt a. M. 1992.
7 Paul Ricœur, Das Rätsel der Vergangenheit. Erinnern – Vergessen – Verzeihen, Göttingen 2000, S. 48.
8 Thomas Schloz, Die Geste des Sammelns. Eine Fundamentalspekulation, Tübingen 2000, S. 3.

FELICITAS HEIMANN-JELINEK

Journey to No End of the World

Judaica from the Gross Family Collection, Tel Aviv

Jewish exile began in 733/32 C.E. That year, the Assyrian king Tiglath-Pileser III invaded Galilee, conquered the northern Kingdom of Israel, and had 13,520 people from that region forcefully transferred to Assyria – mainly to Media – for resettlement. During that period ten of the twelve tribes of Israel were lost. These Lost Tribes would in the future occupy the fantasy of a number of travelers and the inquiring minds of numerous scientists.[1] After the destruction of the First Temple by Nebuchadnezzar's army in 586, again a considerable number of the upper class was deported from Eretz Israel – this time from Judea. Part of them eventually remained there even after in 538 B.C.E. Cyrus had given them permission to return and to rebuild their central sanctuary. The reasons for adopting voluntary exile were probably economic, but there was also doubt regarding the actual fulfillment of the messianic promise. In the course of time, more Jewish communities were created in Asia Minor, Greece, Italy, Egypt, and the Cyrenaica not as a result of war and slavery, but as a consequence of trade relations, diplomatic representations, and cultural exchange. After the lost Jewish war, exile acquired a very different, namely a negative quality. For in the wake of the destruction of the Second Temple in 70 C.E. by the Romans, the conquest of Masada four years later, and the suppression of the Bar Kokhba uprising in 135, the city of Jerusalem and its extended surroundings became prohibited to Jews. Jewish settlement in the province of Syria-Palestine, as it was now called, was limited more or less to Galilee. Hence, Diaspora became the necessary form of existence for the Jews for almost two millenniums.

Where do Jews live? How is one Diaspora different from the other? These are questions that were already asked early on. Thus, from the Early Middle Ages, travelers set out to the most far-flung places, to the "end of the world" in search of Jewish enclaves, and to tell the world about their amazing existence. Their driving force might be called curiosity, love of adventure, scientific aspirations, or a yearning as defined by Max Grunwald: "the yearning that had already befallen Moses to go out and see how the Jewish brothers were faring. A yearning that was nourished by fantastic messages about remainders of Israel's Ten Tribes and about other Jewish dominions in the distant east."[2] To many of these travelers, their voyages were "journeys to the end of the world," whereby the end of the world could be Esfahan for one person and, perhaps, Vienna for the other. One person's "here" is forever the other's "there," and neither "here" nor "there" are absolute. The travelers' points of view depended on their origin. However, they always found, wherever they traveled, a Jewish world, which might have been different from their own on many levels, but was basically always also their own world. What they found was the own in the unknown and, thus, the unknown in the own. Therefore, theirs was not a "journey to the end of the world," but rather a "journey to no end of the world." And indeed, there cannot be a near end of the world in a Jewish-messianic context. Well considered, Menasseh ben Israel wrote in seventeenth century Amsterdam: "It will be only when the Jewish Diaspora reaches from one end of the world to the other that the Jews can be led back from there to the Promised Land."[3] This messianic idea reaches beyond the Jewish future into the future of all of humankind: Because as long as Jews have not fulfilled their role in the history of salvation, Jews will exist and will have to exist at all "ends of the world." That, from a Jewish point of view, it is only possible to endeavor a "journey to no end of the world," is the subject of the same-titled exhibition of Judaica objects from the Gross Family Collection.

In general, Judaica are Jewish ritual objects. In keeping with their holy nature, great importance is attached to the Torah scrolls' furnishing, drapery, and decoration with Torah crowns, finials, and shields. Even though we are not aware of any three-dimensional material evidence of Jewish ritual objects from the time before 1500, their earlier existence can be documented through illuminations in Hebrew manuscripts alone. Besides, the attitude is rooted in the Talmud that for the worship of God, adequately valuable ritual objects are required. In a Talmudic commentary to Exodus 15:2, for instance, it is said: "He is my God, and I will glorify Him." "Because it is taught: 'He is my God, and I will glorify Him,' then glorify Him when observing the commandments. Build in His [honor] a beautiful hut to celebrate, [get] a beautiful and festive bouquet, a beautiful trumpet, beautiful tzitzit, a beautiful Torah scroll, have it written in His name in beautiful ink, with a beautiful pen by a skilled scribe, and drape it in beautiful cloths."[4] The Hebrew version uses na'e for 'beautiful,' and what has been translated as 'skilled scribe' is in the original uman meaning 'artist.' The Hebrew uman is – as in the Greek sense – one whose art comes from skill. He can be the professional architect or the skilled builder, the skilled crafts-man or artist. And the Hebrew na'e means 'beautiful' not only in the sense of 'pretty, handsome, pleasing,' but especially in its nominal form it means, in fact, 'beauty' in the sense of an inner value as Plato and Aristotle have defined the term. The beauty of the furnishings for everything connected to the religious service should, therefore, point not only to the inner value of the Torah, but also to the act of its veneration.

But the degree, to which ritual objects express religious self-understanding, is already reflected in the floor mosaics of synagogues from late antiquity as they are known, for instance, from the excavations in Hamat Tiberias, Bet Alfa, or Isfiya. On these mosaics not only the Torah shrine, but also the Torah curtain, the menorah, the etrog, lulav, shofar, and eternal light are depicted. Finally, the Bible itself should be mentioned – as the oldest testimony to the manu-facturing and use of ritual objects. Particularly the Book of Exodus features detailed descriptions of the creation and use of ritual objects to furnish the tabernacle or the Temple and the religious service conducted there. Thus, pro-duction and use of ritual objects can be traced from biblical to modern times.

The Judaica from the Gross Family Collection cover a period from the Early Modern era to the twentieth century. The collection contains some items that belong to the oldest known Judaica. So what is this collection all about? A collection in general can be any accumulation of objects that are interconnected in any way: for example, the collected items can be of identical origin, they re-present a specific period, they had similar functions, one object complements a group of others, etc. It is possible to collect according to many criteria and probably all of them have their justification. The criterion for the Gross Collection is an object's definition as Judaica. They are interconnected by their origin in a Jewish-religious context. A Judaica collection consists of items that never had any practical-prosaic value, but had been manufactured for a specific ritual purpose. Since they are robbed of their original religious function the moment they are transferred into a collection, they have to assume a different meaning for the collection and the collector. That meaning can be derived from the historic or sociologic context of the objects' origins or else from the relation-ship between collector and collected item. If "we are what we collect,"[5] then a Judaica collector is a "homo judaicus," one who defines himself as a Jew – not necessarily exclusively – through his collection. Judaica collections, then, enable collectors to insert themselves into the chain of Jewish history. By ac-quiring a material part of it, they partake in it on the immaterial level as well. The Gross Collection grew out of passion, passion for Judaism, for Jewish history, for maintaining the memory of it all. In selecting the items, the Judaica collector William Gross has instinctively adhered to an appeal for diversity as Isaiah Berlin has formulated it: "We do not consider diversity to be something that threatens our fundamental unity, on the contrary... ."[6] In that sense, Gross strove to set up a global-Jewish collection to demonstrate the basic unity of Jewish religion and tradition through its variety.

That makes the Gross Family Collection an ideal type of collection for an ex-hibition such as JOURNEY TO NO END OF THE WORLD, which presents thirty-three places of Jewish life near and far – always depending on the location of the spectator– places from Frankfurt to Cochin, from Vienna to Aleppo, and from Vilna to Djerba. Each place is represented through several Judaica objects and Hebrew manuscripts. While these are characteristic of the cultural context of their original environment, they are also always characteristic of their traditional-Jewish context. Regarding these objects, their ethnographic aspect is, therefore, by no means in the foreground, but rather the interface between Jewish culture and surrounding cultures.

Each place has a relevant literary-historical testimony attached. It indicates the Jewish history of the place as it presented itself to the traveler. These testimonies stretch from the Middle Ages into the twentieth century, since Jewish tradition is as independent from time as it is from place. Many, far too many places are connected by a similar fate: founding period – peak period – annihilation. But many of the places visited are also connected through their significance as centers of Jewish scholarship, secular science, and economic success. Some of the places visited are connected by their hope for a different future. And so, the journey through space to no end of the world, is also a journey through time to no end of the world.

So that the JOURNEY TO NO END OF THE WORLD may not remain frozen in the historic past, a present-day photograph of its Jewish life forms the basis of each place. Thus, a bridge is built between past and present, between the no-longer-existing and the still- or once-again-existing. This precludes a nostalgic look back into an idealized past. Furthermore, this bridge-building should emphasize that these Judaica objects are not just relics of a past Jewish-religious ritual, but rather natural components of modern Jewish life as well. And this contemporary photograph contains another hint: those people who live in that place should, indeed, have and keep the right to "their" objects, to the objects whose "seat in life" is in their environment, according to their self-understanding, in this place and nowhere else. An object is only authentic in its original place. Obviously, this remark totally contradicts any collecting concept of any cultural-historic museum, of any institutional and private collection.

The exhibition JOURNEY TO NO END OF THE WORLD deals with Jewish traditions in various cultural, social, political, and historical contexts. The objects are the vestiges of history, our warrantors of history. The question, to what degree these warrantors are, in fact, absolute has to remain unanswered. It can be asked, though, whether they give testimony to the past, the present, or the future. They testify to the past since they were created by specific people under specific circumstances for a specific purpose. But that context of people, circumstances, and purpose no longer exists. In some respect they were deprived of their context and simply remained carriers of something past. But they also testify to the present in that they are alienated from their origins at this time, they are "somewhere else," in another present where they have an entirely new place, in a new context, in a place that has nothing in common with their place of origin. And they testify to a future. A future we are unable to predict, but are able to fantasize about. A future where they may well be transferred to another collection, where they may be provided with new a context, where, in any case, they will play a certain role. And this is future: that we do not know what will be in the hope that it will be the way we are wishing for or at least a similar way. Paul Ricœur's "triad of past-present-future" that can be linked to the "triad of the own, the near, and the far"[7] highlights the parallels to the object's meaning since this is what characterizes an object in the confrontation with the observer: the question of the object's time dimension and the question of the object's position in relation to oneself, the possible interaction between oneself and the object. And the presentation of this slice from a collection wants to show this, too: That something used to be, which is now something else, and which will be something else yet, in the future. And that we, the observers, have to develop an approach to this – although we shall probably never be able to grasp the objects in their totality, in all their inherent dimensions.

Hence, the Gross collection, which formed the basis for the JOURNEY TO NO END OF THE WORLD, also shows us that the objects are relative but that our position as observers of the collection is only a relative one too, faced with the unknowable content of each individual item in this collection: "The One – searched for, found, discovered – is well worth the amazement. Such One is All in the face of None. A Manifold-One in the face of One already is – we are amazed, we grasp, we experience – something overwhelming. A Manifold-One wherein even the 'One' is Manifold can take our breath. It is as if our inner time had stopped – in the face of the experience of temporality in which the own horizon becomes but a futile pathway."[8]

1 Cf., e.g., Sarah Harel-Hoschen/Yossi Avner (eds.), Beyond the Sambatyon. The Myth of the Ten Lost Tribes, Tel Aviv 1991.

2 Max Grunwald, Anteil der Juden an den geographischen Entdeckungen, in: Menorah, IV. vol., no.8, 1926, p.427–442, p. 427.

3 My gratitude to Johannes Reiss for pointing out to me this formulation by Manasseh ben Israel.

4 Babylonian Talmud, Shabbat 133b.

5 Boris Groys, Logik der Sammlung. Am Ende des musealen Zeitalters, Munich-Vienna 1997, p. 48.

6 Isaiah Berlin, Das krumme Holz der Humanität, Frankfurt/Main 1992.

7 Paul Ricœur, Das Rätsel der Vergangenheit. Erinnern – Vergessen – Verzeihen, Göttingen 22000, p. 48.

8 Thomas Schloz, Die Geste des Sammelns. Eine Fundamentalspekulation, Tübingen 2000, p.3.

EVA GRABHERR

Gegenstände des Exils

Ich habe jenen Augenblick des Zerstreuens von Menschen durchlebt, der zu anderen Zeiten und an anderen Orten,
in den Nationen anderer zu einer Zeit des Sammelns wird. Homi K. Bhabha

REISE AN KEIN ENDE DER WELT erzählt von dieser „Zeit des Sammelns", „zu anderen Zeiten", „an anderen Orten" und „in den Nationen anderer": in Kuba, Izmir, Joannina, Fez, Gibraltar, London, Amsterdam, Nürnberg, Wien, Wilna, New York etc. Die Ausstellung erzählt jüdische Weltgeschichte auf die wahrscheinlich einzig mögliche Art, ein solches Unternehmen anzugehen, konzentriert auf die Mikrogeschichte jüdischer Gemeinschaften an den Orten, die sich diese in den letzten 2000 Jahren gesucht haben und in denen sie auch aufgenommen wurden, und aufmerksam für den jeweiligen nichtjüdischen Kontext, in dem sich jüdisches Leben realisierte. Das Leben in der Zerstreuung, an „anderen Orten" und „in den Nationen anderer", ist für jüdische Existenz kein Übergangsstadium; zumindest nicht in „dieser Zeit" (sman hase). Die „Einsammlung der Exilierten" (qibbutz galujot), ein entscheidendes Motiv jüdischer Messiaserwartung seit dem Babylonischen Exil, findet in der „kommenden Zeit" (sman haba) statt. Gegenwart bedeutet, nicht angekommen zu sein, in Differenz zu leben, also Diaspora, und die hat in jeder Zeit ihren tieferen Sinn: „Um unserer großen Sünden willen" in der Vormoderne;[1] um ein „Licht zu sein unter den Völkern" in der Sprache der Vertreter der Wissenschaft des Judentums im säkularisierten 19. Jahrhundert.

Diese Existenz in der Diaspora ist kulturbildend für Judentum, eingeschrieben in die materiellen wie immateriellen Hervorbringungen der Menschen, die diese Kultur einerseits schaffen, ihr andererseits unterliegen, also von ihr mit geschaffen werden; eingeschrieben in literarische und künstlerische Werke, Gegenstände, Symbole, Lebensformen, Rituale, Institutionen etc. dieser Gruppe; kurz: in die „Gesamtheit der Hervorbringungen des Menschen auf allen Gebieten des Lebens", wie Max Weber Kultur definiert.[2] Die kulturelle Dimension dieser „Hervorbringungen" ist, daß sie Resultate sozialen Handelns sind, also nicht lediglich subjektiven Sinn und individuelle Positionen repräsentieren. Sie verkörpern Positionen und Stellungnahmen, die aus der Kommunikation und Auseinandersetzung innerhalb einer Gruppe wachsen; ihnen unterliegt ein sozial verbindlicher Sinn, eine Bedeutung, über die soziale Einigung besteht.

Die kulturelle jüdische Dimension von zwei Leuchtern auf einem gedeckten Tisch, die zum „Erew Schabbat" angezündet werden, ist – abgesehen von allen expliziten Hinweisen, die vorkommen können, wie eine hebräische Inschrift – ihre sozial anerkannte und verbindliche Bedeutung im Ritual des jüdischen Ruhetages. Die in verschiedenen Techniken, Materialien und Formen ausgeführten Misrach-Tafeln an der Jerusalem zugewandten Wand jüdischer Häuser, wo immer die auch stehen, sind auch Monumente individueller künstlerischer und handwerklicher Fertigkeit; ihre jüdische Dimension liegt jedoch vor allem darin, daß sie die Hoffnung auf Überwindung der Diaspora in der „kommenden" messianischen Zeit verkörpern. Sie mahnen das Gedenken an die Zerstörung Jerusalems an und verweisen auf die Hoffnung der „Einsammlung der Exilierten" an diesem zentralen Ort jüdischer Erlösungshoffnung.

Objekte sind „vielstimmig" und vielschichtig. Sie repräsentieren individuelle künstlerische und handwerkliche Fertigkeiten, wie sie sozialen Sinn und Bedeutung in ganz unterschiedlichen Feldern repräsentieren. Je nach Fragen und Interessen, mit denen wir an sie herantreten, bieten sie je andere Lesarten und Antworten. Auch wenn uns ihre kulturelle Dimension interessiert, das Faktum also, daß sie Resultate sozialen Handelns sind, Ausdruck menschlicher Fähigkeit, „bewußt zur Welt Stellung zu nehmen und ihr einen Sinn zu verleihen" (Max Weber),[3] lassen sie sich nicht auf einen einzigen Erschließungskontext reduzieren. Die Schabbat-Leuchter von Ludwig Yehuda Wolpert (Sammlung Gross, 012.001.004), die dieser in den 1960er Jahren in den USA schuf, sind sowohl in einem jüdisch-rituellen Kontext lesbar, als auch innerhalb eines Kunstdiskurses. In letzterem repräsentieren sie Fragestellungen und Debatten, welche die Bauhaus-Tradition begründeten. Der strenge Funktionalismus, den ihre Form repräsentiert, sowie der expressive Ausdruck der hebräischen Schriftzeichen auf ihrem Schaft lassen sie in diesem Kontext lesen. Über den Kern der jüdischen kulturellen Dimension dieser Leuchter lernen wir vielleicht am meisten, wenn wir sie in ein spekulatives historisches Szenario setzen. In welcher Zeit (im Sinne von Epoche) erschließen diese Objekte für wen welchen Sinn? Stellen wir uns zunächst einmal jüdische Akteure des 15. Jahrhunderts vor.[4] Die Inschrift auf den Leuchtern sowie ihr Vorkommen im Paar würden sie für diese recht eindeutig dem Schabbat-Ritual zuweisen lassen. Eine (im traditionellen Sinne gut erzogene) jüdische Frau dieser Zeit wüßte ungefragt, wie mit ihnen zu verfahren. Sie wüßte, zu welchem Zeitpunkt diese Leuchter zum Einsatz kommen, würde den Segensspruch kennen, den sie vor dem Anzünden der Kerzen zu sprechen hätte etc. Kurz: Jüdische Akteure des 15. Jahrhunderts wären in der Lage, über die pragmatische Funktion der beiden Leuchter als Lichtspender hinaus deren Sinn und Bedeutung zu entschlüsseln. So fremd ihnen vielleicht die äußere Form dieser Gegenstände wäre, so nahe wäre ihnen doch deren Sinn und rituelle Funktion. Dasselbe dürfte auch für jüdische Akteure – sagen wir – des späten 21. Jahrhunderts gelten. Wenn wir jetzt einmal alle kulturkritischen Anwandlungen beiseite lassen, ist anzunehmen, daß die beiden Leuchter – wenn auch in der Stilsprache des 20. Jahrhunderts gestaltet – für diese jüdischen Akteure des 21. Jahrhunderts doch noch klar auf ihren jüdischen Sinn und ihre Funktion im religiösen Ritual lesbar wären.

Wechseln wir auf die nichtjüdische Seite: Würden Akteure dieser Gruppe im 15. Jahrhundert mit den beiden Wolpert-Leuchtern des 20. Jahrhunderts konfrontiert werden, würde sich ihnen vielleicht noch die pragmatische Funktion dieser Gegenstände als Halter von Wachskerzen erschließen; aber auch dem würde die Fremdheit und Nichtlesbarkeit des Stils vielleicht entgegen stehen, und auch die Inschrift würde diese Gegenstände diesen Akteuren nicht vertrauter, sondern vielmehr noch fremder machen. Anders im 20. Jahrhundert: Nichtjüdische Akteure dieser Zeit, die über eine kunsthistorische Basisbildung verfügen, könnten die beiden Wolpert-Leuchter wahrscheinlich recht schnell der Bauhaus-Tradition zuordnen, und dasselbe ist für nichtjüdische kunsthistorisch bewußte Akteure und Akteurinnen des 21. Jahrhunderts anzunehmen. Ob sich ihnen die jüdische kulturelle Dimension der Gegenstände erschließen würde, wäre abhängig vom Umfang ihres interkulturellen Wissens.

Es gibt selbstverständlich unzählige Spielarten solcher Szenarien. Für meine Fragestellung hier ist entscheidend, daß Wissen und somit die Entschlüsselung kultureller Phänomene eine soziale Dimension hat. Wissen ist gruppenabhängig und gruppenbildend. Die kulturellen Dimensionen von Objekten erschließen sich in erster Linie nach dem Vorwissen ihrer BenutzerInnen und BetrachterInnen; welche kulturellen Dimensionen eines Gegenstandes man kennt, wie das Objekt zu einem spricht, ist auch abhängig von sozialer Zugehörigkeit. Mich interessiert hier in erster Linie die jüdische kulturelle Dimension der Gegenstände, die an ihre Produktion und Verwendung in einem Traditionszusammenhang gebunden ist. Lassen wir also das wissenschaftlich generierte und tradierte Wissen über die Dinge, wie wir den Zugang der nichtjüdischen Akteure unserer Szenarien zusammenfassen könnten, einmal beiseite. Eine Erkenntnis aus den oben beschriebenen spekulativen historischen Szenarien ist, daß den Wolpert-Schabbatleuchtern, die uns hier zur Anschauung dienen, zwei zeitliche Dimensionen eingeschrieben sind. Die eine läßt sich als vertikale Dimension beschreiben, die andere als horizontale Dimension.

Es ist die vertikale zeitliche Dimension, welche die Objekte über ihre spezifische Zeit und ihren spezifischen Ort hinaus in einem Traditionszusammenhang verankert. Ihr verdanken die Schabbatleuchter in dem spekulativen Szenario, mit dem wir hier arbeiten, ihre Zeiten- und Orte-übergreifende Lesbarkeit für Mitglieder der Traditionsgemeinschaft. Durch diese vertikale Dimension werden sie für diese lesbar, im 15. wie im 20. Jahrhundert, aber auch von Wien über Bagdad bis Melbourne. Festmachbar ist diese Zeitdimension kultureller Produkte, wie auch Gegenstände sie darstellen, an ihrer Funktion im religiösen Ritual und deren Legitimation durch die Rückbindung an die zentralen Quellen der Tradition, die Hebräische Bibel und die darauf begründenden autoritativen Texte. Sichtbar wird diese den Objekten eingeschriebene Dimension dort, wo sich die äußere Form der rituellen Funktion und deren Legitimation in den Quellen verdankt. Bei den Schabbatleuchtern z.B. ist das ihr Auftreten im Paar (entscheidend ist, daß es sich um mehr als eine Lichtquelle handelt) oder die Inschrift in hebräischer Schrift und Sprache (in welcher sprachlichen Umgebung auch immer Juden leben), welche die Objekte eindeutig einer rituellen Funktion zuordnen.[5] Die Wolpert-Leuchter sind aber auch „ein Kind" ihrer spezifischen Zeit und ihres spezifischen Ortes. Das bezeichnet die horizontale Dimension dieser Objekte. Der strenge funktionalistische Stil läßt die Herkunft ihres Künstlers aus der Bauhaustradition erkennen, und auch die expressive Schriftgestalt der hebräischen Buchstaben sind der Zeit ihrer Entstehung verpflichtet. Es ist diese horizontale Dimension der Objekte, die sie zu kulturellen Hervorbringungen ihrer Zeit und ihres Ortes macht, und damit die Menschen, die sie schaffen und verwenden, in ihrer spezifischen Gegenwart verankert.

REISE AN KEIN ENDE DER WELT versammelt Judaica-Objekte aus Gemeinden aus (beinahe) der ganzen jüdischen Welt unterschiedlichster Entstehungszeit und setzt diese durch Gegenwartsfotografien von den Herkunftsorten in ihren jeweiligen lokalen Kontext. Die Zusammenschau dieser Objekte lädt geradezu ein, die Frage nach dem „Eigenen" und dem „Anderen" in der jüdischen Kulturproduktion zu stellen, wobei das „Eigene" und das „Andere" sich leicht in das Bild von der vertikalen und der horizontalen Dimension, die sich in diesen Produkten kreuzen, übersetzen läßt. Die Channukkiot aus Wien, Bagdad, Fez in Marokko und Italien, die in der Ausstellung gezeigt werden, verbindet ihre Funktion im Ritual des Lichterfestes Chanukka, wo immer und wann immer Juden dieses Fest gefeiert haben: im Wien des frühen 19. Jahrhunderts, in Bagdad um 1920, in Fez um 1930 oder in Italien um 1700. Ihre Bedeutung erhalten sie durch ihre Bindung an die noch allen gemeinsame Geschichte der Traditionsgemeinschaft (des Makkabäeraufstandes gegen die Seleukiden 165 v.d.Z. und die Wiedereinweihung des Tempels in Jerusalem). Rituell legitimiert werden sie durch die Rückbindung an Erzählungen und Motive aus den autoritativen Quellen der Tradition, z.B. an die Erzählung im Babylonischen Talmud, Schabbat 21b, vom letzten Krüglein reinen Öls, das im entweihten Tempel gefunden wurde und die Tempel-Menora wundersamerweise für acht Tage brennen ließ. Am Objekt sichtbar wird diese vertikale Dimension in den acht auf einer Ebene gesetzten Lichtquellen, die allen Chanukkiot gemeinsam sind. Darüber hinaus sind diese Leuchter aber genauso Produkte ihrer Zeit und ihres Ortes. Die Wiener Chanukkia ist in der Form eines Biedermeiersofas des frühen 19. Jahrhunderts gestaltet; die Rückwand des italienischen Leuchters zeigt den unverkennbaren Wandaufbau und das Tor repräsentativer italienischer Stadtarchitektur der Renaissance, und den Leuchter aus Bagdad dekorieren u.a. die Übel-abwehrenden Hände (Chamsa), ein Motiv der islamischen Umgebungskultur dieser Gemeinde.

Weder das „Eigene" noch das „Andere" sind jedoch essentielle Größen. Was das „Eigene" ist und was das „Andere", wird festgelegt, ist somit gemacht. Die Grenzen zwischen diesen Dimensionen fließen und können sich verschieben. Die deutsche Schabbatlampe der Sammlung Gross aus Nürnberg, entstanden um 1800, ist ein prägnantes Beispiel solcher Grenzverschiebungen zwischen dem „Eigenen" und dem „Anderen", zwischen der vertikalen und der horizontalen Dimension. Während Funktion und Bedeutung des Gegenstandes tief im Ritual des jüdischen Ruhetages verankert sind, entspricht die Form dieser Lampe dem im Mittelalter weitverbreiteten Typus der sternförmigen Öllampe. Ab dem 16. Jahrhundert fand dieser Typus dann beinahe ausschließlich bei der jüdischen Schabbatlampe Verwendung; ein Umstand, der ihm in der Folge den Namen „Judenstern" eintrug.[6] Hier wurde etwas zum „Jüdischen" par excellence, das ursprünglich aus der Umgebungsgesellschaft übernommen, dann jedoch als „spezifisch Jüdisches" in der jüdischen Kultur konserviert und tradiert wurde.

Die jüdische Kulturgeschichtsschreibung des 19. und frühen 20. Jahrhunderts stand unter großem Druck, die von der Diaspora-Existenz geprägte Kultur des Judentums vom Vorwurf, eine Mischkultur zu sein, zu befreien. Das dominante Paradigma des Nationalen dieser Jahrzehnte forderte die Suche nach der spezifischen nationalen Kultur, die sich in erster Linie in der Abgrenzung von anderen ethnischen und nationalen Kulturen definierte. Diesem Paradigma hatte sich auch die jüdische Kultur zu stellen, was sie im Kern ihrer Existenz traf. Die kulturelle Leistung, Elemente der jeweiligen Umgebungskultur zu integrieren und dennoch das Bewußtsein für das eigene Jüdische und die Differenz zu bewahren, setzte sie nun dem Verdikt aus, eine „Mischkultur" zu sein, sowie dem Vorwurf der „doppelten Loyalität". Paradigmatisch für die Abwertung des nachbiblischen und -talmudischen „Jüdischen" als Mischkultur war die Reserviertheit der kulturellen Eliten der nichtjüdischen Mehrheitsgesellschaft, aber auch der Maskilim, der jüdischen Aufklärer, gegenüber der jiddischen Sprache im ausgehenden 18. und im 19. Jahrhundert. Das Jiddische entsprach in keiner Weise dem von der Aufklärung informierten Ideal der „reinen Sprache", was die Maskilim veranlaßte, für ein „gereinigtes" Hebräisch sowie die nationale Sprache der Mehrheitsgesellschaft als Sprachen der Juden zu plädieren. Durch alle Werke der Sprachwissenschaftler zur jiddischen Sprache im 19. und 20. Jahrhundert zieht sich die Auseinandersetzung um die Rehabilitierung und Etablierung des Jiddischen als einer eigenständiger und vor allem spezifisch jüdischen Sprache. Den Komponentencharakter der jüdischen Sprachen konnten auch die Verteidiger des Jiddischen als eigenständiger Sprache nicht leugnen; sie retteten sich aber mit einer Umwertung in der Frage, was denn nun das Eigentliche einer Kultur und damit auch einer Sprache ausmache. Das Eigentliche liege eben nicht in den Elementen unterschiedlichster Herkunft, sondern in dem System, das die Integration dieser verschiedenen Elemente schaffe. Jüdische Sprachen seien Fusionssprachen, und es sei die Integrationsleistung, so der große Sprach- und Kulturwissenschaftler des Jiddischen, Max

Weinreich, die das entscheidende kulturelle Moment ausmache, an dem das spezifisch Jüdische festmachbar sei.[7]

Max Weinreich und in seiner Nachfolge auch Andrew Sunshine wenden das Modell der vertikalen und horizontalen Dimension auch auf die Beschreibung der jüdischen Sprachen an. Der vertikalen Dimension entspricht die Verwendung des hebräischen Schriftsystems für alle jüdischen Sprachen, worauf auch immer deren Lexik basiert, sowie die Elemente aus dem Hebräischen und Aramäischen, die sich in allen diesen Sprachen finden. Die hebräische Alphabetisierung der Juden über Jahrtausende in der Diaspora in den unterschiedlichsten sprachlichen Umgebungen ermöglichte die Kommunikation in die zeitliche Tiefe mit den Quellen der Traditionsgemeinschaft, erleichterte aber auch die innerjüdische Kommunikation in der Zeit über alle Sprachgrenzen hinweg. Der horizontalen Dimension der jüdischen Sprachen entspricht die Übernahme von Lexik und auch grammatikalischen Strukturen aus ihrer jeweiligen sprachlichen Umgebung. Daß das jiddische „goles" und das Judezmo-Wort „galut", beide hebräisch-aramäischen Ursprungs und mit der Bedeutung „Exil", einerseits völlig unterschiedlich ausgesprochen, andererseits jedoch vollkommen ident in hebräischen Buchstaben geschrieben werden, vermittle etwas Entscheidendes über die jüdische Sprachkultur, so Andrew Sunshine.[8] Diese These läßt sich auch in das Feld der jüdischen Objektkultur übersetzen, was die Beispiele der Chanukkiot aus Wien, Bagdad, Fez und Italien gezeigt haben. Das Leitmotiv dieser Reise an kein Ende der Welt ist die Integrationsleistung, die jüdische Kultur ausmacht: erzwungen und ermöglicht durch die Existenz in einem Exil, das notwendig Exil bleiben muss.

1 „Um unserer großen Sünden willen" („bavoynese'ynu ho ra'bim" in jiddischer Transkription der hebräischen Phrase) ist eine Formel, die in vielen Texten der frühen Neuzeit zu finden ist, und zwar im Kontext der Nennung von Schicksalsschlägen gegen Juden. Sie ist nicht als Schuldeingeständnis in dem konkreten Fall zu verstehen, in dessen Zusammenhang die Formel ausgesprochen oder geschrieben wird, sondern zielt vielmehr auf das Problem der Theodizee: Gott ist dennoch gut und gerecht, auch wenn er dem jüdischen Volk ein Leben in der Zerstreuung auferlegt. Dieses Leben wird nämlich als Strafe für fortwährende Verletzungen des Bundes zwischen Gott und seinem Volk rezipiert.

2 Zitiert nach Otto Gerhard Oexle, Geschichte als Historische Kulturwissenschaft, in: Wolfgang Hardtwig/Hans-Ulrich Wehler (ed.): Kulturgeschichte heute (Geschichte und Gesellschaft, Sonderheft 16), Göttingen 1996, S. 14–40, S. 25.

3 Zitiert nach Oexle, Geschichte, S. 24.

4 Auch wenn das Szenario spekulativ ist, sollte es einen historischen Kern haben. Der Gegenstand, den ich einsetze, sollte in der Zeit bekannt gewesen sein. Eine Abbildung aus dem Rothschild-Gebetbuch, Ferrara (1470–1480), zeigt einen Mann und eine Frau an einem gedeckten Schabbattisch mit einem zweiarmigen Leuchter in der Mitte. Abb. in Bracha Yaniv/Zohar Hanegbi, Sabbath Candles, Bar-Ilan University, 1995, S. 9.

5 Zur Frage, warum am Schabbat zwei oder mehrere Lichter angezündet werden, siehe: Yaniv/Hanegbi, Sabbath Candles, S. 11, und Alfred J. Kolatsch, Jüdische Welt verstehen, Wiesbaden 1996, S. 191–192.

6 Siehe Annette Webers Beschreibung der Schabbat-Lampe, in: Eva Grabherr (ed.), Geschichten von Gegenständen. Judaika aus dem Beziehungsraum der Hohenemser Juden. The Gross Family Collection (Tel Aviv), Hohenems 1994, S. 141.

7 Max Weinreich, History of the Yiddish Language, Chicago and London 1980 (in Jiddisch 1973), S. 205–207.

8 Andrew Lloyd Sunshine, Opening the Mail. Interpersonal Aspects of Discourse and Grammar in Middle Yiddish Letters, PhD Columbia University 1991, S. 10–11.

Objects of Diaspora

I have known that moment of scattering of people, which at different times and at different places turns
into a time of gathering in the nations of others. Homi K. Bhabha

JOURNEY TO NO END OF THE WORLD tells about this "time of gathering" "at different times", "at different places" and "in the nations of others:" in Kuba, Izmir, Ioannina, Fez, Gibraltar, London, Amsterdam, Nuremberg, Vienna, Vilna, New York, etc. The exhibition tells Jewish world history probably in the only way such an undertaking can possibly be approached: focused on the micro-history of Jewish communities in those places which they have found for them-selves in the past two thousand years and in which they have been accepted, and sensitive to the non-Jewish context within which Jewish life has taken place. Life in dispersion, "in different places" and "in the nations of others" is not a transitional stage in Jewish existence; at least not "in this time" (zman haze). The "ingathering of the exiled" (qibbuts galuyot), a crucial motif of Jewish Messianic expectation since the Babylonian exile, will take place in the "time to come" (zman haba). The present means to not have arrived, to live in the difference, that is, in the Diaspora, which in every period has its own deeper meaning: "Owing to our great sins" in the pre-modern era;[1] to be "a light unto the nations" in the language of the representatives of the Wissenschaft des Judentums (scientific investigation of Judaism) in secular nineteenth century.[4] Diaspora existence shapes Jewish culture. It is etched into the material and immaterial manifestations of people who form that culture, but are formed by it as well; etched into this group's literary and artistic works, objects, symbols, ways of life, rituals, institutions, etc.; in short: "the totality of human manifes-tations in all areas of life," as Max Weber defines culture.[2] The cultural dimen-sion of these "manifestations" is that they are the result of social action, that is, they go beyond subjective meaning and individual positions. They represent positions and statements that grow out of communication and interaction within a group; they have an underlying, socially binding meaning based on social consensus. The Jewish cultural dimension of two candlesticks on a set table that are lit for "Erev Shabbat" is – apart from all possible explicit hints, such as a Hebrew inscription – their socially recognized and binding significance for the ritual of the Jewish day of rest. Executed in various techniques, materials,

and shapes, the Mizrah-tablets in Jewish homes on the walls facing Jerusalem are, wherever they may be, testimony of individual artistic skill and crafts-manship; however, their Jewish dimension lies in their epitomizing the hope of overcoming the Diaspora in the Messianic time "to come." They demand to remember the destruction of Jerusalem and refer to the hope of the "ingathering of the exiled" in this place so central to Jewish hope for redemption.

Objects are "multivoiced" and multilayered. They represent individual artistic skill and craftsmanship as they represent social meaning and significance in entirely varying fields. Depending on the questions and interests with which we approach them, they offer different readings and answers. Even though we are interested in their cultural dimension – that is, in the fact that they are the result of social action, expression of the human ability to "consciously relate to the world and provide it with meaning" (Max Weber)[3] – they cannot be reduced to a single interpretative context. Ludwig Wolpert's Shabbat candle-sticks (Gross collection, 012.001.004), which he had created in the 1960s in the United States, can be read in a Jewish-ritual context as well as within a discourse on art. Within the latter, they represent questions and debates that have launched the Bauhaus tradition. The strict functionalism as represented by their shape as well as the expressiveness of the Hebrew letters on their shaft allow for the reading in such a context.

We may perhaps learn the most about the core of these candlesticks' Jewish cultural dimension if we place them in a speculative historic scenario. In which time (that is, era) offer these objects what meaning to whom? Let's start by envisaging Jewish protagonists of the fifteenth century.[4] The inscription on the candlesticks as well as their occurrence in a pair would have them rather clearly assign them a place within the Shabbat ritual. A (in the traditional sense well educated) Jewish woman of that time would have known right away how to handle them. She would have known when to use these candlesticks, which blessing to say before lighting the candles, etc. In short: Jewish protagonists of the fifteenth century would be able to decipher meaning and significance of these two candlesticks beyond their pragmatic function as providers of light. As alien as the external shape of these objects may have possibly been to them, their meaning and ritual function would have been familiar to them. The same is probably true for Jewish protagonists of the – let's say – late twenty-first century. If we put aside all culture-critical impulses for now, it can be assumed that these two candlesticks – although designed in the stylistic language of the twentieth century – would still be clearly comprehensible for these Jewish protagonists of the twenty-first century regarding their Jewish meaning and function in the religious ritual.

Let's change over to the non-Jewish side: If fifteenth-century protagonists from this group were to be confronted with the two Wolpert candlesticks, these objects' pragmatic function as candleholders might still be apparent to them; but perhaps even that might be put into question by the style's strangeness and illegibility. Rather than bringing them closer, the inscription would render these objects even more alien to these protagonists. That is all different in the twentieth century: Non-Jewish protagonists of that era who have basic knowledge of art history probably would be able to swiftly attribute the two Wolpert candlesticks to the Bauhaus tradition. The same can be assumed of non-Jewish protagonists of the twenty-first century somewhat acquainted with art history. Whether the Jewish cultural dimension of the objects is apparent to them would be dependent on the extent of their inter-cultural knowledge.

Obviously, there are innumerable variations to such scenarios. For my question here, it is decisive that knowledge and, thus, the decoding of cultural phenomena have a social dimension. Knowledge is group-dependent and group-forming; the cultural dimensions of objects reveal themselves first and foremost according to the pre-existing knowledge of their users and viewers; someone's awareness of the cultural dimensions of an object and its appeal to that person are dependent on social affiliation as well. In this context I am particularly interested in the objects' Jewish cultural dimension, which is tied

to its production and use in a traditional context. So let's put aside for the moment the scientifically generated and passed on knowledge on how to sum up the approach of our scenarios' non-Jewish protagonists. One finding from the speculative historic scenarios described above would be that the Wolpert Shabbat candlesticks, which serve us here as examples, have two time dimensions inherent. One could be described as vertical dimension; the other as horizontal dimension.

It is the vertical time dimension that places the objects in a traditional context and enables those who are part of that tradition to comprehend the Shabbat candlesticks within the speculative scenario we are working with, beyond their specific time and place. Through that vertical dimension they become comprehensible, in the fifteenth as in the twentieth century, but also from Vienna via Baghdad to Melbourne. The time dimension of cultural products, as represented, for instance, by objects, manifests itself in their function within the religious ritual and their legitimization through the connection back to the central sources of tradition, the Hebrew Bible and the authoritative texts based on it. This dimension, etched into the objects, becomes visible where the external form of ritual function and its legitimization are derived from the sources: in the case of the Shabbat candlesticks, for instance, it is their occurrence in a pair (essentially, more than one source of light is required) or the inscription in Hebrew letters and language (independent of the linguistic environment in which Jews live), which clearly assign these objects a ritual function.[5] However, the Wolpert candlesticks are also "children" of their specific time and place – an indication of their horizontal dimension. The strict functionalistic style reveals the artist's origin in the Bauhaus-tradition, and the expressive lettering of the Hebrew characters is a contemporary feature as well. It is this horizontal dimension of the objects that makes them cultural manifestations of their time and place and, thus, anchors those who create and use them in their specific present time.

JOURNEY TO NO END OF THE WORLD assembles Judaica-objects from communities of (almost) the entire Jewish world and from various times of origin and sets them in their respective local context through present-day photographs of their places of origin. The panorama of these objects invites to ask the question of the "own" and the "other" in Jewish cultural production, whereby the "own" and the "other" can be easily converted into the picture of the vertical and horizontal dimensions, which intersect in these products. Their function in the Hanukkah ritual, the festival of light, connects the hanukkioth from Vienna, Baghdad, Fez in Morocco, and Italy – shown in the exhibition – wherever and whenever Jews have celebrated this feast: in early nineteenth century Vienna, in Baghdad around 1920, in Fez around 1930, or in Italy around 1700. They derive meaning from their connection to the history still common to all those sharing the tradition (of the Maccabees' uprising against the Seleucides in 165 B.C.E. and the rededication of the Temple in Jerusalem); and they are ritually legitimized by their ties back to the narratives and motifs from the traditional authoritative sources, e.g., the account in the Babylonian Talmud, Shabbat 21b, of the last jar of purified oil, which was found in the desecrated Temple, and which miraculously kept the menorah burning for eight days. This vertical dimension becomes visible in the eight sources of light set on one level, which is common to all hanukkioth. Beyond that, these lamps are products of their times and places as well. The Viennese hanukkiah is designed in the shape of an early nineteenth century Biedermeier sofa; the back wall of the Italian lamp displays the unmistakable wall construction and the gate representative of Italian Renaissance city architecture, while the lamp from Baghdad is decorated, among others, with the hands (hamsah) that avert bad luck, a motif from the community's surrounding Islamic culture.

However, neither the "own" nor the "other" are essential dimensions. The "own" and the "other" are determined, therefore made. The borders between these dimensions are fluid and shifting. The Gross collection's German Shabbat lamp from Nuremberg, made around 1800, is an example of such shifting borders between the "own" and the "other," between the vertical and the horizontal dimension. While function and meaning of the object are deeply rooted in the ritual of the Jewish day of rest, the lamp's shape is characteristic of the star-shaped oil lamp so widespread in the Middle Ages. From the sixteenth century onward, this type was used almost exclusively for the Jewish Shabbat lamp; that brought about its name "Jewish Star."[6] Here, something became "Jewish" par excellence that had originally been adopted from the surrounding culture, but later was preserved and conveyed as "typically Jewish" in Jewish culture. Jewish cultural historiography of the nineteenth and early twentieth century was heavily pressured to liberate Jewish culture, molded by Diaspora existence, from the stigma of being a mixed culture. The paradigm of the national, dominating these decades, required to search for the specific national culture, which chiefly defined itself by drawing boundaries to other ethnic and national cultures. Jewish culture had to deal with this paradigm as well, which was a blow to the core of its existence: the cultural achievement to integrate elements of the particular surrounding culture and to preserve, nonetheless, the awareness of its own Jewishness and difference, subjected it now to the verdict of being a "mixed culture" as well as to the accusation of "double loyalty." The reserved attitude of the cultural elite of society's non-Jewish majority, but also of the Maskilim, the representatives of Jewish Enlightenment, toward the Yiddish language in the late eighteenth and in the nineteenth century, was paradigmatic of the devaluation of postbiblical and post-Talmudic Jewish culture as "mixed." Yiddish did not meet the ideal of a "pure language," as advanced by Enlightenment, which lead the Maskilim to plead for a "purified" Hebrew as well as for the adoption of the national language of the majority as the language of the Jews. The argument around the rehabilitation and establishment of the Yiddish language as a separate and specifically Jewish language runs through all works of linguists on Yiddish language in the nineteenth and twentieth century. Even the defenders of Yiddish as a separate language, though, were unable to deny the composite character of the Jewish languages; but they saved themselves by reassessing the question on what, in fact, constitutes the essence of a culture and, thus, a language. The essence lies, after all, not in the elements of various origins, but rather in the system that brings about the integration of these various elements. Jewish languages are fusion languages, according to Max Weinreich, the eminent expert on Yiddish linguistics and culture, and the achievement of integration is the critical cultural factor that identifies them as specifically Jewish.[7]

Max Weinreich and his successor Andrew Sunshine apply the model of vertical and horizontal dimension to the description of Jewish languages as well. Corresponding to the vertical dimension, is the use of the Hebrew writing system in all Jewish languages, independent of their lexical basis, as well as the Hebrew and Aramaic elements inherent in all those languages. The Hebrew alphabetization of the Jews over thousands of years in the Diaspora in the most different linguistic environments enabled the communication into the depth of time with the sources of tradition, but also facilitated intra-Jewish contemporaneous communication beyond all language barriers. Corresponding to the horizontal dimension of Jewish languages is the adoption of lexis and grammar structure from their linguistic environment. The fact that the Yiddish word "goles" and the Judesmo word "galut," both of Hebrew-Aramaic origin and with the meaning "exile," are, on the one hand, pronounced completely differently and, on the other hand, are spelled entirely identically in Hebrew letters, imparts something crucial about Jewish linguistic culture, according to Andrew Sunshine. This thesis can be translated into the field of Jewish object culture as well, which has been shown in the examples of the hanukkioth from Vienna, Baghdad, Fez, and Italy. The leitmotiv of this Reise an kein Ende der Welt is the achievement of integration, which is the essence of Jewish culture: forced and enabled through existence in exile that necessarily must remain exile.

1 "Owing to our great sins" ("bavoynese'ynu ho ra'bim" in the Yiddish transcription of the Hebrew phrase) is a formula that can be found in numerous texts of the Early Modern period in accounts of strokes of fate against Jews. It is not to be taken as an admission of guilt in the concrete case where it is mentioned, but rather touches on the problem of theodicy: God is still kind and just, even if he imposes a life in dispersion on the Jewish people. That life is understood as a punishment for continuous breaches of the covenant between God and His people.

2 Quoted from Otto Gerhard Oexle, Geschichte als Historische Kulturwissenschaft in: Wolfgang Hardtwig/Hans-Ulrich Wehler (eds.), Kulturgeschichte heute (Geschichte und Gesellschaft, special issue 16), Göttingen 1996, p. 14–40, p. 25.

3 Quoted from Oexle, Geschichte, p. 24.

4 Even if the scenario is speculative, it should still have a historical core. The object I use should have been known at the time. An illustration from the Rothschild prayer book, Ferrara (1470–1480), shows a man and a woman at a set Shabbat table with a two-branch candelabrum in the center. Ill. in Bracha Yaniv/Zohar Hanegbi, Sabbath Candles, Bar-Ilan University 1995, p. 9.

5 On the question why two or more lights are lit, see: Yaniv/Hanegbi, Sabbath Candles, p. 11, and Alfred J. Kolatsch: Jüdische Welt verstehen, Wiesbaden 1996, p. 191–192.

6 See Annette Weber's description of the Shabbat lamp, in: Eva Grabherr (ed.), Geschichten von Gegenständen. Judaika aus dem Beziehungsraum der Hohenemser Juden. The Gross Family Collection (Tel Aviv), Hohenems 1994, p. 141.

7 Max Weinreich, History of the Yiddish Language, Chicago and London 1980, (in Yiddish 1973), p. 205 – 207.

8 Andrew Lloyd Sunshine, Opening the Mail. Interpersonal Aspects of Discourse and Grammar in Middle Yiddish Letters, PhD Columbia University 1991, p. 10-11.

Gestaltungsidee

Architektonisches Charakteristikum der Ausstellung REISE AN KEIN ENDE DER WELT, die Judaica aus unterschiedlichen Orten und Zeiten zeigt, ist eine Vielzahl von Inseln, insgesamt rund 33. Diese Inseln konstituieren geographische Räume, Orte auf der ganzen Welt, wo jüdische Gemeinden lebten und leben, einst wie heute. Obwohl sie sich alle um Judaica gruppieren, die sich in Funktion und Erscheinung ähneln mögen, bildet jeder Ort für sich selbst eine eigene kleine Welt. Diese kleinen Welten sind als Inseln gewissermaßen in Bewegung und ignorieren ganz bewusst jedwede geographische Ordnung. Jeder Ort kann zum „Weltende" werden, für den Betrachter wie den Betrachteten, den staunenden Reisenden und den Bewohner der Enklaven.

Zeitgenössische Fotografien aus den jeweiligen Orten werden als kreisrunde liegende Scheiben mit einem Durchmesser von 165 cm am Boden situiert. Aus diesen Abbildungen heraus erheben sich schlichte Stelen. Diese sind Träger von Vitrinen, welche die jeweiligen Objekte des entsprechenden „Weltenden-Ortes" enthalten. Die Vitrinen sind in ihrer Dimension auf das kleinstmögliche Maß reduziert und transportieren so den Gedanken eines Minimalismus, der Portabilität für den Reisenden – doch auch für den Flüchtenden – als zwingende Notwendigkeit vermittelt. Literarische Zitate von Reisenden, die seit dem Mittelalter jüdische Enklaven auf der ganzen Welt besuchten, stehen ortsbezogen außen um das Rund der Fotos. Ihre Mehrsprachigkeit – Deutsch, Englisch, Hebräisch – zeigt sowohl die Unterschiedlichkeit und Vielfalt der Sprachen, die der Reisende wie auch der Besucher der Ausstellung in den diversen Umgebungssprachen der jüdischen Inseln erfährt, als auch die verbindende Gemeinsamkeit des Hebräischen, das die Kommunikation zwischen dem Reisenden und den besuchten Gemeinden erst ermöglichte.

Diese spezifische Art einer szenographischen Gestaltung soll dem Ausstellungsbesucher eigenwillige Zugänge ermöglichen. Er wirkt als wichtiger Mitspieler der Installation, die mehr als einen individuellen Kosmos generiert.

Die Ausstellung REISE AN KEIN ENDE DER WELT ist selbst eine Reisende. Sie soll in Wien, Tel Aviv, Frankfurt am Main und New York zu sehen sein, und wurde somit als Ausstellung für viele Orte, viele „Weltenden", konzipiert.

Martin Kohlbauer Architekt

INSTI
ORT.

·R·A·K·E·O·W.   20.3.98

Exhibition Design Concept

A variety of thirty-three islands is the distinctive architectural mark of the exhibition JOURNEY TO NO END OF THE WORLD, which presents Judaica from various places and times. These islands stand for geographic areas, for places from all over the world where Jewish communities once lived or still live. Although all of them are based on Judaica of similar shapes and functions, each place is a small world of its own. In a way, these small worlds are islands in motion and consciously reject any notion of geographic order. Each of these places can turn into an "end of the world" for the visitors and the visited, the amazed travelers and the residents of those enclaves.

Contemporary photographs from the respective places are placed on the floor in circles of 165 cm diameter. Simple, unadorned steles with glass cabinets rise from these pictorial disks, which contain objects from their places at the "end of the world." These cabinets are reduced to their smallest possible dimensions, thus conveying the idea of minimalism – the concept of portability, equally necessary for both traveler and fugitive. Quotations from travelers, who visited Jewish enclaves all over the world since medieval times are placed around the pictorial circles. Their multilingualism – German, English, Hebrew – reminds both traveler and visitor of the linguistic variety that surrounds the Jewish islands and it reminds at the same time of the unifying function of Hebrew by which alone communication between visitors and visited was rendered possible.

This specific scenographic design was chosen to allow the visitor individual approaches to the exhibition. He plays an important part in this installation, which generates more than just an individual cosmos.

The exhibition JOURNEY TO NO END OF THE WORLD is a traveler itself. It will be shown in Vienna, Tel Aviv, Frankfurt am Main, and New York and is, therefore, designed as an exhibition for many places, for many "ends of the world."

Martin Kohlbauer Architect

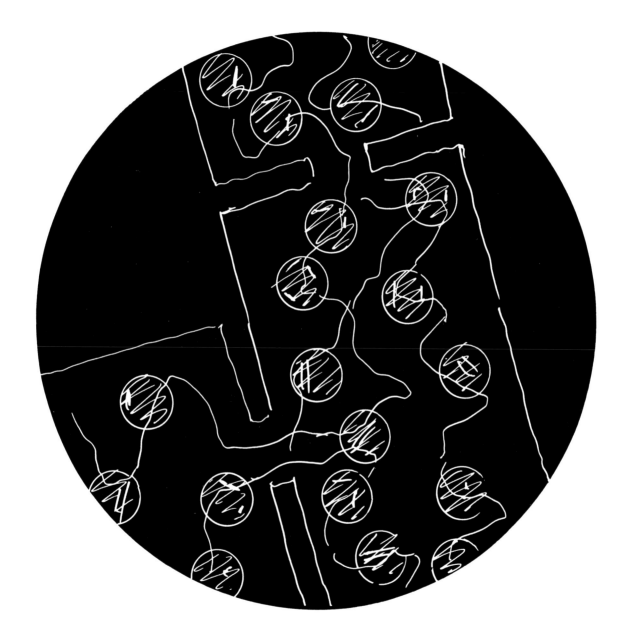

Martin Kohlbauer, „Weltendenkosmos", 2000

Katalog Catalogue

Aleppo. „Es gibt etwa 600 israelitische Familien einheimischen und europäischen Ursprungs, darunter viele sehr gebildete und gute Menschen und viele von ihnen sind reiche und bedeutende Kaufleute. Sie haben eine große Synagoge, die von König David errichtet wurde, in welcher sich sechsundzwanzig weiße Marmorsäulen und eine Kanzel aus weißem Marmor befinden."

R. David d'Beth Hillel, um 1830*

In der zweitgrößten Stadt Syriens lebten Juden ohne Unterbrechung seit der Römerzeit. Sie hielten immer engen Kontakt zu den Gemeinden Palästinas und Bagdads. Die Mongolen, die 1260 Aleppo eroberten, töteten viele Juden, wurden aber noch im selben Jahr von den Mamelucken geschlagen, unter deren Herrschaft die jüdische Gemeinde zunächst eine erneute Blüte erlebte. Die von den Machthabern in Kairo und Damaskus praktizierte religiöse Intoleranz beeinträchtigte jedoch auch das Gemeindeleben der Juden Aleppos. Die Eroberung Aleppos durch Tamerlan im Jahre 1400 führte abermals zu einem blutigen Desaster, von dem sich die Gemeinde erst in der zweiten Hälfte des 15. Jahrhunderts erholte. Bald darauf kamen exilierte spanische Juden nach Aleppo und übernahmen allmählich die spirituelle und intellektuelle Führung in der Gemeinde. Unter osmanischer Herrschaft unterhielten die Juden Aleppos enge Kontakte mit den großen Gemeinden Konstantinopels. Ihre Handelsbeziehungen reichten bis Persien und Indien. Die erste Hälfte des 19. Jahrhunderts brachte den ökonomischen und kulturellen Niedergang der jüdischen Gemeinden Syriens, die durch die Damaskus-Affäre diffamiert und isoliert wurden. Gleichzeitig verschärften sich die Gegensätze zwischen den diversen religiösen Gruppen Syriens. Nach dem Ersten Weltkrieg lebten in Syrien noch 30.000 Juden, davon über 6.000 Juden in Aleppo. Nach der Gründung des Staates Israel und den israelisch-arabischen Kriegen emigrierten 90% der Juden aus Syrien.

HÜLLE FÜR ESTHER-ROLLE
Aleppo/Syrien, um 1875
Silber, Laubsägearbeit
L: 21,5 cm; Dm: 3 cm
Inv.Nr. 080.001.007[1]

KETUBBA/HEIRATSVERTRAG
Aleppo/Syrien, 1867
Pergament, Tusche, Wasserfarben
Braut: Reina Bat Schalom Mizrachi
Bräutigam: Schlomo Ben Abraham Schemaa Halevi
H: 70 cm; B: 40 cm
Inv.Nr. 035.012.013[2]

RIMMONIM/TORA-AUFSÄTZE
Syrien, um 1920
Silber
H: 29,5 cm; Dm: 6,2 cm
Inv.Nr. 050.001.077[3]

S/W Foto S. 33: Robert Lyons, In der Talmud-Tora-Ben-Maimon-Schule, Damaskus, Syrien, 1994

* David d'Beth Hillel, Travels from Jerusalem through Arabia, Kurdistan, Part of Persia and India to Madras 1824-32, Madras 1832.
1 Allgemein zu Judaica aus Aleppo s. Treasures of the Aleppo Community. Zu ähnlichen Stücken vgl. Sotheby's Tel Aviv, May 1987, lot 151; ders., April 1990, lot 242; ders., October 1993, lot 276 u. 92; ders., Sassoon Family Estate, October 2000, lot 42.
2 Zu vorliegender Ketubba s. Sotheby's New York, June 1996, lot 83. Zu einer anderen zeitgleichen syrischen Ketubba vgl. Mazal Tov, Nr. 17.
3 Zu vergleichbaren Stücken s. Sotheby's Tel Aviv, Sassoon Family Estate, October 2000, lot 33.

Aleppo. "There are about 600 families of native and European Israelites, many of them are very learned and kind people, and many of them are rich and great merchants. They have a large synagogue, which was built by King David, of large hewn stones of marble, in which are twenty-six white marble pillars and a pulpit of a white marble stone."

R. David d'Beth Hillel, c. 1830*

From Roman times Jews have lived continuously in this second largest Syrian city. All along they maintained close contact to the communities in Palestine and Baghdad. The Mongolians, who conquered Aleppo in 1260, killed many Jews, but were defeated that same year by the Mamluks under whose rule the Jewish community initially flourished again. However, the religious intolerance practiced by the ruling powers in Cairo and Damascus harmed the community life of Aleppo's Jews as well. The conquest of Aleppo by Tamerlan in 1400 led to another bloody disaster, from which the community recovered only in the second half of the 15th century. Soon thereafter, exiled Spanish Jews came to Aleppo and gradually took over the community's spiritual and intellectual leadership. Under Ottoman rule the Jews of Aleppo maintained close contact to the large communities of Constantinople. Their trade relations reached to Persia and India. The first half of the 19th century brought in its wake the economic and cultural decline of Syria's Jewish communities, who were defamed and isolated as a result of the Damascus affair. At the same time, antagonism between the various religious groups in Syria increased. After World War I, 30,000 Jews were still living in Syria, 6,000 of them in Aleppo. After the founding of the State of Israel and the Israeli-Arab wars, 90% of the Jews emigrated from Syria.

B/W Photo p. 33: Robert Lyons, In the Talmud-Torah-Ben-Maimon-School, Damaskus, Syria, 1994

CASE FOR ESTHER SCROLL
Aleppo/Syria, c. 1875
Silver, fretwork
Length: 21.5 cm; Diameter: 3 cm
No. 080.001.007[1]

KETUBAH/MARRIAGE CONTRACT
Aleppo/Syria, 1867
Parchment, ink, water colours
Bride: Reina Bat Shalom Mizrahi
Groom: Shelomo Ben Avraham Shema'a Halevi
Height: 70 cm; Width: 40 cm
No. 035.012.013[2]

RIMMONIM/TORAH FINIALS
Syria, c. 1920
Silver
Height: 29.5 cm; Diameter: 6.2 cm
No. 050.001.077[3]

Interior of the Synagogue in Aleppo, Syria, c. 1910. *Ben Zvi Institute, Jerusalem/Beth Hatefutsoth Photo Archive, Tel Aviv*

Innenansicht der Synagoge in Aleppo, Syrien, um 1910. *Ben-Zvi-Institut, Jerusalem/Beth Hatefutsoth Foto-Archiv, Tel Aviv*

* David d`Beth Hillel, Travels from Jerusalem through Arabia, Kurdistan, Part of Persia and India to Madras 1824–32, Madras 1832.
1 For Judaica from Aleppo in general, see Treasures of the Aleppo Community. For similar items, cf. Sotheby's Tel Aviv, May 1987, lot 151; ibid., April 1990, lot 242; ibid., Tel Aviv, October 1993, lot 276, lot 92, ibid. Sassoon Family Estate, October 2000, lot 42.
2 For this ketubah, see Sotheby's New York, June 1996, lot 83. For another contemporaneous Syrian ketubah, cf. Mazal Tov, no. 17.
3 For comparable items, see Sotheby's Tel Aviv, Sassoon Family Estate, October 2000, lot 33.

MESACHEKET BA-TEVEL/AUF DIE WELT LACHEN
Ethisch-philosophischer Traktat
Amsterdam/Holland, um 1675
Handschrift auf Papier, Tusche; dekoriert, kalligraphische Initialworte
Autoren: Elija Chajim, Isaak Abravanel, Isaak Arama et al.
38 Seiten
H: 19,7 cm; B: 13 cm
Inv.Nr. HO.011.003 [4]

BUCHEINBAND
(für ein Frauengebetbuch?)
Amsterdam/Holland, 1765
Silber
Künstler: Jan Aarnout Bos
H: 16,2 cm; B: 10,7 cm; T: 3 cm
Inv.Nr. 025.001.022 [5]

PESACH-HAGGADA
Amsterdam/Holland, 1712
Illustrationen: Kupferstiche von Abraham Bar Ja'akow (basierend auf den Bibelillustrationen von Matthäus Merian)
H: 40 cm, B: 25 cm
Inv.Nr. B. 96 [6]

RIMMONIM/TORA-AUFSÄTZE
Amsterdam/Holland, 1650
Silber, teilweise vergoldet
Künstler: Jan van De Velde
H: 40 cm; Dm: 11,6 cm
Inv.Nr. 050.001.043 [7]

Amsterdam. „Es wohnen heute in Amsterdam an 60000 Juden. Hauptstraßen des Judenviertels sind die Jodenbree- und die Weesperstraat. Zahlreiche Gassen und Gässchen zweigen von ihnen ab und münden auf dem Jonas Daniel Meijer Plein, an dem die Portugiesische Synagoge liegt."

Ernst Altkirch, 1910*

Im letzten Viertel des 16. Jahrhunderts fanden Marranen von der Iberischen Halbinsel Aufnahme in Amsterdam, wo es keine Inquisition wie in Spanien oder Portugal gab. Sie lebten jedoch vorerst weiterhin nicht offiziell als Juden. Erst auf das Jahr 1602 geht die Gründung der ersten Amsterdamer jüdischen Gemeinde zurück, die getragen war von einer portugiesischen Einwanderergruppe um Mosche Uri haLevi aus Emden herum, der sich viele der Marranen anschlossen. 1635 wurde auch eine aschkenasische Gemeinde gegründet und wenige Jahre später das jüdische Viertel eingerichtet. Das intellektuelle Image des jüdischen Amsterdam war einerseits geprägt von Autoritäten wie Menasse Ben Israel, andererseits von philosophischen Rebellen wie Uriel da Costa und Baruch Spinoza. 1796 erhielten die holländischen Juden die bürgerliche Gleichstellung, ein rundes Jahrhundert früher als die preußischen oder habsburgischen Untertanen. Als Hitler-Deutschland die Niederlande besetzte, lebten in Amsterdam 80.000 Juden; von ihnen überlebten nur 10.000 die Schoa.

S/W Foto S. 36: Han Singels, Jugendliche auf einem Tourboot in den Kanälen Amsterdams, Amsterdam, Holland, 1996

* Ernst Altkirch, Die Portugiesische Synagoge in Amsterdam, in: Ost und West, Jahrgang X, 1910, S. 726.
4 Abb. dieser Handschrift in: Christie's London, December 1981, lot 302. Zu Handschriften von Jehuda Machabeu, dem einige Illustrationen des vorliegenden Manuskripts zugeschrieben werden könnten, s. Bibliotheca Rosenthaliana, Treasures, In 1655, 1664.
5 Zum Meisterzeichen s. Citroen, Nr. 388.
6 Abb. dieser Haggada in: Reise nach Jerusalem, Nr. 4/9. Zu dieser Haggada-Ausgabe s. Illustrations of the Amsterdam Haggadah, Kommentar zur Faksimile-Ausgabe; Jüdische Buchkunst II, S. 67ff.
7 Zum Typus vgl. Jewish Museum London, S. 102, 111, 113, 115, Pl. LX. Zu vergleichbaren Aufsätzen s. Sotheby's Tel Aviv, Sassoon Family Estate, October 2000, lot 36 (allerdings filigran); Christie's New York, October 1980, lot 193; Collector's Guide, Abb. 90; Crowning Glory, Nr. 383, Abb. 16; Joods Historisch Museum, S. 34 u. 88f. Zum Meisterzeichen s. Citroen, Nr. 1000.

MESACHEKET BA-TEVEL/LAUGHING AT THE WORLD
Ethico-philosophical treatise
Amsterdam/Holland, c. 1675
Manuscript on paper, ink; with decorations and calligraphy
Authors: Elija Hayim, Isaac Abravanel, Isaac Arama et al.
Pages: 38
Height: 19.7 cm; Width: 13 cm
No. HO.011.003 [4]

BOOK COVER
(for a woman's prayer book?)
Amsterdam/Holland, 1765
Silver
Artist: Jan Aarnout Bos
Height: 16.2 cm; Width: 10.7 cm; Depth: 3 cm
No. 025.001.022 [5]

PASSOVER HAGGADAH
Amsterdam/Holland, 1712
Illustrations: copper plate engravings by Abraham Bar Ya'akov (based on the Bible illustrations by Matthäus Merian)
Publisher: Solomon Proops
Height: 40 cm; Width: 25 cm
No. B. 96 [6]

RIMMONIM/TORAH FINIALS
Amsterdam/Holland, 1650
Silver, parcel gilt
Artist: Jan van De Velde
Height: 40 cm; Diameter: 11.6 cm
No. 050.001.043 [7]

Amsterdam. "Today about 60,000 Jews live in Amsterdam. The main streets of the Jewish quarter are the Jodenbree- and the Weesperstraat. Numerous lanes and alleys branch off them and lead into the Jonas Daniel Meijer Plein where the Portuguese Synagogue is located."

Ernst Altkirch, 1910*

In the last quarter of the 16th century, Marranos from the Iberian Peninsula found refuge in Amsterdam from the Inquisition in Spain and Portugal. At first, however, they did not live as Jews officially. Only in 1602 did Portuguese immigrants around Moshe Uri haLevi from Emden, who were joined by a large number of the Marranos, establish the first Jewish community in Amsterdam. In 1635 an Ashkenazic community was established as well and a few years later the Jewish quarter was set up. Scholars such as Menasseh ben Israel on the one hand, and philosophical rebels such as Uriel da Costa and Baruch Spinoza on the other hand, shaped the intellectual image of Jewish Amsterdam. Dutch Jews obtained equal civil rights in 1796, a full century earlier than the subjects of the Prussian and Habsburg monarchs. At the time Hitler occupied the Netherlands, 80,000 Jews lived in Amsterdam; only 10,000 of them survived the Shoah.

B/W Photo p. 36: Han Singels, Roundship in the canals of Amsterdam by young boys, Amsterdam, Holland, 1996

On the left the Portuguese and on the right the two Ashkenasic Synagogues of Amsterdam, Etching by Adolf van der Laan, c. 1710
Jewish Historical Museum, Amsterdam/courtesy of Bibliotheca Rosenthaliana, Amsterdam

Links die portugiesische Synagoge, rechts die beiden aschkenasischen Synagogen von Amsterdam, Stich von Adolf van der Laan, um 1710. *Joods Historisch Museum, Amsterdam/Leihgabe Bibliotheca Rosenthaliana, Amsterdam*

* Ernst Altkirch, Die Portugiesische Synagoge in Amsterdam, in: Ost und West, Jahrgang X, 1910, p. 726
4 Illustration of this manuscript in: Christie's London, December 1981, lot 302. For manuscripts by Yehuda Machabeu, to whom some of the illustrations in the manuscript on hand can be attributed, see Bibliotheca Rosenthaliana, Treasures, In 1655, 1664.
5 For maker's mark, see Citroen, no. 388.
6 Illustration of this Haggadah in: Reise nach Jerusalem, no. 4/9. For this Haggadah edition, see: Illustrations of the Amsterdam Haggadah, Commentary on the facsimile edition; Jüdische Buchkunst II, p. 67ff.
7 For type, cf. Jewish Museum London, p. 102, 111, 113, 115, Pl. LX. For comparable finials, see Sotheby's Tel Aviv, Sassoon Family Estate, October 2000, lot 36 (although filigree); Christie's New York, October 1980, lot 193; Collector's Guide, fig. 90; Crowning Glory, no. 383, fig. 16; Joods Historisch Museum, p. 34, 88f. For maker's mark, see Citroen, no. 1000.

Bagdad. „In Bagdad leben etwa vierzigtausend Juden. Unter der Herrschaft des Kalifen leben sie in Sicherheit, Ruhe und Anerkennung. Unter den Juden gibt es große Gelehrte, die Oberhäupter der Jeschiwot, die mit der Tora befaßt sind. In der Stadt gibt es zehn Jeschiwot."

Benjamin von Tudela, um 1170*

Die Geschichte der jüdischen Gemeinde im Irak reicht 2700 Jahre zurück, in die Zeit der ersten Zwangsumsiedlungen von Israeliten nach Babylonien. Die arabische Eroberung, nach der das Land „Irak" genannt wurde, wurde von den Juden primär begrüßt. Nach Bagdad, wo der Sitz des Exilarchen war, wurden Ende des 9. Jahrhunderts die berühmten Lehrhäuser von Sura und Pumbedita transferiert. Die Gemeinde prosperierte ökonomisch und kulturell bis zur Eroberung Bagdads durch Tamerlan, wonach es für ein Jahrhundert kein jüdisches Leben in der Stadt gab. Die Neuzeit brachte für die Juden Bagdads wechselhafte Bedingungen. Wurden sie von den schiitischen Persern unterdrückt, so verbesserte sich ihre Situation wesentlich unter den verschiedenen osmanischen Herrschaftsperioden. Im 18. und 19. Jahrhundert hatte die Gemeinde hervorragende Gelehrte und Rabbiner und enge Verbindungen wurden zu den Juden Palästinas und anderer Länder geknüpft. Während des ersten Weltkriegs veränderte sich das Verhältnis zur Regierung radikal zum Schlechteren und die Eroberung durch Großbritannien wurde freudig begrüßt. Mit der Entlassung des Irak in die Unabhängigkeit begann eine Zeit offener Judenfeindschaft, die sich nach der Gründung des Staates Israel immer weiter verschärfte und von zahlreichen Pogromen begleitet war. In großen Operationen wurde die jüdische Bevölkerung des Irak daher von Israel evakuiert. 1947 lebten noch 77.000 Juden in Bagdad, heute nur mehr 60.

S/W Foto S. 39: Schamasch der Meir-Toeg-Synagoge, Bagdad, Irak, 1989; Beth Hatefutsoth Foto-Archiv, Tel Aviv

---

TORA-TIK/HÜLLE MIT RIMMONIM/TORA-AUFSÄTZEN
Hülle: Bagdad/Irak, 1885/86
Silber, teilweise vergoldet, Korallen
Hebräische Widmungsinschrift; a) am oberen Außenrand: „Dieser Tik mit der Torarolle wird gewidmet der Seele des edlen Esra Jecheskiel Josef Esra Kalif, möge seine Seele eingebunden sein im Bündel des Lebens, im Jahr 646 der kleinen Zeitrechnung" (i.e.1885/86). b) innen: „Dieser Tik mit der Torarolle wurde von Jecheskiel seinem Vater gewidmet, dem verstorbenen Esra Jecheskiel Josef Esra Kalif/Deut. 4:44, 45"
H: 93,5 cm; Dm: 25,5 cm
Inv.Nr. 045.001.003 [8]
Aufsätze: Bagdad(?)/Irak, um 1925
Silber
Hebräische Widmungsinschrift; auf Aufsatz a): „Gestiftet von Frau Chahla No'om Mizrachi", auf Aufsatz b): „Der heiligen Gemeinde Serach Bogdadai. Mein Bruder Tzalah besorgte die Stiftung."
H: 22 cm; Dm: 5,5 cm
Inv.Nr. 050.001.049

CHANUKKA-LEUCHTER
Bagdad/Irak, um 1925
Messing
H: 28 cm; B: 48,5 cm; T: 8,5 cm
Inv.Nr. 010.002.027 [9]

ILAN AROCH
Wörtlich: „Langer Baum"; Inhalt: theoretische Kabbala
Irak, 1820/21
Pergament, Tusche
Autor: Sassoon Mordechai
Kolophon: „Das ist der größte Baum im Wald ..."
H: 29,5 cm; L: 1048 cm
Inv.Nr. 028.012.009 [10]

KIDDUSCHBECHER
Mit Deckel und Unterteller
Irak, um 1925
Silber, H: 13,2 cm; Dm: 8,2 cm
Inv.Nr. 017.001.042 [11]

---

* Benjamin von Tudela/Petachja von Regensburg, Jüdische Reisen im Mittelalter, Köln 1998, S. 67

8 Zu vergleichbaren Hüllen s. Jewish Museum London, S. 17, Pl. LIII; Collection juive du musée de Cluny, S. 120; For Every Thing a Season, S. 7; Ohel Moshe, Abb. 27–29; Synagoga, Recklinghausen, C 20.

9 Zu ähnlichen Chanukka-Leuchtern vgl. Hanukkah Lamp, Nr. 165, Pl. LVIII; Chanukah Menorah, Abb. 1; Symbols, S. 30; Joodse Feestdagen, Chanoeka, S. 40; Feuchtwanger Collection, Nr. 386.

10 Bereits in dem kabbalistischen Buch Bahir, das im letzten Viertel des 12. Jhs. in Südfrankreich erschien, war vom Baum Gottes, vom Weltenbaum die Rede, der die mythische Struktur von Gottes schöpferischen Kräften widerspiegelt. Im Laufe der Zeit wird dieser Baum zum Inbegriff des theologischen Erkenntniswillens der Kabbalisten. „Aus seiner Verborgenheit heraus erscheint Gott in seinen Potenzen, im Stamm und den Ästen des theogonisch-kosmogonischen ‚Baumes', und wirkt seine Kraft in immer weiteren Sphären aus" erklärte Scholem den kabbalistischen Ilan: als System, die gesamte Schöpfung mit ihren Brüchen, dem Chaos und auch dem Nichts als in Gottes Wesen liegend zu begreifen. Der vorliegende überlange Baum versucht, dieses System zu visualisieren. Zu einem weiteren Ilan s. Le'or ha-menora, S. 129.

11 Zu diesem Kidduschbecher s. auch Sotheby's Tel Aviv, May 1987, lot 89; Jüdische Lebenswelten, Nr. 3/38.

מסתדם מאיר אברהם טייגנע
‏תשי״ד — ‏יח

Baghdad. "About forty thousand Jews live in Baghdad. Under the caliph's reign they live in safety and peace and are held in esteem. Among the Jews there are eminent sages, heads of Yeshivot, who study the Torah. There are ten Yeshivot in town."

Benjamin of Tudela, around 1170*

The history of the Jewish community in Iraq reaches back to the first forced resettlement of Israelites to Babylon 2700 years ago. The Arab conquest – thereafter the country was called "Iraq" – was well received by the Jews. At the end of the 9th century the famous academies of Sura and Pumbedita were transferred to Baghdad, the seat of the exilarch. The community prospered economically and culturally until Tamerlan's conquest of Baghdad. Thereafter, Jewish life in the city ceased to exist for a century. The Modern era brought volatile conditions for Baghdad's Jews. While they were oppressed by the Shiite Persians, their situation improved considerably under the various periods of Ottoman rule. In the 18th and 19th century the community had outstanding scholars and rabbis and had close connections to the Jews of Palestine and other countries. During World War I the relationship to the government drastically deteriorated and the British conquest was received with joy. With the onset of Iraq's independence began a period of open hostility toward Jews that further intensified after the founding of the State of Israel and was accompanied by numerous pogroms. In large operations, Israel evacuated Iraq's Jewish population. In 1947 there still lived 77,000 Jews in Baghdad, today not more than 60.

B/W Photo p. 39: Shamash of the Meir Toeg Synagogue, Baghdad, Iraq, 1989; Beth Hatefutsoth Photo Archive, Tel Aviv

Interior view of the Albert Sassoon Synagogue, Baghdad, Iraq, 1927. Ben Zvi Institute, Jerusalem/Beth Hatefutsoth Photo Archive, Tel Aviv

Innenansicht der Albert-Sassoon-Synagoge, Bagdad, Irak, 1927. Ben-Zvi-Institut, Jerusalem/Beth Hatefusoth Foto-Archiv, Tel Aviv

TORAH TIK/CASE WITH RIMMONIM/TORAH FINIALS
Tik: Baghdad/Iraq, 1885/86
Silver, parcel guilt, coral
Hebrew dedication inscription; a) around the top rim: "This tik and the Torah scroll within are dedicated to the soul of the exalted Ezra Yechezkiel Yoseph Ezra Kalif, may he rest in Eden, may his soul be bound in the bond of life, the year 646 (i.e. 1885/86) according to the minor reckoning"; b) inside: "This tik and the Torah scroll inside were dedicated by Yechezkiel for his father the deceased Ezra Yechezkiel Yosef Ezra Kalif. 'And this is the law which Moses set before the children of Israel). These are the testimonies and the statutes and the judgements'/Deut. 4:44,45."
Height: 93.5 cm; Diameter: 25.5 cm
No. 045.001.003[8]
Finials: Baghdad (?)/Iraq, c. 1925
Silver
Hebrew dedication inscription; on finial a): "Dedicated by the woman Mrs. Chalah No'om Mizrachi"; on finial b): "To the holy congregation of Serach Bogdadai. My brother Tzalah arranged their donation."
Height: 22 cm; Diameter: 5.5 cm
No. 050.001.049

HANUKKAH LAMP
Baghdad/Iraq, c. 1925
Brass; Height: 28 cm; Width: 48.5 cm; Depth: 8.5 cm
No. 010.002.027[9]

ILAN AROCH
Literally: "long tree"; theoretical Kabbalah
Iraq, 1820/21
Parchment, ink
Author: Sassoon Mordechai
Cholophon: "This is the greatest tree in the forest …"
Height: 29.5 cm; Length: 1048 cm
No. 028.012.009[10]

WINECUP
With cover and saucer
Iraq, c. 1925
Silver
Height: 13.2 cm; Diameter: 8.2 cm
No. 017.001.042[11]

* Benjamin von Tudela/Petachja von Regensburg, Jüdische Reisen im Mittelalter, Köln 1998, p. 67

8 For comparable Torah cases, see Jewish Museum London, p. 17, Pl. LIII; Collection juive du musée de Cluny, p. 120; For Every Thing a Season, p. 7; Ohel Moshe, fig. 27–29; Synagoga, Recklinghausen, C 20.

9 For similar Hanukkah lamps, cf. Hanukkah Lamp, no. 165, Pl. LVIII;Chanukah Menorah, fig. 1; Symbols, p. 30; Joodse Feestdagen, Chanoeka, p. 40; Feuchtwanger Collection, no. 386.

10 Already the kabbalistic book Bahir, published in southern France in the last quarter of the 12th c., mentions the tree of God, the tree of the world, which reflects the mythical structure of God's creative forces. In the course of time, this tree becomes the quintessence of the kabbalists' theological quest for knowledge. "Out of his hiddenness, God appears in his potencies in the trunk and the branches of the theogonic-cosmogonic 'tree' and exerts his strength in ever so far-reaching spheres," as Scholem explained the kabbalistic Ilan: as a system to understand the entire creation with its ruptures, the chaos, and also the nothingness being in God's essence. The overly long tree on hand tries to illustrate this system. For another Ilan, see Le'or ha-menora, p. 129.

11 For this wine cup, see also Sotheby's Tel Aviv, May 1987, lot 89; Jüdische Lebenswelten, no. 3/38.

DIE BINDUNG ISAAKS

Wandbehang

Jerusalem/Erez Israel, um 1900

Filz, Seidengarn

Hebräische Inschrift: „Jeden Tag soll seine Nachkommenschaft der Bindung Isaaks innig geden-
ken/Jerusalem, die Heilige Stadt/Strecke deine Hand nicht gegen den Knaben aus (1. Buch Mose,
22,12)/Jischmael, Elieser/bleibt mit dem Esel hier (1. Buch Mose, 22,5)/Hier sind Abraham, das
Feuer und die Bäume".

H: 54,8 cm; B: 81,5 cm

Inv.Nr. 003.016.001[12]

KIDDUSCHBECHER

Mit Darstellungen der Heiligen Stätten

Safed/Erez Israel, 1880/81

Silber

Hebräische Inschrift: „Elijahu Zwi, Sohn des Schmuel Leib, aus der Heiligen Stadt Jerusalem,
möge sie erbaut und errichtet werden, schnell, in unseren Tagen, amen. Im Jahr 5641 (i.e.1880/81)".

H: 7 cm; Dm: 6,1 cm

Inv.Nr. 017.001.075[13]

PIJJUTIM/LITURGISCHE POESIE

Jerusalem/Erez Israel, um 1850

Handschrift auf Papier, farbige Tusche

Schreiber: Chaim Israel Meir Mizrachi

142 Seiten

H: 18,2 cm; B: 9,6 cm; T: 1,5 cm

Inv.Nr. El.011.010[14]

CHANUKKA-LEUCHTER

Jerusalem/Israel, 1980

Silber

Künstler: Yakov Greenvurcel

H: 12 cm; B: 12cm; T: 12 cm

Inv.Nr. 010.001.005[15]

Jerusalem. „Jerusalem ist zum größten Teil desolat und in Ruinen. Seine Einwohner zählen, wie man mir berichtet, etwa 4000 Familien. Was Juden betrifft, so sind etwa siebzig Familien des ärmsten Standes verblieben."

Obadja da Bertinoro, 1487–90[*]

Nach der Zerstörung des Zweiten Tempels in Jerusalem durch die Römer im Jahr 70 d.Z. begann für die Juden die Diaspora, die Zerstreuung unter die Völker. Eine kleine jüdische Gemeinschaft blieb jedoch immer in Erez Israel, so in Jerusalem, Hebron, Safed und Tiberias. Immer wieder zogen Fromme ins Land der Väter, immer wieder kamen messianische Ideen an eine Heimkehr auf. Dementsprechend gab es immer ein jüdisch-kulturelles Leben in Palästina, getragen von einer sehr unterschiedlichen Schicht von Handwerkern bis zu Kabbalisten. Doch politisch wirksam wurde erst der Zionismus des ausgehenden 19. Jhs., der große Einwanderungswellen mit sich brachte. Als das Land nach dem Ersten Weltkrieg britisches Völkerbundmandat wurde, wuchs die Zuversicht auf die Schaffung einer jüdischen Heimstätte. Unüberwindliche Probleme wie die – aus britischer Sicht – illegalen Einwanderungen von europäischen Juden in und nach dem Zweiten Weltkrieg, die kriegerischen Auseinandersetzungen zwischen Juden und Moslems, sowie v.a. die Erkenntnisse über das Ausmaß der Schoa, ließen England das Mandat abtreten; und die UN-Vollversammlung stimmte der Gründung des Staates Israel im Mai 1948 zu.

S/W Foto S. 42: David Harris, Gebete an der Westmauer am Abend des Tisha B' Av, Jerusalem, Israel, 1979

---

* Elkan Nathan Adler (ed.), Jewish Travellers. A Treasury of Travelogues from 9 Centuries, New York 1966, S. 234

12 Abb. des Textils in: Sotheby's Tel Aviv, May 1987, lot 83.

13 Zwei vergleichbare, allerdings spätere Safed-Becher befinden sich ebenfalls in der Gross Family Collection: Inv.Nr. 017.001.037, 017.001.010. Zu dem vorliegenden Becher s. Sotheby's New York, June 1985, lot 149; Reise nach Jerusalem, Nr. 3/28; Spirit and Matter, S. 15. Zu weiteren ähnlichen Stücken s. Collector's Guide, Abb. Nr. 38, 39; Jewish Museum London, S. 405, Pl. CXIX.

14 Die meisten Pijjutim in dieser Handschrift wurden von dem damaszenischen Dichter Israel Ben Mosche Najara verfasst, der in der 2. H. des 16. und im 1. V. des 17. Jhs. lebte. Zur obigen Handschrift s. Christie's Amsterdam, December 1990, lot 446.

15 Zu weiteren Objekten von Greenvurcel s. beispielsweise Continuity and Change, Nr. 42, 71; Dort und Jetzt, Nr. 4 u. 12; Judenfragen, S. 44.

THE BINDING OF ISAAC
Textile wall hanging
Jerusalem/Eretz Israel, c. 1900
Felt, thrown silk
Hebrew inscription: "Every day his seed shall remember the binding of Isaac with compassion/
Jerusalem, the Holy City, lay not thy hand upon the lad (Genesis 22:12)/Yishmael, Eliezer, abide
ye here with the ass (Genesis 22:5)/here are Abraham, Isaac, the fire and the trees".
Height: 54.8 cm; Width: 81.5 cm
No. 003.016.001[12]

WINECUP
With representations of the Holy places
Safed/Eretz Israel, 1880/81
Silver
Hebrew inscription: "Eliyahu Tzvi, son of Shmuel Leib, from the Holy city of Jerusalem, may it be
built and established speedily in our time, amen. The year 5641 (i.e. 1880/81)".
Height: 7 cm; Diameter: 6.1 cm
No. 017.001.075[13]

PIYUTIM/LITURGICAL POETRY
Jerusalem/Eretz Israel, c. 1850
Manuscript on paper, colored ink
Scribe: Chaim Israel Meir Mizrachi
Pages: 142
Height: 18.2 cm; Width: 9.6 cm; Depth: 1.5 cm
No. El.011.010[14]

HANUKKAH LAMP
Jerusalem/Israel, 1980
Silver
Artist: Yakov Greenvurcel
Height: 12 cm; Width: 12 cm; Depth: 12 cm
No. 010.001.005[15]

Jerusalem. "Jerusalem is for the most part desolate and in ruins. Its inhabitants, I am told, number about 4000 families. As for Jews, about seventy families of the poorest class have remained."

Obadja da Bertinoro, 1487– 90*

With the destruction of the Second Temple by the Romans in 70 C.E. began
for the Jews the Diaspora, the dispersion among the nations. A small Jewish
community, however, remained in Eretz Israel at all times, such as in Jerusalem,
Hebron, Safed, and Tiberias. Time and again religious Jews moved back to the
land of their ancestors, time and again messianic ideas about a return came
up. Accordingly, there always existed a Jewish cultural life in Palestine carried
by people from various walks of society, from craftsmen to Kabbalists. However,
only Zionism in the late 19th century became politically effective, which brought
in its wake large waves of immigration. When the country came under British
League-of-Nations mandate after World War I, confidence in the establishment
of a Jewish homeland grew. But insurmountable problems arose, such as the
– from a British standpoint – illegal immigration of European Jews during and
after World War II, the violent confrontations between Jews and Moslems and,
in particular, the exposure of the Shoa's extent. Eventually, England returned
the mandate and the UN-General Assembly agreed to the establishment of the
State of Israel in may 1948.

B/W Photo p. 42: David Harris, Prayers at the Western Wall on the eve of Tisha B' Av, Jerusalem,
Israel, 1979

* Elkan Nathan Adler (ed.), Jewish Travellers. A Treasury of Travelogues from 9 Centuries, New York 1966, p. 234
12 Illustration of the textile in: Sotheby's Tel Aviv, May 1987, lot 83.
13 Two comparable, but later Safed cups are also in the Gross Family Collection: Inv. no. 017.001.037, 017.001.010. For this cup,
see Sotheby's New York, June 1985, lot 149; Reise nach Jerusalem, no. 3/28; Spirit and Matter, p. 15. For further similar items,
see Collector's Guide, fig. 38, 39; Jewish Museum London, p. 405, Pl. CXIX.
14 The Damascus poet Israel Ben Moshe Najara, who lived in the second half of the 16th c. and first quarter of the 17th c. wrote most
of the piyutim in this manuscript. For the above manuscript, see Christie's Amsterdam, December 1990, lot 446.
15 For further objects by Greenvurcel, see, for instance, Continuity and Change, no. 42, 71; Dort und Jetzt, no. 4 and 12; Judenfragen,
p. 44.

Interior of the Rabbi Yohanan ben Zakkai Synagogue, Jerusalem,
c. 1925. *Central Zionist Archives, Jerusalem/Beth Hatefutsoth
Photo Archive, Tel Aviv*

Innenansicht der Rabbi-Yohanan-ben-Zakkai-Synagoge,
Jerusalem, um 1925. *Central Zionist Archives, Jerusalem/ Beth
Hatefutsoth Foto-Archiv, Tel Aviv*

Fez. „In den Mellahs der den Europäern geöffneten Hafenstädte dürften durchschnittlich 5-7000 Juden wohnen, in Tanger, Fez und Marrakesch je 8000, und Tausende leben außerdem bei den Araberstämmen, von denen sie sich den Mezrag, d.h. den Schutz durch teures Geld erkaufen müssen."

Ernst von Hesse-Wartegg, 1907*

Mit fast 20.000 Mitgliedern stellt Marokko heute die größte jüdische Gemeinde in den arabischen Ländern. Bereits vor der Zerstörung des Zweiten Tempels siedelten hier Juden. Von wenigen Ausnahmen abgesehen, waren sie auch unter islamischer Herrschaft hier sicher und konnten frei ihre Religion ausüben. So floh beispielsweise im 12. Jh. die Familie des Maimonides vor den Almohaden nach Marokko und das Land nahm im 15./16. Jh. zahllose Flüchtlinge aus Spanien und Portugal auf. Zwar erfolgte um diese Zeit auch die Gettoisierung der Juden in Mellahs, doch lebten sie immer unter liberaleren Bedingungen als in Europa. Zur selben Zeit wurde Fez, ein wichtiges Zentrum der islamischen Welt, auch ein ökonomisches und spirituelles Zentrum der ibero-jüdischen. Die Kolonisation durch Frankreich änderte an den günstigen Bedingungen zwar im Prinzip nichts, doch förderte sie durch die Übernahme der Oberhoheit antieuropäische, antichristliche und antijüdische Ausschreitungen, die in Fez zur blutigen Zerstörung der Mellah führten, die 1925 wieder aufgebaut war. Während des Zweiten Weltkriegs verhinderte Sultan Mohammed V. die Deportation der marokkanischen Juden durch das mit Nazi-Deutschland kollaborierende Vichy-Regime. Nach der Unabhängigkeit Marokkos 1956 wurden die Juden gleichberechtigte Staatsbürger. Trotzdem verließen viele das Land. In Fez beispielsweise, wo 1951 über 12.000 Juden lebten, fand sich 1969 nur mehr eine Gemeinde von 1.000.

S/W Foto S. 45: Rose-Lynn Fisher, Fez Mellah, Marokko, 1995

ESTHER-ROLLE MIT HÜLLE
Meknes/Marokko, um 1925
Silber, Email
H: 18,7 cm; Dm: 3,2 cm
Inv.Nr. 080.001.032

SYNAGOGEN- (MEMORIAL-) LAMPE
Tanger/Marokko, 1924
Glas, goldbemalt
Chamsa-Aufhängung mit Kette:
Meknes/Marokko
Silber, emailliert
Hebräische Beschriftung: „Für den Frieden des ehrbaren Rabbi Abraham Nahon, möge er in Eden ruhen, der verstarb am 27. Tag des Monats Schewat im Jahr 724 der kleinen Zeitrechnung (i.e. 1924), möge seine Seele eingebunden sein im Bündel des Lebens."
H: 97,5 cm; Dm: 24 cm
Inv.Nr. 012.001.010[16]

CHANUKKA-LEUCHTER
Fez/Marokko, um 1930
Silber, Laubsägearbeit
H: 33 cm; B: 22 cm
Inv.Nr. 010.001.004[17]

MESUSA
Fez/Marokko, um 1930
Silber
H: 27,2 cm; B: 18,3 cm
Inv.Nr. 040.001.003[18]

* Ernst von Hesse-Wartegg, Die Juden von Marokko, in: Ost und West, 1907, S. 732

16 Zu vergleichbaren, jedoch wesentlich einfacheren Stücken s. auch: In the Paths, S. 114f.; Sotheby's London, February 1986, lot 579; Sotheby's Tel Aviv, April 1997, lot 22; Vie juive au Maroc, Nr. 42; Magic and Superstition, Nr. 130.

17 Zum Typus dieses Fez-Leuchters vgl. u.a. auch: Vie juive au Maroc, Nr. 121; Furman Collection, S. 172; Kleine Geschichte, Abb. 3; Sotheby's New York, Fine Judaica, June 1982, lot 459.

18 Vergleichsstücke u.a. in: Feuchtwanger Collection, Nr. 106; Vie juive au Maroc, Nr. 90; Jewish Life in Art and Tradition, S. 62; Sotheby's Tel Aviv, October 1993, lot 268.

Fez. "In the Mellahs of those ports that are open to the Europeans reside probably 5–7000 Jews on average, in Tangier, Fez, and Marrakech 8000 each. Besides, thousands of Jews live among the Arab tribes from whom they have to buy their mezrag, i.e., protection, dearly."

Ernst von Hesse-Wartegg, 1907*

With almost 20,000 members, Morocco has today the largest Jewish community of all the Arab countries. Jews have settled here already before the destruction of the Second Temple. Apart from a few exceptions, they were safe also under Islamic rule and were free to practice their religion. In the 12th century, for instance, the family of Maimonides escaped from the Almohads to Morocco and the country absorbed numerous refugees from Spain and Portugal in the 15th and 16th century. Although around that time began the ghettoization of the Jews in Mellahs, they still lived under more liberal conditions than in Europe. At the same time Fez – an important center of the Islamic world – became also an economic and spiritual center of the Ibero-Jewish world. French colonization principally did not change the favorable conditions, but by gaining controlling power it enhanced anti-European, anti-Christian, and anti-Jewish excesses. In Fez, the Mellah was destroyed under bloodshed, but was re-established in 1925. During Word War II Sultan Mohammed V prevented the deportation of Moroccan Jewry by the Vichy-regime, which collaborated with Nazi-Germany. After Morocco's independence in 1956, the Jews became citizens with equal rights. Nevertheless, many left the country. In Fez, for instance, where over 12,000 Jews had lived in 1951, only a community of 1,000 was left by 1969.

B/W Photo p. 45: Rose-Lynn Fisher, Fez Mellah, Morocco, 1995

Interior of the Sabah Synagogue, Fez, Morocco, c. 1920
Alex Kaufmann/Beth Hatefutsoth Photo Archive, Tel Aviv

Innenansicht der Sabah-Synagoge, Fez, Marokko, um 1920
Alex Kaufmann/Beth Hatefutsoth Foto-Archiv, Tel Aviv

ESTHER SCROLL WITH CASE
Meknes/Morocco, c. 1925
Silver, Enamel
Height: 18.7 cm; Diameter: 3.2 cm
No. 080.001.032

SYNAGOGUE (MEMORIAL) LAMP
Tangier/Morocco, 1924
Glass with gold paint
Chain with hamsah holder:
Meknes/Morocco
Silver, enamelled
Hebrew inscription: "For the repose of the honorable Rabbi Avraham Nahon, may he rest in Eden, who passed away on the 27th day of the month of Shevat, in the year 724 according to the minor reckoning (i.e. 1924), may his soul be bound up in the bond of life."
Height: 97.5 cm; Diameter: 24 cm
No. 012.001.010[16]

HANUKKAH LAMP
Fez/Morocco, c. 1930
Silver, fretwork
Height: 33 cm; Width: 22 cm
No. 010.001.004[17]

MEZUZAH
Fez/Morocco, c. 1930
Silver
Height: 27.2 cm; Width: 18.3 cm
No. 040.001.003[18]

* Ernst von Hesse-Wartegg, Die Juden von Marokko, in: Ost und West, 1907, p. 732
16 For comparable, but much simpler items, see also: In the Paths, p. 114f.; Sotheby's London, February 1986, lot 579; Sotheby's Tel Aviv, April 1997, lot 22; Vie juive au Maroc, no. 42; Magic and Superstition, no. 130.
17 For this type of Fez-lamp, cf., a.o., also: Vie juive au Maroc, no. 121; Furman Collection, p. 172; Kleine Geschichte, fig. 3; Sotheby's New York, Fine Judaica, June 1982, lot 459.
18 Comparable items, int.al., in: Feuchtwanger Collection, no. 106; Vie juive au Maroc, no. 90; Jewish Life in Art and Tradition, p. 62; Sotheby's Tel Aviv, October 1993, lot 268.

BUCHEINBAND FÜR EIN GEBETBUCH

Lemberg/Galizien, 1774/75

Silber, teilweise vergoldet

Inschrift: vorne: „Die Fünf Bücher Mose; Mose, Aharon; Zehn Gebote."

Rückseitig: „Im Jahr 535 nach der kleinen Zählung (i.e.1774/75)."

H: 14,5 cm; B: 8,5 cm; T: 5 cm

Inv.Nr. 025.001.003[19]

SEDER-TELLER

Mit der Darstellung des Auszugs aus Ägypten und den Illustrationen zu den zehn Plagen

Lemberg/Galizien, um 1805

Silber, teilweise vergoldet

H: 24,3 cm; B: 34,3 cm

Inv.Nr. 022.001.004[20]

BSAMIM-/GEWÜRZTURM

Lemberg/Galizien, um 1780

Silberfiligran

H: 38 cm; B: 10 cm

Inv.Nr. 015.001.001[21]

HÜLLE FÜR EINE ESTHER-ROLLE

Mit reichem, für Galizien typischem Dekor

Lemberg/Galizien, um 1800

Silber, teilweise vergoldet

L: 24 cm; Dm: 4,8 cm

Inv.Nr. 080.001.013[22]

Lemberg. „In Lemberg sind die Juden unter sich. Sie sind achtzigtausend gegen zweihunderttausend Polen. Das polnische Lemberg ist eine hübsche Stadt. Doch wir sind wegen des anderen Lemberg hier. Es liegt genau am anderen Ende der Legionenallee, hinter dem Theater, der Grenzstein. Das Leben, das sie dort führen ist infernalisch. Alle hoffen auf Flucht."

Albert Londres, 1929*

Erste Spuren jüdischer Siedlungen in Lemberg gehen auf byzantinische Zeit zurück. Sehr früh entwickelte sich Lemberg zu einem wichtigen Handelszentrum und einer Drehscheibe zwischen Orient und Okzident. Mit der Eroberung der Stadt durch den polnischen König Kasimir III. im Jahr 1340 kamen zahlreiche Juden aus Deutschland und Böhmen nach Lemberg. Im 14. Jahrhundert bestanden in Lemberg zwei jüdische Gemeinden, eine innerhalb und eine außerhalb der Stadtmauern, die jeweils eine separate Verwaltung hatten und nur den Friedhof miteinander teilten. Schwer getroffen wurden die Lemberger Juden durch den Kosakenaufstand des Jahres 1648, als Chmielnitzkis Truppen brandschatzend und mordend durch die polnischen Städte und Dörfer zogen. Nach den polnischen Teilungen gegen Ende des 18. Jahrhunderts fielen Galizien und seine Hauptstadt Lemberg an die Österreichisch-Ungarische Monarchie. In der österreichischen Zeit wuchs die jüdische Bevölkerung der Stadt auf über 57.000 an, doch die Zeit relativer Ruhe und Prosperität war nicht von langer Dauer. Der Ausbruch des Ersten Weltkriegs führte zu einer massenhaften Flüchtlingsbewegung in Galizien, und nach 1918 gerieten die Lemberger Juden ins Kreuzfeuer zwischen ukrainischen und polnischen Truppen, die um die Vorherrschaft in Galizien kämpften. Beim Pogrom im November 1918 wurden allein in Lemberg mehr als 70 Juden ermordet. 1941 eroberten die Deutschen die Stadt und begannen mit der systematischen Vernichtung der jüdischen Bevölkerung. Nur wenige Lemberger Juden erlebten die Befreiung der Stadt durch die Sowjetarmee. Heute ist die jüdische Gemeinde in Lemberg verschwindend klein.

* Albert Londres, Ahasver ist angekommen. Eine Reise zu den Juden im Jahre 1929, München 1998, S. 112–113

19 Zu vergleichbaren galizianischen Einbänden s. Jewish Ceremonial Art, Nr. 177; Jewish Life in Art and Tradition, S. 62; Furman Collection, S. 220.

20 Abb. dieses Tellers in: The Jews and Europe, S. 137. Zu einem Vergleichsstück s. Stieglitz Collection, Nr. 211.

21 Zu diesem Turm s. Zwischen Ost und West, S. 142f.

22 Zur typisch jüdisch-galizischen Formensprache allg. s. Yiddishe Folks-Ornament. Zu diesem Objekt s. Zwischen Ost und West, S. 140f.

S/W Foto S. 48: Andrzej Polec, Alte jüdische Dame aus Lemberg, 2000

BOOK COVER FOR A PRAYER BOOK

Lemberg/Galicia, 1774/75

Silver, parcel gilt

Hebrew inscription: Front: "The Five Books of Moses; Moshe; Aaron; Ten Commandments."

Back: "In the year 535, according to the minor reckoning (i.e. 1774/75)."

Height: 14.5 cm; Width: 8.5 cm; Depth: 5 cm

No. 025.001.003 [19]

PASSOVER PLATE

With the depiction of the exodus from Egypt and the depiction of the ten plagues

Lemberg/Galicia, c. 1805

Silver, parcel gilt

Height: 24.3 cm; Width: 34.3 cm

No. 022.001.004 [20]

B'SAMIM/SPICE-TOWER

Lemberg/Galicia, c. 1780

Silver filigree

Height: 38 cm; Width: 10 cm

No. 015.001.001 [21]

CASE FOR ESTHER SCROLL

With elaborate typically Galician ornamentation

Lemberg/Galicia, c. 1800

Silver, parcel gilt

Length: 24 cm; Diameter: 4.8 cm

No. 080.001.013 [22]

Lemberg. "In Lemberg the Jews are among themselves. They number eighty thousand against two hundred thousand Poles. Polish Lemberg is a charming city. However, we came for the other Lemberg. It is exactly at the opposite end of the Legionenallee, behind the theater – the boundary stone. The life they lead there is hell. Everybody hopes for escape."

Albert Londres, 1929*

The first traces of Jewish settlements in Lemberg go back to Byzantine times. Early on Lemberg developed into an important center of commerce and became a meeting point for Orient and Occident. In the wake of the city's conquest by the Polish king Kasimir III in 1340, many Jews from Germany and Bohemia came to Lemberg. Two Jewish communities existed in Lemberg in the 14th century, one inside and one outside the city walls. Each had a separate administration and they just shared a common cemetery. In 1648 the Jews of Lemberg were severely hit by the uprising of the Cossacks when Chmielnitzki's troops roamed through Polish towns and villages, pillaging and murdering. After the Polish partitions toward the end of the 18th century, Galicia and its capital Lemberg fell to the Austro-Hungarian Monarchy. During the Austrian period the city's Jewish population grew to over 57,000, but the time of relative peace and prosperity was brief. The outbreak of World War I brought about throngs of refugees in Galicia. After 1918, the Lemberg Jews came under cross fire from Ucranian and Polish troops, who fought for predominance in Galicia. During the pogrom in November 1918, seventy Jews were murdered in Lemberg alone. The Germans conquered the city in 1941 and started with the systematic annihilation of the Jewish population. Just a few Lemberg Jews lived to see the liberation of the city by the Soviet army. Today, only a tiny Jewish community exists in Lemberg.

B/W Photo p. 48: Andrzej Polec, Old Jewish Lady from Lemberg, 2000

* Albert Londres, Ahasver ist angekommen. Eine Reise zu den Juden im Jahre 1929, München 1998, p. 112–113

19 For comparable Galician covers, see Jewish Ceremonial Art, no. 177; Jewish Life in Art and Tradition, p. 62; Furman Collection, p. 220.

20 Illustration of this plate in: The Jews and Europe, p. 137. For a comparable item, see Stieglitz Collection, no. 211.

21 For this tower, see Zwischen Ost und West, p. 142f.

22 For typical Jewish-Galician forms in general, see Yiddishe Folks-Ornament. For this object, see Zwischen Ost und West, p. 140f.

The synagogue on Boznicza/Sans'ka, which was burnt in the November Pogroms 1918, Lemberg, Ucraine. *Historic Museum Vienna*

Die beim Pogrom im November 1918 verbrannte Synagoge in der Boznicza/Sans'ka, Lemberg, Ukraine. *Historisches Museum Wien*

Sanaa. „Plötzlich sehen wir im Glanz der Abendsonne das weiße Sanaa vor uns liegen, unvergleichlich schön und anmutig. Ich sehe auch schon, daß eine Menge zerlumpter Juden auf uns zukommt. Trotz ihres Elends, ihres kläglichen Aussehens kann ich nicht finden, daß die Leute wie die Wilden sind. Im Gegenteil!"

Jomtob Semach, 1910*

Wie die Bibel berichtet, soll es bereits zu Zeiten Salomos Kontakte zwischen Israel und dem Jemen gegeben haben. Belegt ist eine jüdische Ansiedlung im Jemen seit dem 3. Jahrhundert d.Z. durch verschiedene archäologische Funde. Um 400 soll der König der Chima, die einen Großteil Südarabiens kontrollierten, mit seinem Volk zum Judentum konvertiert sein, was die starke Präsenz von Juden im Jemen erklärbarer machen würde. Im ersten Viertel des 6. Jahrhunderts soll diese jüdische Herrschaft geendet haben. Die Juden des Jemen hatten enge Kontakte zur irakischen Gemeinde. Insbesondere von Sanaa aus wurden die irakisch-babylonischen Akademien unterstützt. Durch die Verlagerung der rabbinischen Zentren wurde später der Kontakt nach Fostat enger. Obwohl es einige Vertreibungen aus Sanaa gab, besaß das jüdische Viertel an die 30 Bethäuser und obwohl die Juden als „Dhimmis" diskriminiert waren, zählte die jüdische Gemeinde 1948 hier 6.000 Personen. Die Auswanderungswilligen wurden in mehreren Aktionen, von denen die berühmteste die „Operation Magic Carpet" war, nach Israel geholt. 1968 lebten in Sanaa noch 150 Juden. Da sie unter einer sehr restriktiven Politik leben müssen, hat sich ihre Zahl weiter verringert.

S/W Foto S. 51: Zion Ozeri, Haidan Ash-Sham, Jemen, 1992

TALLIT/GEBETSSCHAL
Jemen, 1947
Baumwolle, mehrfarbig
Eingewebt auf arabisch: „Elias Lemama (?)"
L: 248 cm; B: 105 cm
Inv.Nr. 047.015.001[23]

BUCHEINBAND IN SCHATULLENFORM
Sanaa/Jemen, 1937
Bemaltes Textil, Silber, vergoldet
Eingebundene Handschrift: Gebetbuch, ausgeführt von dem Schreiber Shalom Karach
H: 27 cm; B: 20 cm; T: 3,1 cm
Inv.Nr. 025.001.021

RIMMONIM/TORA-AUFSÄTZE
Sanaa/Jemen, um 1900
Silberfiligran, teilweise vergoldet, Glasperlen
Hebräische Inschrift: „Keter Tora" (Krone der Tora)
H: 38,5 cm; Dm: 5 cm
Inv.Nr. 050.001.002[24]

CHUMASCH-HANDSCHRIFT/DIE FÜNF BÜCHER MOSE
(unvollständig)
Jemen, um 1500
Papier, Tusche, Wasserfarben; jemenitischer Schriftduktus, illuminiert, Massora-Ornamentik
149 Seiten
H: 25 cm; B: 19 cm; T: 3,5 cm
Inv.Nr. YM.011.054

* Jomtob Semach, Eine Alliance-Expedition nach dem Yemen, in: Ost und West, Jahrgang X, 1910, S. 390–391
23 Vergleichsstücke: Jewish Folk Art, S. 67; The Yemenites, S. 78, Nr. 2.
24 Abb. der Aufsätze in: Pe'amim Nr. 85, S. 11; zu vergleichbaren Rimmonim s. Pe'amim Nr. 11, S. 4; Crowning Glory, Nr. 371; Yemenite Jewry, Poster Nr. 10; zu solchen, die in Israel von jemenitischen Silberschmieden gearbeitet werden, s. Stieglitz Collection, Nr. 18; Art and Tradition, Nr. 87.

Sana'a. "All of a sudden we see, drenched in the glow of the evening sun, white Sana'a spreading out in front of us – supremely beautiful and enchanting. I can already see a number of ragged Jews approaching us. Their misery, their lamentable appearances notwithstanding, I am unable to conceive of these people as savages. On the contrary!"

Yomtov Semach, 1910*

According to the Bible, contacts between Israel and Yemen have existed already during Solomon's time. A Jewish settlement in Yemen is documented since the 3rd century C.E. through various archeological findings. Around 400, the king of the Chima, who controlled a large part of southern Arabia, is supposed to have converted to Judaism together with his people, which would explain the strong presence of Jews in Yemen. Supposedly in the first quarter of the 6th century this Jewish rule came to an end. Yemenite Jews were in close contact with the Iraqi community. The community in Sana'a, in particular, supported the Iraqi-Babylonian academies. Later, when the rabbinical centers shifted, the contact to Fostat became closer. Although there were some expulsions from Sana'a, the Jewish quarter had almost thirty houses of prayer and although the Jews were discriminated as Dhimmis, the Jewish community here numbered 6,000 persons in 1948. Those prepared to emigrate were brought to Israel in several operations, the most famous of them being "Operation Magic Carpet." In 1968, 150 Jews were still living in Sana'a. Since they have to live under severe restrictions, their number has been further decreasing.

B/W Photo p. 51: Zion Ozeri, Haidan Ash-Sham, Yemen, 1992

The Damari Synagogue, Sana'a, Yemen, c. 1930
Hermann Burchardt, Museum of Ethnography, Hamburg/Beth Hatefutsoth Photo Archive, Tel Aviv

Die Damari Synagoge, Sana'a, Jemen, um 1930
Hermann Burchardt, Museum für Völkerkunde Hamburg/Beth Hatefutsoth Foto-Archiv, Tel Aviv

TALLIT/PRAYER SHAWL
Yemen, 1947
Cotton, colored threads
Interwoven in Arabic: "Elias Lemamah (?)"
Length: 248 cm; Width: 105 cm
No. 047.015.001[23]

BOX-SHAPED COVER FOR A MANUSCRIPT
Sana'a/Yemen, 1937
Painted cloth, silver, gilt
Manuscript inside: prayer book written by the scribe Shalom Karach
Height: 27 cm; Width: 20 cm; Depth: 3.1 cm
No. 025.001.021

RIMMONIM/TORAH FINIALS
Sana'a/Yemen, c. 1900
Silver filigree, parcel gilt, glass beads
Hebrew inscription: "Keter Torah" (crown of the Torah)
Height: 38.5 cm; Diameter: 5 cm
No. 050.001.002[24]

PENTATEUCH MANUSCRIPT
(incomplete)
Yemen, c. 1500
Paper, ink, watercolors; Yemenite script, illuminated, Massorah ornamentations
Pages: 149
Height: 25 cm; Width: 19 cm; Depth: 3.5 cm
No. YM.001.054

*   Jomtob Semach, Eine Alliance-Expedition nach dem Yemen, in: Ost und West, Jahrgang X, 1910, p. 390–391
23 Comparable items: Jewish Folk Art, p. 67; The Yemenites, p. 78, no. 2.
24 Illustration of the finials in: Pe'amim no. 85, p. 11; for comparable rimmonim, see Pe'amim no. 11, p. 4; Crowning Glory, no. 371; Yemenite Jewry, poster no. 10; for those that are manufactured in Israel by Yemenite silversmiths, see Stieglitz Collection, no. 18; Art and Tradition, no. 87.

SEFER JOSIPPON
Gedruckt in Frankfurt a.M./Deutschland, 1706/07
Illustrierte Ausgabe in jiddischer Sprache, vermutlich für eine weibliche Leserschaft
Herausgeber: Zeligman Reiss
Originaler Ledereinband
H: 17,5 cm; B: 11 cm; T: 6,5 cm
Inv.Nr. B. 1497 [25]

TAS/TORASCHILD MIT JAD/TORAZEIGER
Frankfurt a.M./Deutschland, 1904
Künstler: Leo Horovitz
Tas: Silber, teilweise vergoldet
Hebräische Inschrift: „Nicht durch Macht, nicht durch Kraft, allein durch meinen Geist!"
(Zacharia 4,6)
H: 26,3 cm; B: 31,8 cm
Inv.Nr. 051.001.035
Jad: Silber, teilweise vergoldet
L: 24 cm; Dm: 3 cm
Inv.Nr. 052.001.061 [26]

CHANUKKA-LEUCHTER
Frankfurt a.M./Deutschland, 1924
Messing, Patina
Künstler: Ludwig Yehuda Wolpert
H: 34 cm; B: 38 cm
Inv.Nr. 010.002.045 [27]

HAWDALA-KOMPENDIUM
(Kombination von einem Gewürzbehältnis und einem Kerzenhalter für die Hawdala-Zeremonie)
Frankfurt a.M./Deutschland, um 1775
Silber
Künstler: Johann Jacob Leschhorn
H: 23,9 cm; Dm: 9,1 cm
Inv.Nr. 015.001.053 [28]

Frankfurt. „Die Frankfurter Jüdische Gemeinde besaß Gewicht und Charakter. In ihr aufzuwachsen, bewahrte einen vor Minderwertigkeitskomplexen. Es war die Welt einer gesicherten jüdischen Gemeinschaft, die sich verwurzelt und stark fühlte und nicht daran dachte, ihr Judentum zu verleugnen."

Nachum Goldmann, um 1920[*]

Die Geschichte der jüdischen Gemeinde Frankfurt am Main reicht bis ins 12. Jahrhundert zurück. Neben den Verfolgungen der Jahre 1241 und 1349 kam es zu einem der schwersten Pogrome im Zusammenhang mit dem Fettmilch-Aufstand Anfang des 17. Jahrhunderts. Seit der Mitte des 15. Jahrhunderts siedelte die Gemeinde in der „Judengasse", aus der das Getto entstand. Erst 1864 wurde den Juden die bürgerliche Gleichstellung gewährt. Zum bekanntesten Exponenten der Emanzipation in Frankfurt wurde Ludwig Börne. Einer der bedeutendsten Frankfurter Rabbiner des 19. Jahrhunderts war Samson Raphael Hirsch, der die neoorthodoxe „Israelitische Religionsgesellschaft" gründete und später die Anerkennung der Austrittsgemeinde durchsetzen konnte. Seine Gegenspieler waren der nicht weniger bedeutende Reformer Abraham Geiger und der liberale Rabbiner Leopold Stein. Zahlreiche philanthropische Einrichtungen wurden gegründet, die meisten unterstützt von der Familie Rothschild. 1920 richtete Franz Rosenzweig das Institut für Jüdische Studien ein. 30.000 Mitglieder zählte die Gemeinde im Jahr 1925. 1941, als die Deportationen nach Lodz, Minsk, Riga und Theresienstadt begannen, hatten zwei Drittel von ihr die Stadt verlassen können. 1943 war ihre Zahl brutal auf 600 reduziert worden. 1945 gründete sich eine neue jüdische Gemeinde in Frankfurt, die bis in die neunziger Jahre auf mehr als 1.000 Personen angewachsen war.

S/W Foto S. 53: Martin Kohlbauer, Alte Oper Frankfurt am Main, Deutschland, 2000

[*] Nahum Goldmann, Mein Leben als Deutscher und Jude, Frankfurt am Main / Berlin / Wien 1983, S. 45

[25] Das Sefer (Buch) Josippon gehört zur Gattung der erzählenden jüdischen Geschichtsschreibung. Der Verfasser des im Original hebräisch verfassten Werkes ist anonym, etliches weist jedoch darauf hin, dass es in Italien verfasst wurde. Als historische Hauptquellen wurden die Arbeiten des Flavius Josephus verwendet sowie die Apokryphen, weiters verschiedene frühmittelalterliche Chroniken. Im 14. Jh. edierte Juda Leon Mosconi das Werk mit weiteren Zusätzen. Diese Ausgabe wurde Grundlage für alle folgenden. In zahlreiche Sprachen übersetzt war der Josippon bis zum Beginn der Neuzeit für Viele eine der wichtigsten historischen Quellen.

[26] Zum Künstler Leo Horovitz, Sohn des Frankfurter Rabbiners Marcus Horovitz, s. Der Bildhauer Leo Horovitz; Moderne israelitische Kunst, Abb. 33–38; German Jewish Heritage, S. 114f. Zu dem vorliegenden Schild s. Synagogale Kunst, Leo Horovitz, Abb. VII; In the Light of the Menorah, Abb. 6; Jewish Home, S. 14. Weitere Judaica von Horovitz auch in: Zedaka, A36; Feast of Freedom, S. 50, Abb.18; Christie's New York, October 1982, lot 47; Sotheby's London, February 1987, lot 244, 248; Sotheby's New York, December 1986, lot 244.

[27] Zu Wolpert s. Wolpert. A Retrospective; Sermon in Metal; Jüdische Kunst, S. 178f., Abb. 74 u. 75. Zu Schabbat-Leuchtern des Künstlers, nach der erzwungenen Emigration gefertigt, s. Index, Gross Family Collection No. 012.001.004, hier im Katalog mit weiteren Hinweisen.

[28] Zum Künstler s. Scheffler, Hessen, S. 312, Nr. 480. Ähnliche Frankfurter Kompendien u.a. in: Jewish Ceremonial Art and Religious Observance, Abb. 111; Parke Bernet New York, November 1955, lot 90; Sotheby's New York, December 1988, lot 238. Zur Stadt-Punze s. Scheffler, Hessen, S. 54, Nr. 145.

SEFER YOSIPPON
Printed in Frankfurt a.M./Germany, 1706/07
Illustrated edition in Yiddish, probably for female readers
Publisher: Zeligman Reiss
Original leather binding
Height: 17.5 cm; Width: 11 cm; Depth: 6.5 cm
No. B.1497[25]

TAS/TORAH SHIELD WITH TORAH POINTER
Frankfurt a.M./Germany, 1904
Artist: Leo Horovitz
Shield: Silver, parcel gilt
Hebrew Inscription: "Not by might nor by power but by my spirit" (Zech. 4:6)
Height: 26.3 cm; Width: 31.8 cm
No. 051.001.035
Pointer: Silver, parcel gilt
Length: 24 cm; Diameter: 3 cm
No. 052.001.061[26]

HANUKKAH LAMP
Frankfurt a.M./Germany, 1924
Brass, patina
Artist: Ludwig Yehuda Wolpert
Height: 34 cm; Width: 38 cm
No. 010.002.045[27]

HAVDALAH SET
(combining a spice box and a candle holder for the kindling of the light in the havdala ceremony)
Frankfurt a.M./Germany, c. 1775
Silver
Artist: Johann Jacob Leschhorn
Height: 23.9 cm; Diameter: 9.1 cm
No. 015.001.053[28]

Frankfurt. "The Frankfurt Jewish community had weight and character. To grow up in it prevented from developing inferiority complexes. This was the world of a secured Jewish community that deemed itself rooted and strong and that did not even think of denying its Jewishness."

Nahum Goldmann, c. 1920*

55

The history of the Jewish community in Frankfurt am Main reaches back to the 12th century. Besides the persecutions of 1241 and 1349, one of the most severe pogroms occurred in connection with the Fettmilch-uprising at the beginning of the 17th century. Since the mid-15th century, the community lived in the Judengasse (street of the Jews), which eventually became the ghetto. Only in 1864 the Jews were granted equal civil rights. One of the best known representatives of Emancipation became Ludwig Börne. Samson Raphael Hirsch, a preeminent Frankfurt rabbi in the 19th century, founded the neo-orthodox "Israelitische Religionsgesellschaft" (Israelite religious society), but was later unable to obtain recognition for the secessionist congregation. His opponents were the equally important reformer Abraham Geiger and the liberal rabbi Leopold Stein. Numerous philanthropic institutions were founded, most of them with the support of the Rothschild family. Franz Rosenzweig established the Institute of Jewish Studies. In 1925 the community numbered 30,000 members. By 1941, when the deportations to Lodz, Minsk, Riga, and Theresienstadt began, two thirds of them had been able to leave the city. By 1943 their number was brutally reduced to 600. A new Jewish community was founded in Frankfurt in 1945, which had increased to over 1,000 persons by the 1990s.

B/W Photo p. 53: Martin Kohlbauer, Old Opera, Frankfurt am Main, Germany, 2000

* Nahum Goldmann, Mein Leben als Deutscher und Jude, Frankfurt am Main/Berlin/Wien 1983, p. 45
25 The sefer (book) Yosippon belongs to the genre of narrative Jewish historiography. The author of this work, originally written in Hebrew, is anonymous. But there are indications that it was written in Italy. The works of Flavius Josephus as well as the Apocrypha and also various chronicles from the Early Middle Ages were the main historic sources used. Juda Leon Mosconi edited this work in the 14th c. with further additions. It became the basis for all the following editions. Translated into numerous languages, the Yossipon became for many one of the most important historical sources until the onset of the Modern era.
26 For artist Leo Horovitz, son of the Frankfurt rabbi Marcus Horovitz, see: Der Bildhauer Leo Horovitz, fig. 33–38; German Jewish Heritage, p. 114f. For shield and pointer on hand, see Synagogale Kunst, Leo Horovitz, fig. VII; In the Light of the Menorah, fig. 6; Jewish Home, p. 14. Further Judaica by Horovitz also in: Zedaka, A36; Feast of Freedom, p. 50, fig.18; Christie's New York, October 1982, lot 47; Sotheby's London, February 1987, lot 244, 248; Sotheby's New York, December 1986, lot 244.
27 On Wolpert, see Wolpert. A Retrospective; Sermon in Metal; Jüdische Kunst, p. 178f., fig. 74 and 75. For Shabbat lamps by the artist, manufactured after the forced emigration, see Index, Gross Family Collection, no. 012.001.004, in this catalogue with further remarks.
28 For artist, see Scheffler, Hessen, p. 312, no. 480. Similar Frankfurt compendiums, int. al., in: Jewish Ceremonial Art and Religious Observance, fig. 111; Parke Bernet New York, November 1955, lot 90; Sotheby's New York, December 1988, lot 238. On city-hall-mark, see Scheffler, Hessen, p. 54, no. 145.

Synagogue at the Friedberger grounds, Frankfurt am Main, c. 1910. *Postcard, Jewish Museum Vienna, Collection Stern*

Synagoge an der Friedberger Anlage, Frankfurt am Main, um 1910. *Postkarte, Jüdisches Museum Wien, Sammlung Stern*

Kuba. „Die Juden hier sind arm aber nicht unzufrieden. Ihr Minhag ist der des italienischen gedruckten Gebetbuches. Aber sie erfreuen sich der stolzen Auszeichnung, von den Russen als ‚gorskische‘ oder ‚Bergjuden‘ angesehen zu werden. Baku ist ihr Hauptquartier, und sie haben Gemeinden und Synagogen nicht nur hier und in Petrowsk, Derbend und Grosnyi, sondern auch in Kuba und Bakuba.“

E.N. Adler, um 1890*

Jüdische Siedlungen in Aserbaijan hat es wohl gegeben, seit Juden in Persien leben. Belegt ist ihre Präsenz allerdings erst mit dem 12. Jahrhundert. Die jüdischen Bewohner des später russischen Teils Aserbaijans und Daghestans werden mit einem Begriff, der aus der Zeit der Annexion dieser Gebiete durch das Zarenreich stammt, als „Bergjuden“ bezeichnet. Sie selbst nennen sich Juhur. Sprachlich (Judeo-Tat) sind sie dem westiranischen Raum zuzurechnen. Ihre wichtigsten Siedlungszentren in Aserbaijan sind Baku und vor allem Kuba. In Daghestan sind es Derbent, Makhachkalah und Buynaksk. Eine beträchtliche Zahl von „Bergjuden“ lebt auch außerhalb Aserbaijans und Daghestans in Nalchik und Grosny. Die Einwanderung von Juden aus Persien und aus zum byzantinischen Reich gehörigen Gebieten nach Aserbaijan dürfte mit der arabischen Invasion begonnen haben. Unter dem Druck von Turkstämmen scheinen „Bergjuden“ nach Daghestan ausgewichen zu sein, wo sie in Kontakt mit Khazaren kamen, die schon im 8. Jahrhundert das Judentum angenommen hatten. Als in der zweiten Hälfte des 18. Jahrhunderts Russland, Persien, die Türkei und lokale Machthaber um die Herrschaft in der Region rangen, gerieten die „Bergjuden“ zwischen die Fronten, und eine längere Periode relativen Friedens und Wohlstandes war damit zu Ende. Den Drangsalierungen durch islamische Machthaber und russische Autoritäten folgten die sowjetrussischen Bestrebungen, die jüdische Identität der Juhur auszulöschen. Ihre Zahl wurde für das Jahr 1970 auf 50.000 bis 70.000 geschätzt. Seit den achtziger Jahren sind mindestens 30.000 von ihnen hauptsächlich nach Israel ausgewandert.

S/W Foto S. 57: Michael Keyfets, Kaukasus, Kuba, Aserbaijan, 1989

RIMMONIM/TORA-AUFSÄTZE
Madjelis/Daghestan/Aserbaijan, um 1900
Silber, Niello
Hebräische Stiftungsinschrift: „Dies sind die Tora-Aufsätze des Elkana, Sohn von … Schlomo … Menjelis, möge Er unsere Stadt wiedererrichten, amen.“
H: 29 cm; Dm: 10 cm
Inv.Nr. 050.001.068[29]

PRAKTISCHE KABBALA
Kuba/Aserbaijan, 1861–1866
Handschrift auf Papier, Tusche, Wasserfarbe; mit Illustrationen von Amuletten und magischen Formeln
67 Seiten
Kolophon (S. 20): „Der junge Schreiber Ruben, Sohn des ehrbaren Rabbi Abraham, möge sein Fels und Erlöser ihn beschützen, schrieb bis hierher die Absätze der Goralot des weisen Josef Chaim, möge sein Fels und Erlöser ihn beschützen, Einwohner der heiligen Stadt Tiberias. Möge Er seine Stadt bauen, möge sie rasch gebaut und errichtet werden in unserer Zeit, amen; im Jahr 621 (i.e. 1861) … Kuba. Möge sie rasch gebaut und errichtet werden in unserer Zeit, amen.“
H: 20,7 cm; B: 16,7 cm. T: 0,8 cm
Inv.Nr. AZB.011.001[30]

JAD/TORA-ZEIGER
Kuba/Aserbaijan, 1923/24
Silber, Karneol
Hebräische Widmungsinschrift: „Für das Licht der Tora ist dies gestiftet, im Andenken und zur Erlösung der Seele des jungen Mannes, Rafael, Sohn unseres Lehrers Elkana, möge er in Eden ruhen. Dieser silberne Zeiger (das hier verwendete hebr. ‚etzba‘ ist eigentlich ‚Finger‘) ist gestiftet und gewidmet der Erlösung der Seele des jungen Mannes, der getötet wurde im Krieg zwischen Soldaten, … der ehrbare Rafael, Sohn von Elkana, möge er in Eden ruhen. Möge der Herr sein Blut diesen Tag rächen. Josef, Sohn des guten David Lematmeonim (?), im Jahr … 684 der kleinen Zeitrechnung (i.e. 1923/24).“[31]
L: 26,5 cm; B: 3,7 cm
Inv.Nr. 052.001.067[32]

* Elkan Nathan Adler, Von Ghetto zu Ghetto. Reisen und Beobachtungen von Elkan Nathan Adler, Stuttgart 1909, S. 125–126

29 Zu zwei fast identischen Aufsätzen s. 50 Rimmonim, S. 7; Sotheby's Tel Aviv, October 1993, lot 234. Ein sehr ähnliches Paar aus Tiflis in: Sotheby's New York, December 1987, lot 313.

30 Der Begriff „Kabbala“ bedeutet ursprünglich einfach „Überlieferung“ und bezeichnete ganz allgemein die traditionelle religiöse Überlieferung. Erst im Mittelalter, als das Sefer ha-Bahir und der Zohar als Hauptwerke einer neuen esoterisch-mystischen Theologie verfasst wurden, erhielt der Begriff die Bedeutung einer verborgenen Geheimlehre. Im südfranzösisch-katalonischen Raum seine Anfänge habend, dehnte sich das aktive Interesse an der Kabbala bis zur Neuzeit über ganz Europa und den Vorderen Orient aus. Man unterscheidet zwischen theoretischer und praktischer Kabbala. Während die theoretische Kabbala nach höheren theologisch-philosophischen Erkenntniszusammenhängen sucht, ist die praktische Kabbala von volkstümlichem Charakter und hatte großen Einfluss sowohl auf die verschiedenen messianischen Bewegungen als auch auf den modernen Chassidismus.

31 Der Text lässt vermuten, dass der junge Mann während des russischen Bürgerkrieges umgekommen ist.

32 Abb. des vorliegenden Stückes in: Judaica Jerusalem, March 1994, lot 363. Zu einem weiteren Zeiger aus Kuba s. Mirror of Jewish Life, Nr. 42.

Kuba. "The Jews here are poor but not necessarily discontent. Their minhag follows the Italian printed prayer book. But they delight in the proud honor to be regarded as 'Gorsk' Jews or 'Mountain Jews' by the Russians. With Baku as their center, they have communities and synagogues not only here and in Petrowsk, Derbend, and Groznyj, but also in Kuba and Bakuba."

E.N. Adler, c. 1890*

Jewish settlements seem to have existed in Azerbaijan since Jews have lived in Persia. However, their presence is documented only from the 12th century. The Jewish inhabitants of the later on Russian parts of Azerbaijan and Daghestan are called "Mountain Jews," a term that originates from the time when czarist Russia annexed these areas. The Jews call themselves Juhur. Linguistically (Judeo-Tat) they belong to the west Iranian region. Their main centers of settlement in Azerbaijan are Baku and, in particular, Kuba. In Daghestan these are Derbend, Makhachkalah, and Buynaksk. A significant number of "Mountain Jews" also lives outside of Azerbaijan and Daghestan, in Nalchik and Grosnyi. The immigration of Jews from Persia and from parts of the Byzantine Empire to Azerbaijan started probably with the Arab invasion. It seems that under the pressure of Turkic tribes, "Mountain Jews" retreated to Daghestan where they came in touch with Khazares who had converted to Judaism already in the 8th century. When in the second half of the 18th century, Russia, Persia, Turkey, and local rulers fought over control of the region, the "Mountain Jews" got between all the fronts and thus, a rather long period of peace and prosperity ended. The harassments of Islamic rulers and Russian authorities were followed by Soviet attempts to eradicate the Jewish identity of the Juhur. Their estimated number for 1970 is between 50,000 to 70,000 persons. Since the 1980s, at least 30,000 of them have emigrated, mainly to Israel.

B/W Photo p. 57: Michael Keyfets, Caucasus, Kuba, Azerbaijan, 1989

The synagogue of Kuba, Azerbaijan, early 20th century. *Postcard, Beth Hatefutsoth Photo Archive, Tel Aviv*

Die Synagoge von Kuba, Aserbaijan, Anfang 1900. *Postkarte, Beth Hatefutsoth Foto-Archiv, Tel Aviv*

RIMMONIM/TORAH FINIALS

Madjelis/Daghestan/Azerbaijan, c. 1900

Silver, Niello

Hebrew inscription: "These are the Torah finials of Elkanah son of … Shlomo … Menjelis, may he rebuild our city, amen".

Height: 29 cm; Diameter: 10 cm

No. 050.001.068 [29]

BOOK OF PRACTICAL KABBALAH

Kuba/Azerbaijan, 1861–1866

Manuscript on paper, ink, water color; illustrations of charms and amulets

Pages: 67

Colophon (p. 20): "The young scribe, Reuven, son of the honorable Rabbi Avraham, may his rock and redeemer protect him, wrote the paragraphs of the Goralot by the wise Yoseph Haim, may his rock and redeemer protect him, citizen of the holy city of Tiberias, may He build His city, may it be built and established speedily in our time, amen, the year 621 (i.e. 1861) … Kuba, may it be built and established speedily in our time, amen."

Height: 20.7 cm; Width: 16.7 cm; Depth: 0.8 cm

No. AZB. 011.001 [30]

YAD/TORAH POINTER

Kuba/Azerbaijan, 1923/24

Silver, Carnelian

Hebrew Inscription: "For the light of the Torah, this is dedicated to the memory and salvation of the soul of the young man, Rafael, son of our teacher Elkanah, may he rest in Eden. This silver Torah pointer ('etzba') is dedicated and presented for the salvation of the soul of the young man, killed in the war between soldiers, … the eminent Rafael, son of Elkanah, may he rest in Eden. May the Lord avenge his blood this day. Yosef, son of the dear David Lematmeonim (?), the year 684 (i.e. 1923/24) according to the minor reckoning." [31]

Length: 26.5 cm; Width: 3.7 cm,

No. 052.001.067 [32]

* Elkan Nathan Adler, Von Ghetto zu Ghetto. Reisen und Beobachtungen von Elkan Nathan Adler, Stuttgart 1909, p. 125–126

29 For two almost identical finials, see 50 Rimmonim, p. 7; Sotheby's Tel Aviv, October 1993, lot 234. A very similar pair from Tbilisi in: Sotheby's New York, December 1987, lot 313.

30 Originally, the term "Kabbalah" means simply "tradition," indicating religious tradition in general. Only in the Middle Ages, when the *Sefer ha-Bahir* and the Zohar were written as main works of a new esoteric-mystic theology, did the term acquire the meaning of a hidden occult doctrine. Originating in the area of southern France and Catalonia, active interest in the Kabbalah spread, up to the Modern era, all over Europe and the Near East. The theoretical and the practical Kabbalah can be distinguished. While the theoretical Kabbalah searches for higher theological-epistemological connections, the practical Kabbalah is of more popular character and had a large influence on the various messianic movements as well as on modern Hassidism.

31 The text suggests that the young man lost his life during the Russian Civil War.

32 Illustration of this item in: Judaica Jerusalem, March 1994, lot 363. For another pointer from Kuba, see Mirror of Jewish Life, no. 42.

JAD/TORA-ZEIGER
Podolien, 1871/72
Holz, geschnitzt
Hebräische Inschrift: „Sei geschwind wie der Adler, schnell wie die Gazelle und mutig wie der Löwe, dem Willen des Herrn nachzukommen[33]/ (5)632 (i.e. 1871/72)"; sowie die Anfangsbuchstaben der Zehn Gebote
L: 33,2 cm; B: 2,5 cm
Inv.Nr. 052.008.004[34]

KETER/TORA-KRONE
(oberer Teil fehlend)
Ukraine, um 1850
Silber
Hebräische Inschrift: „Dies ist die Krone der Tora, die aus einem gesegneten Schekel angefertigt wurde"[35]
H: 14,3 cm; Dm: 19,2
Inv.Nr. 053.001.007[36]

MISRACH
Und Jahrzeit-Erinnerung
Krenetz/Ukraine, 1925/26
Wolle, farbige Baumwollfäden, gestickt
Hebräische Inschrift: „Wisse vor wem du stehst, vor dem höchsten König der Könige, dem Heiligen, gepriesen sei er.[37] Misrach – Osten – von hier kommt der Geist des Lebens, die Krone der Tora./Sei geschwind wie der Adler, mutig wie der Löwe, stark wie der Leopard und schnell wie die Gazelle.[38]/Ich habe den Herrn allzeit vor Augen.[39]/Der Mensch sorgt sich um den Verlust seines Wohlstands und sorgt sich nicht um den Verlust seiner Tage. Sein Wohlstand wird ihm nicht zu Hilfe kommen. Die Tage seines Lebens kommen nicht zurück.[40]/Der Jahrzeittag meines Vaters Aharon Mosche ist der 10. Ijjar./Der Jahrzeittag meiner Mutter Sara ist der 15. Cheschwan/Das Jahr 686 (i.e. 1925/26). Krenetz".
H: 60 cm; B: 44,5 cm
Inv.Nr. 056.016.001

TAS/TORA-SCHILD
Raschkov Velechisch/Podolien, 1820/21
Silber, teilweise vergoldet
Hebräische Inschrift, vorne: „Das Jahr (5)581 (i.e. 1820/21). Chana, Tochter des Meir", rückseitig: „Aus der Synagoge von Raschkov Velechisch".
H: 29,3 cm; B: 22,4 cm
Inv.Nr. 051.001.039[41]

Podolien. „Wir hielten vor der Schenke. Mit einem flackernden Talglicht in der Hand kam uns der Wirt entgegen, ein ältliches, verwachsenes Männchen, ein Jude natürlich, wie fast alle Schenkwirte in Podolien."

Karl Emil Franzos, um 1870*

Die Geschichte Podoliens war wesentlich durch die Grenzsituation zwischen dem polnisch-litauischen und dem osmanischen Reich geprägt. Raschkow war eines der typischen jüdischen Schtetl in Podolien. Die Bevölkerung war ländlich, und die Juden lebten zumeist vom Kleinhandel, als Pächter oder Gastwirte. Im 17. und 18. Jahrhundert wurden die Juden Podoliens von den messianischen Bewegungen Schabtai Zwis und Josef Franks erfaßt. Podolien galt auch als die Wiege des Chassidismus. Sein Begründer, der berühmte Israel Baal Schem Tow, lebte und starb im podolischen Städtchen Medzibosch, und auch andere berühmte chassidische Zaddikim wie Nachman von Bratslav ließen sich in der Region nieder. 1793 fiel der Großteil Podoliens an das Russische Reich, ein kleiner Teil im Westen an Österreich-Ungarn. Die jüdische Bevölkerung Podoliens litt im Laufe der Jahrhunderte unter den zahlreichen Pogromen, vom Bogdan-Chmielnitzki-Aufstand bis zum russischen Bürgerkrieg. Während des Zweiten Weltkriegs wurden zahlreiche podolische Juden in den Lagern Transnistriens ermordet. In Raschkow wie in den meisten ehemaligen Schtetln gibt es heute keine jüdische Gemeinde mehr.

S/W Foto S. 60: Andrzej Polec, Letzter Jude von Raschkow in den Ruinen der Synagoge, Raschkow, Ukraine, 1997

---

* Karl Emil Franzos, Der Schnapsgraf, in: Aus Halbasien. Kulturbilder aus Galizien, der Bukowina, Südrußland und Rumänien, Stuttgart und Berlin 1901, S. 227
33 Mischna, Awot V, 20 (unvollständiges Zitat).
34 Zur Holzschnitz-Kunst in der Ukraine vgl. Wooden Lecterns and Torah Pointers. Abb. des vorliegenden Zeigers in: Sotheby's Tel Aviv, April 1994, lot 130.
35 Im chassidischen Milieu Osteuropas ließen sich die Gläubigen oftmals Münzen von einem Zaddik oder Wunderrabbi segnen und schmolzen sie ein, um das Silber für die Herstellung eines Kultgegenstandes zu verwenden. Vgl. Heilige Gemeinde Wien, 2/2.12; Zwischen Ost und West, S. 128.

36 Zu den Tierornamenten, insbesondere zum Einhorn s. Gestalten und Symbole der jüdischen Kunst, S. 58f. Abb. der vorliegenden Krone in: Siddur Klal Jisrael, S. 40 u. 222.
37 Mischna, Awot III, 1/III, 22/bTalmud, Berakhot 28b.
38 Beginn von Mischna, Awot V, 20.
39 Psalm 16,8.
40 Sefer haChajim, 10,1.
41 Zu der typischen Tier-Ornamentik auf osteuropäischen Judaica vgl. Zauber der Volkskunst; Gestalten und Symbole der jüdischen Kunst, S. VII.

TORAH POINTER

Podolia, 1871/72

Wood, carved

Hebrew inscription: "Be swift as an eagle, fast as a gazelle, brave as a lion to do the will of the Lord [33]/(5)632 (i.e. 1871/72)/" and the first letters of the Ten Commandments on the tablets of the law.

Length: 33.2 cm; Width: 2.5 cm

No. 052.008.004[34]

TORAH CROWN

(upper part missing)

Ucraine, c. 1850

Silver

Hebrew inscription: "This is the crown of the Torah which is made from the blessed shekel (coin?)"[35]

Height: 14.3 cm; Diameter: 19.2 cm

No. 053.001.007[36]

MIZRAH

Also serving as a Kaddish reminder

Krenetz/Ucraine, 1925/26

Wool, colored cotton thread, embroidered

Hebrew inscription: "Know before whom you are standing, before the supreme king of kings, the holy one, blessed by he.[37] Mizrah – east – from this direction comes the spirit of life the crown of torah./Be swift as the eagle, brave as the lion, strong as the leopard and fleet as the gazelle.[38]/I have set the Lord always before me.[39]/Man worries over the loss of his wealth but not over the loss of his days. His wealth will not come to his aid. The days of his life will not return.[40]/The memorial day of my father Aharon Moshe is the 10th day of the month of Iyar./The memorial day of my mother Sarah is the 15th day of the month of Cheshvan./The year (5)686 (=1925/26). Krenetz".

Height: 60 cm; Width: 44.5 cm

No. 056.016.001

TORAH SHIELD

Rashkov Velechish/Podolia, 1820/21

Silver, parcel gilt

Hebrew inscription: Front: "The year (5)581 (i.e.1820/21). Hanah, daughter of Meir", in back: "From the synagogue in Rashkov Velechish".

Height: 29.3 cm; Width: 22.4 cm

No. 051.001.039[41]

* Karl Emil Franzos, Der Schnapsgraf, in: Aus Halbasien. Kulturbilder aus Galizien, der Bukowina, Südrußland und Rumänien, Stuttgart und Berlin 1901, p. 227

33 Mishna, Avot V, 20 (quotation incomplete).

34 For the art of woodcarving, cf. Wooden Lecterns and Torah Pointers. Illustration of this pointer in: Sotheby's Tel Aviv, April 1994, lot 130.

35 In the Hassidic milieu of eastern Europe, the faithful frequently had coins blessed by a zaddik or wonder rabbi and melted them down to use the silver for the manufacturing of ritual objects. Cf. Heilige Gemeinde Wien, 2/2.12; Zwischen Ost und West, p. 128.

36 For the animal ornamentation, especially the unicorn, see Gestalten und Symbole der jüdischen Kunst, p. 58f. Illustration of this crown in: Siddur Klal Jisrael, p. 40 and 222.

37 Mishna, Avot III, 1/III, 22/bTalmud, Berakhot 28b.

38 Beginning of Mishna, Avot V, 20.

39 Psalm 16:8.

40 Sefer HaHaim, 10,1.

41 For the typical animal ornamentation on Eastern European Judaica, cf. Zauber der Volkskunst; Gestalten und Symbole der jüdischen Kunst, p. VII.

Podolia. "We stopped in front of the tavern. A flickering tallow candle in his hand, the proprietor came up to us, an elderly, deformed man, a Jew, of course, as are almost all tavern keepers in Podolia."

Karl Emil Franzos, c. 1870*

Podolia's history was marked essentially by its border situation between the Polish-Lithuanian realm and the Ottoman Empire. Rashkov was one of those typical Jewish shtetls in Podolia. The population was rural and the Jews mostly worked in retail, as tenants, or innkeepers. In the 17th and 18th century the messianic movements of Shabbtai Zvi and Josef Frank seized Podolia's Jews. Podolia is also considered to be the cradle of Hassidism. Its founder, the legendary Israel Baal Shem Tov, lived and died in the Podolian townlet of Medzibosh and other famous Hassidic zaddikim such as Nahman of Bratslav also settled in this region. In 1793 the larger part of Podolia fell to the Russian Empire, a small part in the west to the Austro-Hungarian Empire. The Jewish population of Podolia suffered from numerous pogroms in the course of the centuries, from the Bohdan Chmielnitzki uprising to Russia's civil war. During World War II numerous Podolian Jews were murdered in the camps of Transnistria. In Rashkov, as in most former shtetls, there no longer exists a Jewish community today.

B/W Photo p. 60: Andrzej Polec, Last Jew of Rashkov in the ruins of the synagogue, Rashkov, Ucraine, 1997

Typical wooden synagogue of Podolia, Ucraine, c. 1911
Technische Universität Wien

Typische Holzsynagoge Podoliens, Ukraine, um 1911
Technische Universität Wien

Afghanistan. „Die Juden Afghanistans sind mit den ‚alten' Juden verwandt, deren Auszug aus dem Lande Israel vor der Zerstörung des Zweiten Tempels begann, im Gegensatz zu den Aschkenasim und den Sephardim, deren Auszug aus dem Lande Israel später war. Diese Juden breiteten sich entlang der alten Handelswege aus, welche bis China reichten, und errichteten große und kleine Gemeinden."

Ben-Zion Jehoschua, 1973*

Frühen karäischen und rabbinischen Traditionen zufolge soll es die verlorenen Zehn Stämme nach Afghanistan verschlagen haben. Afghanische Chroniken weisen ferner einigen afghanischen Stämmen jüdische Wurzeln zu, die in die Zeit König Sauls reichen sollen. Zur Zeit des Babylonischen Exils wurden häufig Personen, die der jüdischen Führung unerwünscht waren, nach Afghanistan verbannt oder zogen sich freiwillig dorthin zurück. Mittelalterliche Quellen nennen verschiedene Zentren jüdischer Siedlung. Die bedeutendste jüdische Siedlung war Balch. Nach persischer und islamischer Tradition wurde Balch von Nebukadnezar gegründet, der exilierte Juden hier angesiedelt haben soll. Ferner soll der Prophet Jeremia hierher geflohen und der Prophet Chesekiel hier begraben sein. Der Mongolensturm stellt einen dramatischen Einschnitt in der Geschichte der jüdischen Gemeinden Afghanistans dar. Bis ins 19. Jahrhundert wissen die Quellen nicht viel zu berichten. Die vor den Zwangsbekehrungen des Jahres 1839 geflohenen Juden Mesheds prägten das kulturelle Leben der Gemeinden. Die Sprache der afghanischen Juden ist deshalb auch nicht Paschto, sondern ein judeo-persischer Dialekt. 1948 lebten noch etwa 5000 Juden in Afghanistan. 1969 waren es nur noch 300.

S/W Foto S. 63: Seder im Hause von Meir Simantov, Kabul, Afghanistan, 1971; Beth Hatefutsoth Foto-Archiv, Tel Aviv

JAD/TORA-ZEIGER
Balch/Afghanistan, um 1890
Silber, Farbsteine
Hebräische Inschrift: „Dies ist der silberne (Tora-Zeiger), der von Baba (?), Sohn des Baki, der Synagoge von Balch gespendet wurde."
L: 28,3 cm; B: 4,6 cm
Inv.Nr. 052.001.039 [42]

SCHABBAT-LEUCHTER
(zur Verwendung von Öl)
Afghanistan, um 1925
Silber
Hebräische Inschrift: „Ein Licht zu Ehren des Schabbat und der Feiertage; Brucha, Gattin von Zwi Bazal, möge sein Fels und Erlöser ihn beschützen."
H: 18,5 cm; B: 20,5 cm; T: 8,8 cm
Inv.Nr. 012.001.05 [43]

WEINBECHER FÜR DIE HAWDALA
Afghanistan, um 1900
Silber
Hebräisch beschriftet mit den Segenssprüchen für die Hawdala/Psalmen 23,5 und 116,13
H: 7,7 cm; Dm: 7,5 cm
Inv.Nr. 017.001.023 [44]

RIMMONIM/TORA-AUFSÄTZE
Afghanistan, um 1880
Silber
Hebräisch beschriftet mit Amulett-Texten, einem Schiwiti (Ps 67) in Form einer Menora, der Anrufung verschiedener Engel, den 42 Buchstaben des Gottesnamens, Segenssprüchen und der Androhung biblischer Verfluchungen an Jedermann, der diese Rimmonim stehlen oder verkaufen sollte. „Gestiftet von Zeruja, Tochter des Abraham, im Namen der Seele von Nissan Bar Jitzchak Bar Jakow …, Gottes Geist wird ihn in den Garten Eden führen, möge seine Seele eingebunden sein im Bündel des Lebens, amen, sela. Gestiftet der Synagoge von David Bar …, seligen Andenkens."
H: 29,7 cm; B: 11 cm
Inv.Nr. 050.001.003 [45]

* Ben Zion Jehuschua, Eine jüdische Hochzeit in Afganistan, Jerusalem, 1973, S. 7
42 Abb. des vorliegenden Zeigers: Afghanistan, Umschlag, im Text S. 35 u. Abb. 21; auch in: Christie's New York, June 1984, lot 197; Sotheby's New York, December 1988, lot 263.
43 Abb. des vorliegenden Leuchters in: Jüdische Lebenswelten, Nr. 3/29; Shabbat Shalom, S. 13. Zum selben Typus vgl. Feuchtwanger Collection, Nr. 209; Jewish Life in Art and Tradition, S. 129; Christie's Amsterdam, December 1986, lot 205.
44 Abb. des vorliegenden Bechers in: Jüdische Lebenswelten, Nr. 3/37; Shabbat Shalom, S. 55. Für ein vergleichbares Stück s. Stieglitz Collection, Nr. 55.
45 Zu afghanischen Judaica allgemein s. Afghanistan; hier sind auch die vorliegenden Aufsätze abgebildet, Nr. 17, Abb. 26; ebenso in: Siddur Klal Jisrael, S. 177; Flat Torah Finials, Abb. 6; Torah and Magic, Abb. 8.

Afghanistan. "Unlike the Ashkenazim and Sephardim whose emigration from the Land of Israel took place later, the Jews of Afghanistan are related to those 'ancient' Jews whose emigration from the Land of Israel started before the destruction of the Second Temple. These Jews spread along the ancient trade routes, which reached China, and established large and small communities."

Ben-Zion Yehoshua, 1973*

According to early Karaite and rabbinic traditions, the lost Ten Tribes ended up in Afghanistan. Afghan chronicles further attribute Jewish roots to some Afghan tribes, which apparently go back to the time of King Saul. At the time of the Babylonian exile, undesired members of the Jewish leadership were frequently banished to Afghanistan or retreated there voluntarily. Medieval sources mention various centers of Jewish settlements the most important of which was Balkh. According to Persian and Islamic tradition, Balkh was founded by Nebuchadnezzar who is said to have settled exiled Jews here. Also, it is said that the prophet Jeremiah took refuge and the prophet Ezekiel was buried here. The Mongolian offensive represented a dramatic turn in the history of the Jewish communities of Afghanistan. The sources hardly mention anything up to the 19th century. The Jews of Meshed who had escaped forced conversions in 1839 shaped the cultural life of the communities. Therefore, the language of Afghan Jews is not Pashto, but a Judeo-Persian dialect. In 1948 there were still some 5,000 Jews living in Afghanistan, by 1969 only 300 remained. Today there are even less.

B/W Photo p. 63: Passover Seder at the home of Meir Simantov, Kabul, Afghanistan, 1971; Beth Hatefutsoth Photo Archive, Tel Aviv

The Mullah Samuel Synagogue, Herat, Afghanistan, c. 1925
Hebrew University of Jerusalem

Die Mullah-Samuel-Synagoge, Herat, Afghanistan, um 1925
Hebrew University of Jerusalem

YAD/TORAH POINTER
Balkh/Afghanistan, c. 1890
Silver, blue stones
Hebrew inscription: "This is the silver (Torah pointer) which was dedicated by Baba (?), son of Baki, to the synagogue of Balch."
Width: 4.6 cm; Length: 28.3 cm
No. 052.001.039 [42]

SHABBAT LAMPS
(for oil)
Afghanistan, c. 1925
Silver
Hebrew inscription: "A light in honour of Shabbats and Holy Days; Brucha, the wife of Tzvi Batzal, may his rock and redeemer protect him."
Height: 18.5 cm; Width: 20.5 cm; Depth: 8.8 cm
No. 012.001.005 [43]

WINECUP FOR HAVDALLAH
Afghanistan, c. 1900
Silver
Hebrew inscription: Blessings for Havdallah/Psalms 23,5 and 116,13
Height: 7.7cm; Diameter: 7.5 cm
No. 017.001.023 [44]

RIMMONIM/TORAH FINIALS
Afghanistan, c. 1880
Silver
Inscribed with amuletic elements, a Shiviti (67th Psalm) in the form of a menorah, the invocation of angels, the 42 letter name of God, several blessings and a call for biblical curses on anyone who steals or sells these finials. Donor: "Dedicated by Tzeruyah, daughter of Abraham, in the name of the soul of Nissan Bar Yitzhak Bar Ya'akov ..., God's spirit will lead him to the garden of Eden, may his soul be bound up in the bond of life, amen, selah. Dedicated to the synagogue of David Bar ... of blessed memory."
Height: 29.7 cm; Width: 11cm
No. 050.001.003 [45]

* Ben Zion Jehuschua, Eine jüdische Hochzeit in Afghanistan, Jerusalem, 1973, p. 7
42 Illustration of this pointer: Afghanistan, cover, in text p. 35 and fig. 21; also in: Christie's New York, June 1984, lot 197; Sotheby's New York, December 1988, lot 263.
43 Illustration of this lamp in: Jüdische Lebenswelten, no. 3/29; Shabbat Shalom, p. 13. For the same type, cf. Feuchtwanger Collection, no. 209; Jewish Life in Art and Tradition, p. 129; Christie's Amsterdam, December 1986, lot 205.
44 Illustration of this cup in: Jüdische Lebenswelten, no. 3/37; Shabbat Shalom, p. 55. For a comparable item, see Stieglitz Collection, no. 55.
45 For Afghan Judaica in general see Afghanistan, here are also the illustrations of the finials on hand, no. 17, Abb. 26; also in: Siddur Klal Jisrael, p. 177; Flat Torah Finials, fig. 6; Torah and Magic, fig. 8.

64

TORA-WIMPEL

Mulhouse/Elsass/Frankreich, 1892

Leinen, bemalt

Hebräische Beschriftung: „Schlomo Ben Mosche Blum" sowie der übliche Wimpel-Text.
Illustrationen: Das Urteil des Salomo (in Anlehnung an den Namen des Kindes), ein Klapperstorch,
ein Rabbiner mit einem Weinglas, ein fischender Junge, die Tora (die er in Hinkunft lernen möge) und ein Traubaldachin (die zukünftige Ehe wünschend).

H: 17,3 cm; L: 322,5 cm

Inv.Nr. 019.014.045 [46]

PAROCHET/TORA-VORHANG

Mit französischer Fahne

Dehlingen/Elsass/Frankreich, 1810/11

Seide

Hebräische Widmungsinschrift: „Meir Cohen/meine Spende 1810/1811/heilige Gemeinde
Dehlingen"

H: 190 cm; B: 110 cm

Inv.Nr. 049.013.002

CHANUKKA-LEUCHTER

Mit zwei Brennleisten, damit Vater und Sohn die Lichter an einer Chanukkia zünden können

Elsass/Frankreich, um 1850

Zinn, Messing

H: 29,6 cm; B: 27,7 cm; T: 11 cm

Inv.Nr. 010.020.002 [47]

TAS/TORA-SCHILD

Strasbourg/Elsass/Frankreich, um 1680

Silber, vergoldet

Künstler: Daniel Hammerer

Inschrift: späterer Zusatz gotisch gehaltener Initialen des 19. Jhs., möglicherweise von einem
Wohltäter, der die Restaurierung des Stückes bezahlt haben mag

H: 20,8 cm; B: 17,8 cm

Inv.Nr. 051.001.022 [48]

---

* Daniel Stauben, Eine Reise zu den Juden auf dem Lande, Augsburg 1986, S. 6
46 Vgl. Imagerie juive d'Alsace, S. 67; Sotheby's Tel Aviv, April 1998, lot 221.
47 Zu Vergleichsstücken s. Das jüdische Jahr, Nr. 51; Juden im Elsaß, Nr. 124; Jüdische Lehre, Nr. 54. Vorliegendes Stück in: Sotheby's
Tel Aviv, April 1995, lot 266.
48 Bei diesem Schild handelt es sich um eine der frühesten Formen aschkenasischer rechteckiger metallener Schilder. Zu elsässischen Judaica allg. s. Juden im Elsass. Abb. des vorliegenden Stückes in: Geschichten von Gegenständen, Nr. 2, Abb. 2; Sotheby's
New York, December 1986, lot 264. Schilder desselben Meisters auch in: Anglo-Jewish Historical Exhibition, nach S. 86; Jewish
Museum London, S. 136, Pl. LXIV. Frankfurter Schilder dieses Typus in: Collector's Room, Nr. 71, Abb. 6; Golden Age, Abb. 4.
Zum Meisterzeichen s. Rosenberg IV, Nr. 6993; zur Stadt-Marke s. ebenda, Nr. 6910.

Elsass. „Haben die Juden unserer elsässer Weiler, die schon Jahrhunderte vor der Eroberung der Franzosen in dieser Gegend ansässig waren, sich in ihr nicht eine besondere Sprache erhalten und haben sie sich dort nicht auch ein ganz besonderes Leben geschaffen, eine eigene Kultur?"

Daniel Stauben, 1860*

Zu den traditionellen jüdischen Siedlungsgebieten in Frankreich gehörte seit dem 12. Jahrhundert das Elsass. Während des 14. Jahrhunderts kam es zu mehreren schrecklichen Pogromen in den elsässischen Gemeinden, trotzdem kam es wenig später zu neuen Ansiedlungen insbesondere auf dem Lande. Im Allgemeinen waren sie hier mit denselben Restriktionen konfrontiert wie im übrigen Aschkenas, doch gab es auch Ausnahmen wie in Mulhouse, wo die Juden ab dem 15. Jh. fast dieselben Rechte genossen wie die Christen. Nachdem das Elsass 1648 französisch geworden war, stieg die Anzahl der Gemeinden stetig, wenn auch im 18. Jahrhundert versucht wurde, ihre Zahl zu reduzieren. Als Napoleon die Emanzipation der französischen Judenheit einleitete, war man zwar aus Gründen der Tradition anfänglich reserviert, doch erkannten die Elsässer schnell die Vorteile der allgemeinen Liberalisierung. Aus Patriotismus und Loyalität zu Frankreich emigrierten viele elsässische Juden, als Deutschland das Elsass 1871 annektierte. 1918 mußte das Elsass wieder an Frankreich abgetreten werden, doch dauerte die Phase der Ruhe nur bis 1940, als Nazi-Deutschland das Gebiet erneut okkupierte. Diejenigen, die sich nicht ins Landesinnere retten konnten, wurden deportiert. Nach 1945 reorganisierten sich die Landgemeinden nicht wieder, wohl aber entstanden wieder städtische, wie in Strasbourg, Colmar, Metz und Mulhouse.

S/W Foto S. 66: Michel Rothé, Jungen am Fuße des Europa Towers in Mulhouse, Frankreich, 1999

TORAH BINDER
Mulhouse/Alsace/France, 1892
Linen, painted
Hebrew inscription: "Shelomo Ben Moshe Blum" and the Wimpel formular
Illustrations: The trial of Shelomo (allegorical for the name of the boy), a stork (that has brought the baby-boy), a Rabbi with a cup of wine, a young boy fishing, the Torah (toward future study) and a huppa (toward future marriage).
Height: 17.3 cm; Length: 322.5 cm
No. 019.014.0 [46]

PAROKHET TORAH CURTAIN
With the French flag
Dehlingen/Alsace/France, 1810/11
Silk
Hebrew inscription: "Meir Cohen/my donation 1810/1811/the holy community of Dehlingen"
Height: 190 cm; Width: 110 cm
No. 049.013.002

HANUKKAH LAMP
With two sets of burners for a father and son to kindle the lights
Alsace/France, c. 1850
Tin, brass
Height: 29.6 cm; Width: 27.7 cm; Depth: 11 cm
No. 010.020.002 [47]

TAS/TORAH SHIELD
Strasbourg/Alsace/France, c. 1680
Silver, gilt
Artist: Daniel Hammerer
Inscription: Later addition of gothic style initials from the 19th century of a donor who may have paid for the restauration of this item.
Height: 20.8 cm; Width: 17.8 cm
No. 051.001.022 [48]

Alsace. "The Jews of our Alsatian hamlets, who have been residing in this area centuries before the French conquered it, have they not maintained a distinct language and have they not created for themselves a very distinct life, a culture of their own?"

Daniel Stauben, 1860*

Alsace is one of the traditional areas in France where Jews have settled since the 12th century. During the 14th century several horrendous pogroms occurred in Alsatian communities. Nevertheless, new settlements were established a short time later, mainly on the countryside. In general, Jews were subjected here to the same restrictions as everywhere else in Ashkenaz, but there were exceptions, such as Mulhouse, where from the 15th century onward, Jews had almost the same rights as Christians. After the Alsace became French in 1648, the number of communities increased continuously, even though there were attempts to reduce them in the 18th century. When Napoleon introduced the emancipation of French Jewry, they received it initially with reservations for reasons of tradition. Rather soon, however, the Alsatians recognized the advantages of general liberalization. Patriotism and loyalty led many Alsatian Jews to emigrate when Germany annexed Alsace in 1871. In 1918 Alsace had to be returned to France, but peace and quiet lasted only till 1940 when Nazi-Germany occupied the area anew. Those who were unable to save themselves into the country's interior were deported. Although rural communities were not re-established after 1945, Jewish communities in cities such as Strasbourg, Colmar, Metz, and Mulhouse were set up again.

B/W Photo p. 66: Michel Rothé, Young boys at the bottom of the Europe Tower in Mulhouse, France, 1999

* Daniel Stauben, Eine Reise zu den Juden auf dem Lande, Augsburg 1986, p. 6
46 Cf. Imagerie juive d'Alsace, p. 67; Sotheby's Tel Aviv, April 1998, lot 221.
47 For comparable items, see Das jüdische Jahr, no. 51; Juden im Elsaß, no. 124; Jüdische Lehre, no. 54. This item in: Sotheby's Tel Aviv, April 1995, lot 266.
48 This shield represents one of the earliest forms of Ashkenasic rectangular metal shields. For Alsatian Judaica in general, see Juden im Elsass. Illustration of this item in: Geschichten von Gegenständen, no. 2, fig.2; Sotheby's New York, December 1986, lot 264. Shields from the same maker also in: Anglo-Jewish Historical Exhibition, after p. 86; Jewish Museum London, p. 136, Pl. LXIV. Frankfurt shields of this type in: Collector's Room, no. 71, fig. 6; Golden Age, fig. 4. For maker's mark, see Rosenberg IV, no. 6993; for city mark, see ibid. no. 6910.

Group-piece with Mme. Hirschler at the synagogue in Mulhouse, France, 1937, Courtesy of Dr. Michel Rothé

Gruppenfoto mit Mme. Hirschler vor der Synagoge in Mulhouse, Frankreich, 1937, Leihgabe Dr. Michel Rothé

Indien. „Ungefähr 20 Meilen von Cranganor sind vier andere Plätze, alle an dem berühmten Cochin-Stauwasser gelegen, wo die schwarzen Juden noch Synagogen haben. Parur, Channamangalam und Malah haben je eine Synagoge; Ernakulam hat zwei und Cochin drei Synagogen, von denen eine den weißen Juden gehört."

E.N. Adler, 1906*

Die jüdische Bevölkerung Indiens unterteilt sich in drei verschiedene Gruppen: die Cochin-Juden, die Bene Israel und die Bagdad-Juden. Die Bagdad-Juden immigrierten im späten 18. Jh. aus dem Irak nach Indien, während die Bene Israel legendären Ursprung haben: Gemäß ihrer Tradition sind sie die Nachkommen von schiffbrüchigen israelitischen Überlebenden, die nach der Zerstörung des Ersten Tempels hierher fanden. Die Cochin-Juden sind in Kerala in Südindien beheimatet. Ihre Gemeinde besteht aus sogenannten „Meschuchrarim" (Freedmen), „schwarzen" und „weißen" Juden. Letztere sind Exilierte aus Cranganora, die sich mit den späteren Einwanderern aus Europa und aus dem Nahen Osten mischten. Die „schwarzen Juden" sehen sich selbst als die ursprünglichen an. Die Meschuchrarim waren ursprünglich offen- sichtlich Sklaven; sie erhielten erst 1932 das Recht, am offiziellen synagoga- len Gottesdienst teilzunehmen. Obwohl in ganz Indien nur noch 6.000 Juden leben, gibt es in Cochin noch zwei funktionierende Synagogen, eine aus dem 16., die andere aus dem 17. Jahrhundert.

S/W Foto S. 69: Leihgabe Dan Kala, Hakkafot während der Simchat-Tora-Feier im Hof der Paradesi Synagoge, Cochin, Indien, 1971; Beth Hatefutsoth Foto-Archiv, Tel Aviv

KETUBBA/EHEVERTRAG
Cochin/Indien, 1790
Papier, Tusche, Farbe, Goldstaub
Braut: Mazla Bat David Cohen
Bräutigam: Abraham Ben Meir
H: 54,8 cm; B: 43 cm
Inv.Nr. 035.011.028 [49]

CHANUKKA-LEUCHTER
Indien, um 1875
Messing
H: 25,6 cm; B: 28,6 cm; T: 8,4 cm
Inv.Nr. 010.002.017 [50]

RIMMONIM/TORA-AUFSÄTZE
In Form einer Lotosblüte
Cochin/Indien, um 1850
Blattgold auf Silber
H: 22 cm; Dm: 9,4 cm
Inv.Nr. 050.021.001 [51]

* Elkan Nathan Adler, Von Ghetto zu Ghetto. Reisen und Beobachtungen von Elkan Nathan Adler, Stuttgart 1909, S. 187

49 An der Rückseite der Ketubba ist ein Teil ihrer Geschichte auf einem angehängten Papier dokumentiert: Sie wurde in der ersten Hälfte des 19. Jhs. von dem Missionar Joseph Wolff in Indien erworben. In England schenkte Wolff sie dem christlichen Hebraisten John Hookham Frere (gest. 1846). Vor rund zehn Jahren tauchte sie auf einer Auktion in England auf. Zu weiteren Ketubbot aus Cochin vgl. Mazal Tov, Nr. 55, Nr. 33. u. Nr. 34 (wobei die beiden letzteren stilistisch völlig „britisch" sind).

50 Die indische Herkunft des Leuchters ist aufgrund seiner Gesamtform wie auch der Form der Brennstellen und der eingearbeiteten Elefanten erkennbar. Metallene Chanukka-Leuchter aus Indien sind ansonsten kaum bekannt.

51 Abb. des vorliegenden Paares in: The Jews of India, S. 61. Ein ähnliches Paar befindet sich im Jewish Museum New York, publiziert in: Treasures of the Jewish Museum, S. 49; Crowning Glory, Nr. 444; Jüdische Lebenswelten, Nr. 4/6. Zu einem weiteren Paar s. Christie's New York, October 1982, lot 160.

India. "Roughly 20 miles from Cranganor there are four other places, all located at the famous Cochin backwaters, where the black Jews still have synagogues. Parur, Channamangalam, and Malah each have a synagogue; Ernakulam has two and Cochin three synagogues, of which one belongs to the white Jews."

E.N. Adler, 1906*

The Jewish population of India is divided into three different groups: the Cochin Jews, the Benei Israel, and the Baghdad Jews. The latter immigrated to India from Baghdad in the late 18th century from Iraq. The Benei Israel are of legendary origin: according to tradition, they are the descendants of shipwrecked Israelite survivors who arrived here after the destruction of the First Temple. The Cochin Jews reside in Kerala in southern India. Their community consists of so-called meshuhrarim (freed men), "black" and "white" Jews. The latter are Jews who were exiled from Cranganore and who mixed with the later immigrants from Europe and the Near East. The "black Jews" consider themselves to have been here first. Apparently, the meshuhrarim were originally slaves; only in 1932 did they obtain the right to attend the official service in the synagogue. Although only 6,000 Jews are still living in the whole of India today, there are still two functioning synagogues in Cochin, one from the 16th, the other from the 17th century.

B/W Photo p. 69: Dan Kala, Hakkafot during Simhat Torah Service at the Paradesi Synagogue yard, Cochin, India, 1971; Beth Hatefutsoth Photo Archive, Tel Aviv

KETUBAH/MARRIAGE CONTRACT
Cochin/India, 1790
Paper, ink, paint, gold dust
Bride: Matzla Bat David Cohen
Groom: Avraham Ben Meir
Height: 54.8 cm; Width: 43 cm
No. 035.011.028 [49]

HANUKKAH LAMP
India, c. 1875
Brass
Height: 25.6 cm; Width: 28.6 cm; Depth: 8.4 cm
No. 010.002.017 [50]

RIMMONIM/TORAH FINIALS
Lotus-blossom-shaped
Cochin/India, c. 1850
Gold leaf on silver
Height: 22 cm; Diameter: 9.4 cm
No. 050.021.001 [51]

Jew Town with the bell tower of the Paradesi Synagogue, Cochin, India, c. 1930. *From: Daniel/Barbara C. Johnson, Ruby of Cochin, Philadelphia/Jerusalem 1995, p. 4*

Judenviertel mit Sicht auf den Glockenturm der Paradesi Synagoge, Cochin, Indien, um 1930. *Daniel/Barbara C. Johnson, Ruby of Cochin, Philadelphia/Jerusalem 1995, S. 4*

* Elkan Nathan Adler, Von Ghetto zu Ghetto. Reisen und Beobachtungen von Elkan Nathan Adler, Stuttgart 1909, p. 187

49 On reverse side of the ketubah, part of its history is documented on an attached paper: It was acquired in India in the first half of the 19th c. by the missionary Joseph Wolff. In England Wolff presented it to the Christian Hebraist John Hookham Frere (d. 1846). Around ten years ago, it appeared at an auction in England. For more *ketuboth* from Cochin, cf. Mazal Tov, no. 55, no. 33, and no. 34 (whereby the latter two are entirely "British" in style).

50 The lamp's Indian origin is evident because of its overall shape as well as the shape of the burning points and the elephants worked into it. Otherwise, metal Hanukkah lamps from India are almost unknown.

51 Illustration of this pair in: The Jews of India, p. 61. A similar pair is in the Jewish Museum New York, published in: Treasures of the Jewish Museum, p. 49; Crowning Glory, no. 444; Jüdische Lebenswelten, no. 4/6. For another pair, see Christie's New York, October 1982, lot 160.

Krakau. „... durch Kazimierz gehe ich. Läden nach Läden, in den Etagen Geschäfte über Geschäfte. Ich lese die Firmenschilder ‚Affenkraut', ‚Stieglitz', ‚Vogelfang', ‚Goldstoff'."

Alfred Döblin, 1924*

Die jüdische Gemeinde in Krakau war eine der ältesten in Polen und wurde erstmals Anfang des 14. Jahrhunderts urkundlich erwähnt. Jüdische Kaufleute und Bankiers spielten eine wichtige Rolle im Geschäftsleben der Stadt. Gegen Ende des 15. Jahrhunderts wurden die Juden auf Druck der christlichen Kaufmannschaft aus der inneren Stadt vertrieben, und sie ließen sich im nahgelegenen Kazimierz nieder, wo sie einen geschlossenen Stadtteil bewohnten. Krakau war auch ein Zentrum jüdischer Gelehrsamkeit, in dem so wichtige Rabbiner wie Moses Isserles, Joel Sirkes, Lipmann Heller und andere wirkten. Unter österreichischer Herrschaft erhielt Krakau Anfang des 19. Jahrhunderts den Status der Autonomie. Die Stadt entwickelte sich zu einem Zentrum der polnischen Nationalbewegung, an der sich auch die polnischen Juden unter dem berühmten Rabbiner Berisch Meisels aktiv beteiligten. Am Vorabend des Zweiten Weltkriegs lebten in Krakau mehr als 60.000 Juden. Nachdem deutsche Truppen die Stadt eingenommen hatten, errichteten sie ein Konzentrationslager in Plaszów. Die Juden mußten ins Getto übersiedeln, und obwohl sich bald eine jüdische Widerstandsbewegung bildete, überlebten nur wenige Krakauer Juden die Schoa. Heute gibt es eine sehr kleine jüdische Gemeinde in Krakau. In der ältesten Synagoge, der „Hoichen Schul", befindet sich ein jüdisches Museum. In der nach Moses Isserles benannten Remu Synagoge werden heute die Gottesdienste abgehalten.

S/W Foto S. 72: Tomasz Tomaszewski, Die Cafeteria im Jüdischen Gemeindezentrum Krakau, Polen, 1984; Beth Hatefutsoth Foto-Archiv, Tel Aviv

---

TUR CHOSCHEN HAMISCHPAT

Mit dem Kommentar „Bet Josef" von Josef Ben Efraim Karo

Krakau/Polen, 1613

Papier, Holzschnitt-Illustrationen

Autor: Jakob Ben Ascher

Druckerei: Isaak Prosstitz Söhne

H: 36 cm; B: 25,5 cm; T: 6,1 cm

Inv.Nr. B.1858[52]

KETER/TORA-KRONE

Mit doppelköpfigen Adlern, einer russischen Münze und einem halben amerikanischen Dollar[53]

Krakau/Polen, um 1800

Silber, teilweise vergoldet

H: 38 cm; Dm: 22 cm

Inv.Nr. 053.001.009[54]

BUCHEINBAND

Krakau/Polen, 1879

Holz, geschnitzt

Künstler: Naphtali Kohav (Stern)

H: 14,5 cm; B: 10 cm; T: 5,5 cm

Inv.Nr. 025.008.004[55]

---

* Alfred Döblin, Reise in Polen, München 1993, S. 266–267

52 Einer der „Arba Turim", der „vier Reihen" des Jakob ben Ascher. Der vierteilige religionsgesetzliche Kodex war das Lebenswerk des in der 2. H. des 13. und in der 1. H. des 14. Jhs. wirkenden Jakob ben Ascher. Im 16. Jh. waren die „Arba Turim" die Grundlage für Josef Karos Gesetzeskodex „Schulchan Aruch", der mit diesem Werk die Turim auf das Wesentlichste reduziert zusammenfasste und autoritativ für die sefardische und orientalische Judenheit wurde. Für die Aschkenasen wurde Karos „Gedeckter Tisch", wie der Kodex heißt, erst mit den Adaptionen an die aschkenasische Tradition und den Zusätzen Rabbi Mose Isserles' bindend.

53 Die russische Münze ist möglicherweise eine Schmira-Münze, die nach chassidischem Brauch von einem Rabbiner gesegnet und vom Besitzer dann in ein Kultgerät integriert wurde. Die Halbdollar-Münze könnte vermuten lassen, dass der Auftraggeber der Krone nach Amerika auswandern wollte und dafür von seinem Rabbiner den Segen erbat.

54 Zur Taxmarke s. Reitzner, S. 204, P 129.

55 Zum vorliegenden Einband s. The Jews and Europe, S. 175; Reise nach Jerusalem, Nr. 3/30; Spirit and Matter, Nr. 23; Sotheby's Tel Aviv, May 1987, lot 101; lot 102 zeigt einen Tora-Zeiger desselben Künstlers.

TUR HOSCHEN HAMISHPAT
With the commentary "Bet Yosef" from Yosef Ben Ephraim Karo
Cracow/Poland, 1613
Paper, woodcut-illustrations
Author: Ya'akov ben Asher
Printer: Sons of Yitzchak Prosstitz
Height: 36 cm; Width: 25.5 cm; Depth: 6.1 cm
No. B.1858 [52]

KETER/TORAH CROWN
With double headed eagles, a Russian coin and an American half-Dollar-coin [53]
Cracow/Poland, c. 1800
Silver, parcel gilt
Height: 38 cm; Diameter: 22 cm
No. 053.001.009 [54]

BOOK COVER
Cracow/Poland, 1879
Wood, carved
Artist: Naphtali Kohav (Stern)
Height: 14.5 cm; Width: 10 cm; Depth: 5.5 cm
No. 025.008.004 [55]

Kraków. "… I walk through Kazimierz. Stores after stores, on the floors shops on top of shops. I read company names like 'Affenkraut', 'Stieglitz', 'Vogelfang', 'Goldstoff.'"

Alfred Döblin, 1924*

The Jewish community in Cracow was one of the oldest in Poland and was first mentioned in a document at the beginning of the 14th century. Jewish merchants and bankers played an important role in the city's economy. Toward the end of the 15th century the Jews were evicted from the inner city under pressure exerted by the Christian merchants and they settled in nearby Kazimierz where they inhabited a closed district. Cracow was also a center of Jewish scholarship with eminent rabbis such as Moses Isserles, Yoel Sirkes, Lipmann Heller, and others. Under Austrian rule, Cracow received autonomous status at the beginning of the 19th century. The city developed into a center of the Polish national movement and Polish Jews under the famous rabbi Berish Meisels were also active in it. On the eve of World War II over 60,000 Jews lived in Cracow. After German troops had occupied the city, they established a concentration camp in Plaszów. The Jews had to move into the ghetto and although a Jewish resistance movement was soon formed, only few Jews from Cracow survived the Shoah. Today there is a tiny Jewish community in Cracow. A Jewish museum exists in the oldest synagogue, the Hoichen Schul. Nowadays services are conducted in the Remu synagogue, named after Moses Isserles.

B/W Photo p. 72: Tomasz Tomaszewski, The Cafeteria at the Cracow Jewish Community Center, Poland, 1984; Beth Hatefutsoth Photo Archive, Tel Aviv

* Alfred Döblin, Reise in Polen, München 1993, p. 266–267
52 One of the Arba Turim, the "Four Rows" by Ya'akov ben Asher. The four-part code of religious law constitutes the life's work of Ya'akov ben Asher, who was active in the second half of the 13th c. and the first half of 14th c. In the 16th c., the Arba Turim became the basis for Yosef Karo's code of law "Shulhan Arukh." That work, in which Karo reduced the Turim codex to its essence, became authoritative for Sephardic and Oriental Jewry. For the Ashkenazim, Karo's "Set Table," as the code is named, became only binding with the adaptations to Ashkenazic tradition and with the additions of Rabbi Mose Isserles.
53 Possibly, the Russian coin is a shmira-coin that was blessed by a rabbi according to Hassidic custom and then was integrated into a ritual object by the owner. The half-dollar coin suggests that the crown's patron wished to emigrate to America and had requested his rabbi's blessing for that purpose.
54 For tax mark, see. Reitzner, p. 204, P 129.
55 For this cover, see The Jews and Europe, p. 175; Reise nach Jerusalem, no. 3/30; Spirit and Matter, no. 23; Sotheby's Tel Aviv, May 1987, lot 101; lot 102 shows a Torah pointer by the same artist.

Interior view of the Remu Synagogue, Cracow, Poland, c. 1920
Postcard, Beth Hatefutsoth Photo Archive, Tel Aviv

Innenansicht der Remu Synagoge, Krakau, Polen, um 1920
Postkarte, Beth Hatefutsoth Foto-Archiv, Tel Aviv

Izmir. „Wir gingen durch Judenviertel der Sephardim und Aschkenasim, die leider in schmutzigen, schmalen, schlechtgepflasterten Straßen wohnen. Es ist ein Viertel armer Leute. Überall wird fleißig gearbeitet, alle Handwerke sind vertreten. Viele sprechen die hebräische Sprache außer ihrer spaniolischen Mundart."

Max Bodenheimer, 1898*

Seit der Antike gab es jüdische Ansiedlungen in Kleinasien. Nach der türkischen Eroberung Konstantinopels im Jahr 1453 erlebten die jüdischen Gemeinden aufgrund der neuen toleranten Religions- und Einwanderungspolitik einen enormen Aufschwung. So nahm das Osmanische Reich gerne einen Hauptstrom von sefardischen Flüchtlingen nach der 1492 erfolgten Vertreibung aus Spanien auf, stellten diese doch als Handwerker, Großhändler, Ärzte, Gelehrte, Buchdrucker sowie als Experten für Feuerwaffen eine ausgesprochene Bereicherung für das dem Westen noch unterlegene Reich dar. Die liberalen Zuwanderungsbedingungen ließen im 17. Jahrhundert auch Portugiesen die jüdische Gemeinde Izmirs gründen, die der Stadt dazu verhalf, nach Saloniki zum zweitwichtigsten Handelszentrum in der Ägäis zu werden. In der jüdischen Welt wurde Izmir als Geburtsort des falschen Messias Schabtai Zwi bekannt. Seit dem 19. Jahrhundert gerieten die Juden immer wieder zwischen die Fronten der Nationalitätenkämpfe innerhalb des großen Reiches. Nach der jungtürkischen Revolution unter Mustafa Kemal Atatürk wurden die Juden den Muslimen gleichgestellt. Als neutraler Staat nahm die Türkei zahlreiche Flüchtlinge aus Nazi-Deutschland auf. Nach der Staatsgründung wanderten Ende der vierziger Jahre 37.000 Juden nach Israel aus. Die jüdische Gemeinde Istanbuls zählte am Ende des 2. Jahrtausends an die 20.000, diejenige Ankaras um 3.000 und die Gemeinde Izmirs um 1.500 Mitglieder.

S/W Foto S. 75: R. Joshua Eli Plaut, Der Stern im Halbmond, Tora Lesepult-Überwurf der ehemaligen Beth-Hillel-Synagoge, Izmir, Türkei, 1987

BUCHEINBAND
Istanbul/Türkei, 1817/18
Silber
Hebräische Inschrift auf dem Rücken: „Ich habe das Vorrecht Seiner Arbeit. Er sei gepriesen/Ich, der junge, einflussreiche und ehrbare Rabbi Mordechai, Sohn des ehrenwerten/Asher Biti. Möge sein Schutz und Erlöser ihn beschützen, im Jahr 5578 (i.e. 1817/18)." Spätere Inschrift auf beiden Deckeln: „Reuvin, möge der Herr ihn schützen und ihm Gunst erweisen/ Abraham Schalchut, 5656 (i.e. 1895/96)."
H: 17,5 cm; B: 12 cm; T: 3,8 cm
Inv.Nr. 025.001.009 [56]

SEDER TEFILLOT JESCHAROT
Kabbalistischer Siddur
Istanbul (?)/Türkei, 1732
Handschrift auf Papier, Tinte, Farbe, Blattgold
Die Illuminationen verweisen auf den typischen Koran-Dekor [57]
114 Seiten
H: 16,2 cm; B: 11,1 cm; T: 3,5 cm
Inv.Nr. OT.011.010 [58]

HÜLLE FÜR MEGILLA/ESTHER-ROLLE
Izmir/Türkei, 1872/73
Gold, Goldfiligran, Perle
Hebräische Inschrift: „Das Rollen-Buch ist ein Geschenk dem liebenswürdigen und einnehmenden Bräutigam, dem Verlobten, dem ehrenwerten Rabbi Senior David Leon, möge der Herr ihn erhalten und beschützen, dem Sohn des vornehmen Senior Jizchak, möge der Gnädige ihn schützen und segnen, möge sein Name auf immer leben, amen. Im Jahr [Chronogramm] 633 nach der kleinen Zeitrechnung (i.e. 1872/73)."
H: 22 cm; Dm: 3,75 cm
Inv.Nr. 080.021.001 [59]

RIMMONIM/TORA-AUFSÄTZE
Bodrum/Türkei, um 1860
Silber
Hebräische Inschrift: „Gestiftet von dem vornehmen Herrn Raw Abraham Galante, Sohn des ehrbaren Mosche. Möge sein Fels ihn schützen und erhalten. Für die heilige Gemeinde Bodrum. Möge Er Seine Stadt erbauen, amen, sela." [60]
H: 30,5 cm; Dm: 8,5 cm
Inv.Nr. 050.001.038 [61]

* Max Bodenheimer u. Henriette Hannah Bodenheimer, Die Zionisten und das kaiserliche Deutschland zur Zeit der Reise Wilhelms II. nach Palästina, Jerusalem 1981, S. 22

56 Technisch und ornamental ist der Einband im typischen Stil der türkischen Spiegel-Rückseiten gearbeitet. Vgl. Jews in the Ottoman Empire, Nr. 28. Zum vorliegenden Stück s. Christie's Amsterdam, December 1982, lot 149.

57 Möglicherweise hat der Schreiber ein für eine Koranhandschrift vorbereitetes Buch erworben.

58 Die Handschrift enthält die Gebete mit den täglichen Kawanot, den Gebeten für Schabbat und Neumond von Chanukka bis Purim. Abb. in: Sotheby's Tel Aviv, October 1993, lot 170.

59 Zur vorliegenden Hülle s. Sephardic Journey, Nr. 85; Jews in the Ottoman Empire, Nr. 23; Jews under Islam, Nr. 52. Zu einem sehr ähnlichen Stück s. Victoria & Albert Museum, Nr. 37. Andere Goldhüllen für Esther-Rollen beispielsweise in: Art in the Jewish Tradition.

60 Aus der Familie Galante stammte einer der bekanntesten Historiker des osmanischen Judentums, Abraham Galante (1873–1961). Möglicherweise handelt es sich bei dem Stifter dieser Rimmonim um dessen Großvater. Gemeinsam mit den Aufsätzen wurde der Bodrumer Synagoge ein Tora-Zeiger gespendet, der sich ebenfalls in der Gross Family Collection befindet.

61 Zu technisch ähnlich gefertigten Objekten vgl. z.B. Crowning Glory, Nr. 245, 400, Abb. 25; Sotheby's New York, November 1982, lot 368; Jewish Life in Art and Tradition, S. 120.

Izmir. "We walked through Jewish quarters of the Sephardim and Ashkenazim, who, unfortunately, live in dirty, narrow, shoddily paved streets. It is a poor men's quarter. People are working hard everywhere, all trades are represented. Apart from their Judeo-Spanish vernacular, many speak the Hebrew language."

Max Bodenheimer, 1898*

Jewish settlements in Asia Minor are in existence since antiquity. Jewish communities soared after the Turkish conquest of Contantinople in 1453 because of the new tolerant policies regarding religion and immigration. The Ottoman Empire willingly accepted a major part of the Sephardic refugees after their expulsion from Spain in 1492. As craftsmen, merchants, physicians, scholars, printers, as well as experts on firearms they represented a real gain for the empire, which was still backward compared to the West. The liberal immigration conditions allowed for the foundation of a Jewish community in Izmir by Portuguese Jews, which launched the city into becoming the second most important commercial center in the Aegean after Salonika. In the Jewish world, Izmir became known as the birthplace of the false Messiah, Shabbtai Zvi. From the 19th century, the Jews kept getting between the battlefronts of the empire's various nationalities. After the Young Turk Revolution under Mustafa Kemal Atatürk, Jews received equal status to Muslims. As a neutral country Turkey accepted numerous refugees from Nazi-Germany. Following the establishment of the State, 37,000 Jews emigrated from Turkey to Israel in the 1940s. At the end of the second millennium, the Jewish community of Istanbul numbers close to 20,000, that of Ankara around 3,000, and the community of Izmir around 1,500 members.

B/W Photo p. 75: R. Joshua Eli Plaut, The star in the crescent, Torah Reader's Table Cover from defunct Beth Hillel Synagogue, Izmir, Turkey, 1987

Bengiat Family at the tomb of Rachelle Bengiat, Izmir, Turkey, c. 1881. *Jewish Museum New York, Bengiat Family Archive*

Familie Bengiat am Grab von Rachelle Bengiat, Izmir, Türkei, um 1881. *Jewish Museum New York, Bengiat Family Archive*

BOOK BINDING

Istanbul/Turkey, 1817/18

Silver

Inscribed on the spine: "I am privileged to have His work. May He be blessed/I, the young prominent and honorable Rabbi Mordechai, son of the honorable/ Asher Biti, may his Rock and Redeemer protect him, the year 5578 (i.e. 1817/18)." Later inscription on both covers: "Reuvin, may the Lord sustain him and grant him favour/Avraham Shalchut, 5656 (i.e. 1895/96)."

Height: 17.5 cm; Width: 12 cm; Depth: 3.8 cm

No. 025.001.009[56]

SEDER TEFILOT YESHAROT

Kabbalistic Siddur

Istanbul (?)/Turkey, 1732

Manuscript on paper, ink, paint, gold leaf, with Koran type illuminations[57]

Pages: 114

Height: 16.2 cm; Width: 11.1 cm; Depth: 3.5 cm

No. OT.011.010[58]

CASE FOR ESTHER SCROLL

Izmir/Turkey, 1872/73

Gold, gold filigree, pearl

Hebrew blessing-inscription: "The scroll book is a gift presented to the kind and charming Bridegroom, the engaged gentleman, the fiancé, the honorable Rabbi Senior David Leon, may the Lord sustain and protect him, the son of the gentleman Senior Yitzchak, may the Merciful one protect him and bless him, may his name live forever, amen. The year [chronogramm] 633 according to the minor reckoning (i.e. 1872/73)."

Height: 22 cm; Diameter: 3.75 cm

No. 080.021.001[59]

RIMMONIM/TORAH FINIALS

Bodrum/Turkey, c. 1860

Silver

Hebrew inscription: "Dedicated by the distinguished gentleman the honorable Rav Avraham Galante, son of the honorable Moshe. May his Rock protect and sustain him. For the Holy Congregation of Bodrum. May He build His city, amen, selah."[60]

Height: 30.5 cm; Diameter: 8.5 cm

No. 050.001.038[61]

* Max Bodenheimer u. Henriette Hannah Bodenheimer, Die Zionisten und das kaiserliche Deutschland zur Zeit der Reise Wilhelms II. nach Palästina, Jerusalem 1981, p. 22

56 The cover is manufactured technically and ornamentally in the style typically of the reverse sides of Turkish mirrors. Cf. Jews in the Ottoman Empire, no. 28. For this item, see Christie's Amsterdam, December 1982, lot 149.

57 Possibly, the writer had acquired a book designed for a Koran manuscript.

58 The manuscript contains prayers with the daily Kavvanot, the prayers for Shabbat and New Moon from Hanukkah to Purim. Illustration in: Sotheby's Tel Aviv, October 1993, lot 170.

59 For this Esther-scroll case, see: Sephardic Journey, no. 85; Sephardi Jews in the Ottoman Empire, no. 23; Jews under Islam, no. 52. For a very similar item, see Victoria & Albert Museum, no. 37. Other gold cases for Esther scrolls, for instance, in: Art in the Jewish Tradition, not paginated; Christie's Amsterdam, May 2000, lot 326.

60 From the Galante family comes one of the most renowned historians of Ottoman Jewry, Abraham Galante (1873–1961). Possibly, his grandfather is the donor of these *rimmonim*. Together with the finials, a Torah pointer was donated to the Bodrum synagogue, which is in the Gross Family Collection as well.

61 For technically similarly manufactured objects, cf., e.g., Crowning Glory, no. 245, 400, fig. 25; Sotheby's New York, November 1982, lot 368; Jewish Life in Art and Tradition, p. 120.

RIMMONIM/TORA-AUFSÄTZE

In Form der Habsburger Krone

Wien/Österreich, 1806

Silber, teilweise vergoldet

Künstler: Franz Lorenz Turinsky

H: 37 cm; Dm: 12 cm

Inv.Nr. 050.001.016 [62]

SEDER TEFILLAT KOL PE

Gebetbuch nach sefardischem Ritus mit einer Übersetzung in Ladino

Wien/Österreich, 1865/66

Papier, farbige Druckerfarben

Druckerei: Josef Alschech

Auf dem Einband die hebräische Inschrift: „Jom Tow Giron, möge der Herr ihn bewahren und schützen. Im Jahr 5626 (i.e. 1865/66)"

H: 22,8 cm; B: 15 cm; T: 3 cm

Inv.Nr. B.997 [63]

CHANUKKA-LEUCHTER

In Form eines Biedermeier-Sofas

Wien/Österreich, 1837

Silber

H: 20 cm; B: 25,5 cm

Inv.Nr. 010.001.011 [64]

TAS/TORA-SCHILD

Mit der Darstellung von Mose und Aaron

Wien/Österreich, 1819

Silber, vergoldet

Künstler: Johann Mayerhofer

Eine ehemalige Inschrift ist nicht mehr lesbar

H: 33 cm; B: 25 cm

Inv.Nr. 051.001.003 [65]

Wien. „Was anbelangt die Juden in dieser Stadt, so sind sie die vornehmsten in ganz Europa. Schulen hat Jedweder in seinem Haus, und auch sind sie alle Diener und Verwalter von einigen Sachen des Kaisers."

Abraham Levi, 1719*

Die Grundlagen für die rechtliche Stellung der Juden in Österreich wurden im 13. Jahrhundert geschaffen, an dessen Ende sich die mittelalterliche Judenstadt in Wien herausbildete. 1420/21 wurde dieser ein mit einer angeblichen Hostienschändung legitimiertes schreckliches Ende gesetzt, und es dauerte 150 Jahre, bis es zu einer neuerlichen jüdischen Siedlung in Wien kam. 1625 wurden die Juden Wiens im Getto im Unteren Werd angesiedelt, 1669/70 aber neuerlich vertrieben. Wenig später kam es zur Vergabe von Einzelprivilegien an jüdische Hoffaktoren, deren Nachkommen um 1800 die Schicht der „Tolerierten" darstellten. Es dauerte bis 1852, daß sich die offizielle Kultusgemeinde konstituieren konnte, und auf die bürgerliche Gleichstellung der Juden in Österreich mußte man bis 1867 warten. Um die Jahrhundertwende boomte nicht nur der Kultur- und Wissenschaftsbereich, beide zu einem großen Teil von Juden getragen, wichtiges Thema war auch die Suche nach der eigenen staatlichen Nation, die Theodor Herzl von Wien aus zu schaffen begann. Die soziale Struktur des jüdischen Wien änderte sich dramatisch mit den Flüchtlingsströmen aus dem Osten, die die antisemitische Propaganda aus-zunutzen wußte. Der Anschluß an Hitler-Deutschland 1938 war dem Großteil der Österreicher willkommen. Von den rund 180.000 Wiener Juden konnten zwei Drittel flüchten. 65.459 österreichische Juden fielen der nationalsozialistischen Vernichtung zum Opfer. Die heutige Wiener Kultusgemeinde hat ungefähr 7.500 Mitglieder.

S/W Foto S. 78: Harry Weber, Bar-Mizwa-Feier auf dem Restaurantschiff Johann Strauß, Donaukanal, Wien, Österreich, 1996

* Bernhard Mandl, Beschreibung Wiens von einem jüdischen Touristen aus dem Jahre 1719, in: Die Neuzeit 40, 2. Oktober 1896, S. 412

62 Zu diesen Aufsätzen s. Geschichten von Gegenständen, Nr. 22, Abb. 22; Perry's Tel Aviv, September 1986, lot 207. Zu weiteren Rimmonim von Turinsky vgl. Möcht' ich ein Österreicher sein, Nr. 3; Crowning Glory, Nr. 323; Jüdisches Museum Wien, Inv.Nr. 7589. Zu anderen Judaica-Objekten von Turinsky vgl. Möcht' ich ein Österreicher sein, Nr. 2, 66; Heilige Gemeinde Wien, Nr. 1/6.9; Sotheby's Tel Aviv, April 1990, lot 256; Das Jüdische Museum in Budapest, Nr. 39. Zu den Silberschmied- und Stadtpunzen vgl. Reitzner, S. 196, Nr. 947, P 119.

63 Im 19. und beginnenden 20. Jh. war Wien ein Publikationszentrum für die judeo-spanische Presse im Habsburgerreich und auf dem Balkan, soweit er dem wachsenden Einfluß des Kaiserreiches unterstand. Auch sefardische Gelehrte aus der Türkei und Nordafrika, insbesondere aus Marokko und Syrien, wandten sich nach Wien, um ihre Schriften hier herauszugeben.

64 Zu dieser Chanukka s. Geschichten von Gegenständen, Nr. 20, Abb. 20; zu weiteren „Sofa"-Leuchtern vgl. Jewish Museum London, S. 271, Abb. Pl. LXXXVIII; Jüdisches Lexikon IV, gegenüber S. 112, CXXII, Nr. 5; Juden im Elsaß, Nr. 135; Möcht' ich ein Österreicher sein, Nr. 39. Zur Stadtpunze s. Reitzner, S. 203, P 125.

65 Zum vorliegenden Schild s. Geschichten von Gegenständen, S. 25, Abb. 25; Index, Gross Family Collection II, Nr. 18. Zu den Silberschmied-, Tax- und Stadtpunzen vgl. Reitzner, S. 207, Nr. 1123; S. 203, P 125; S. 205, P 132.

RIMMONIM/TORAH FINIALS
Habsburg-crown-shaped
Vienna/Austria, 1806
Silver, parcel gilt
Artist: Franz Lorenz Turinsky
Height: 37 cm; Diameter: 12 cm
No. 050.001.016 [62]

SEDER TEFILLAT KOL PE
Prayer book in the sephardic tradition with a translation into Ladino
Vienna/Austria, 1865/66
Paper, colored ink
Publisher: Josef Alschech
Inscribed on binding on binding: "Yom Tov Giron, may the Lord sustain and protect him. The year 5626 (i.e. 1865/66)."
Height: 22.8 cm; Width: 15 cm; Depth: 3 cm
No. B.997 [63]

HANUKKAH LAMP
In form of a Biedermeier-couch
Vienna/Austria, 1837
Silver
Height: 20 cm; Width: 25.5 cm
No. 010.001.011 [64]

TAS/TORAH SHIELD
With the depicition of Moshe and Aharon
Vienna/Austria, 1819
Silver, gilt
Artist: Johann Mayerhofer
Former inscription polished off
Height: 33 cm; Width: 25 cm
No. 051.001.003 [65]

* Bernhard Mandl, Beschreibung Wiens von einem jüdischen Touristen aus dem Jahre 1719, in: Die Neuzeit 40, 2. Oktober 1896, p. 412

62 For these finials, see Geschichten von Gegenständen, no. 22, fig. 22; Perry's Tel Aviv, September 1986, lot 207. For more finials by Turinsky, cf. Möcht' ich ein Österreicher sein, no. 3; Crowning Glory, no. 323; Jüdisches Museum Wien, inv.no. 7589. For other Judaica objects by Turinsky, cf. Möcht' ich ein Österreicher sein, no. 2, 66; Heilige Gemeinde Wien, no. 1/6.9; Sotheby's Tel Aviv, April 1990, lot 256; Das Jüdische Museum in Budapest, no. 39. For silversmith- and city marks, cf. Reitzner, p. 196, no. 947, P 119.

63 In the 19th and early 20th c., Vienna was a publishing center for the Judeo-Spanish press in the Habsburg Empire and on the Balkans as far as the empire's ever-increasing influence reached. Also Sephardic scholars from Turkey and North Africa, particularly from Morocco and Syria, turned to Vienna to have their works published here.

64 For this Hannukiah, see Geschichten von Gegenständen, no. 20, fig. 20; for more "sofa"-lamps, cf. Jewish Museum London, p. 271, fig. Pl. LXXXVIII; Jüdisches Lexikon IV, opposite p. 112, CXXII, no. 5; Juden im Elsaß, no. 135; Möcht' ich ein Österreicher sein, no. 39. For city mark, see Reitzner, p. 203, P 125.

65 For this shield, see Geschichten von Gegenständen, p. 25, fig. 25; Index, Gross Family Collection II, no. 18. For silversmith-, tax- and city marks, cf. Reitzner, p. 207, no. 1123; p. 203, P 125; p. 205, P 132.

Vienna. "As to the Jews in this city of Vienna, they are the most refined in the whole of Europe. They all have private synagogues in their own homes and they all are assistants and administrators of some of the Emperor's affairs as well."

Abraham Levi, 1719*

Foundations for the legal status of the Jews in Austria were laid in the 13th century, thus bringing about the development of Jewish life in Vienna in the Middle Ages. That, however, was cut short by a horrible ending in 1420/21, legitimated by accusing the Jews of Host desecration. It would take another 150 years until another Jewish settlement was established in Vienna. The Jews of Vienna were settled in the ghetto in the Unterer Werd in 1625, but were again expelled in 1669/70. A while later individual privileges were granted to the so-called "court" Jews whose descendants eventually became the "tolerated" Jews around 1800. Only as late as 1852 was it possible to establish an official Jewish community. Jews in Austria had to wait for equal civil rights until 1867. Around the turn of the century arts and sciences were flourishing, both carried to a large extent by Jews. But an important issue was also the search for a sovereign Jewish nation, which Theodor Herzl set out to create from Vienna. The social structure of Jewish Vienna changed dramatically with the arrival of throngs of Jewish refugees from the East, a fact that got widely exploited by anti-Semitic propaganda. The majority of Austrians welcomed the Anschluß to Hitler's Germany in 1938. Of the 180,000 Viennese Jews, two thirds were able to escape. 65,459 Austrian Jews fell victim to National-Socialist extermination. Today's Vienna Jewish Community has approximately 7,500 members.

B/W Photo p. 78: Harry Weber, Bar Mizwa celebration on the restaurant-ship Johann Strauß, Danube-canal, Vienna, Austria, 1996

Opened Thora-shrine of the City Temple at Seitenstettengasse, Vienna, Austria, c. 1915. *Jewish Museum Vienna, Inv.No. 2515*

Geöffneter Tora-Schrein des Stadttempels in der Seitenstettengasse, Wien, Österreich, um 1915. *Jüdisches Museum Wien, Inv.Nr. 2515*

Kurdistan. „Nach der Meinung des Mufti befanden sich hier schon vor 1000 Jahren über 200 christliche Kirchen und viele Synagogen. Während die Juden in Europa vom Handwerk ausgeschlossen sind, müssen sie hier ihr Brot durch ihrer Hände Arbeit verdienen.“

Carsten Niebuhr, um 1765*

Heute teilen sich drei Länder das Gebiet Kurdistans: die Türkei, der Iran und der Irak. Der Großteil der kurdischen Juden lebte im nachmaligen Irak. Der Tradition zufolge sind die Juden Kurdistans Nachfahren der Zehn Stämme aus der Zeit des assyrischen Exils. Die jüdische Bevölkerung vergrößerte sich durch die Nachkommen des Königreichs von Adiabene, das im ersten Jahrhundert geschlossen zum Judentum konvertiert war. Eines der bedeutenden jüdischen Zentren Kurdistans war Amadiya, das im Mittelalter 25.000 jüdische Einwohner gehabt haben soll. Spätere Zentren waren Irbil, Kirkuk, Mosul, Sulaimanija und Sena. Die längste Zeit isoliert, erlebten die kurdischen Juden im 12. Jahrhundert einmal von außerhalb Aufmerksamkeit, als es zu den messianischen Bewegungen unter Menachem ben Solomon ibn Ruchi und David Alroy kam. Etliche kurdische Rabbinen beschäftigten sich mit praktischer Kabbala, und auffällig viele jüdische Kurden waren begabte Paijjtanim, Dichter, die religiöse und säkulare Poesie in hebräischer und aramäischer Sprache schufen. Seit den großen Verfolgungen der vierziger Jahre des 20. Jahrhunderts im Irak und der antizionistischen Propaganda auch im Iran hat der Großteil der jüdischen Kurden die Region verlassen und ist nach Israel ausgewandert.

S/W Foto S. 81: Frits Meyst, Jüdische Frau, Kurdistan, 1990

* Carsten Niebuhr, Entdeckungen im Orient. Reise nach Arabien und anderen Ländern 1761–1767, S. 166–67

66 Die Handschrift enthält religiöse Dichtungen in Hebräisch und Persisch (in hebräischen Lettern geschrieben) von verschiedenen Paijjtanim (Dichtern religiöser Texte und Lieder) wie Menachem Ben Sassoon, Rafael Bar Elijahu Kazin, Israel Najara, Sassoon Ben Mosche, Abdulla Ben Zir, Schmuel Bar Nissim et al. Abb. einer ähnlichen Handschrift in: The Jews of Kurdistan, S. 11.

67 Zur vorliegenden Ketubba s. Index, Gross Family Collection, Nr. 84. Zu vergleichbaren Eheverträgen: The Jews of Kurdistan, S. 24–27. Zu einer weiteren Ketubba aus Sena: Mazal Tov, Nr. 48; zu einem Vertrags-Fragment aus Sena: Ketubbah, Nr. 222. Die obige Handschrift ist ein Geschenk des israelischen Künstlers Litvnovsky an die Gross Family Collection.

PIJJUTIM/RELIGIÖSE DICHTUNG
Kurdistan, 1863/64
Handschrift auf Papier, Tusche, Farbe; mit Teppichseiten und Randdekorationen
Schreiber: Siman Tow Ben Jecheskiel
Kolophon auf fol 64a: „Ich, der gelehrte Schreiber Siman Tow, Sohn des ehrbaren Raw und Gelehrten Jecheskiel, möge der Gnädige ihn beschützen und segnen, geschrieben im Jahr (5)624 (i.e. 1863/64).“
105 Seiten
H: 17,8 cm; B: 11,1 cm; T: 1,2 cm
Inv.Nr. KU.011.001 [66]

KETUBBA/HEIRATSVERTRAG
Sena/Kurdistan, 1872
Papier, Tusche, Wasserfarben
Braut: Jicofa Bat Maschiach
Bräutigam: Jecheskiel Ben Daniel
H: 69,9 cm; B: 44,7 cm
Inv.Nr. 035.011.004 [67]

RIMMONIM/TORA-AUFSÄTZE
Kurdistan, 1924
Silber
Künstler: Chatan Ben Levi
Hebräische Inschrift auf Rimmon 1: „Gewidmet dem Herrn auf Immer/Initialen der ersten und letzten drei Worte von Psalm 145,16/ Initialen der ersten und letzten drei Worte von Psalm 91,11/Sassoon Ben Jissachar, möge der Herr ihn bewahren und schützen.“ Auf Rimmon 2: „4. Siwan, 724 des Jahres Fünftausend (i.e. 1924)/Initialen der ersten Worte von Deuteronomium 33,4/(dies ist) die Arbeit meiner Hände Chatan Ben Levi …“
H: 28 cm; Dm: 7,3 cm
Inv.Nr. 050.001.054 [68]

TORA-PLAKETTE
Amadiya/Kurdistan, um 1924/25
Silber
Hebräische Inschrift auf der Rückseite: „Diese Plakette wurde gestiftet von Nasi Bat Baton für die heilige Gemeinde Amadiya im Jahr 685 der kleinen Zeitrechnung (i.e. 1924/25).“ Auf der Vorderseite sind die Abkürzungen für die Zehn Gebote eingraviert.
H: 13,5 cm; B: 9,1 cm
Inv.Nr. 045.001.001 [69]

68 Die vorliegenden Rimmonim stammen aufgrund ihrer Stilistik vermutlich aus dem irakischen Teil Kurdistans. Vergleichbare Rimmonim in: The Jews of Kurdistan, S. 24. Zur kurdisch-jüdischen Silberschmiedekunst s. Kurdish Jewish Silvercraft.

69 In kurdischen Gemeinden war es üblich, dass der Gabbai eine solche Tora-Plakette demjenigen Teilnehmer am Gottesdienst überreichte, der zur Tora aufgerufen werden sollte. Nach der Tora-Lesung wurde diese Plakette zurückgegeben. Heute wird dieser Brauch in Israel nur mehr selten weitergeführt. Zu vergleichbaren Tora-Plaketten s. The Jews of Kurdistan, S. 31ff.

Kurdistan. "According to the mufti, as much as 1000 years ago there were more than 200 Christian churches and many synagogues in this area. Whereas the Jews of Europe are excluded from the trades, here they have to make their livings by the work of their hands."

Carsten Niebuhr, c. 1765*

Nowadays, three countries share the area of Kurdistan: Turkey, Iran, and Iraq. The majority of Kurdish Jews lived in what later became Iraq. According to tradition, the Jews of Kurdistan are the descendants of the Ten Tribes from the time of the Assyrian exile. Jewish population was boosted by the descendants of the Kingdom of Adiabene, which had converted in a body to Judaism in the 1st century. One of Kurdistan's most important Jewish centers was Amadiya, which supposedly had 25,000 Jewish inhabitants in the Middle Ages. Later centers were Arbil, Kirkuk, Mosul, Sulaimaniya, and Sena. Isolated for the longest time, Kurdish Jews drew for once the outside's attention in the 12th century with the messianic movements of Menahem ben Solomon ibn Ruchi and David Alroy. Several Kurdish rabbinates dealt with practical Kabbalah and a remarkable number of Jewish Kurds were gifted payitanim, poets who wrote religious and secular poetry in Hebrew and Aramaic. Ever since the big persecutions of the 1940s in Iraq and the anti-Zionist propaganda also in Iran, the majority of Jewish Kurds has left the region and immigrated to Israel.

B/W Photo p. 81: Frits Meyst, Jewish lady, Kurdistan, 1990

The Navi Yehezqel Synagogue in Amadiya, Kurdistan, c. 1940.
From: Erich Brauer, The Jews of Kurdistan, Detroit 1993

Die Navi Yehezqel Synagoge in Amadiya, Kurdistan, um 1940.
Aus: *Erich Brauer, The Jews of Kurdistan, Detroit 1993*

PIYUTIM/LITURGICAL POETRY
Kurdistan, 1863/84
Manuscript on paper, ink, paint; with carpet pages and decorations on margins
Scribe: Siman Tov Ben Yechezkiel
Colophon on fol 64a: "I, the learned scribe, Siman Tov, the son of the honorable Rav, the wise Yehezkiel, may the Merciful protect him and bless him, written in the year (5)624 (i.e. 1863/64)."
Pages: 105
Height: 17.8 cm; Width: 11.1 cm; Depth: 1.2 cm
No. KU.011.001 [66]

KETUBAH/MARRIAGE CONTRACT
Sena/Kurdistan, 1872
Paper, ink, watercolors
Bride: Jicofa Bat Mashiach; Groom: Yechezkiel Ben Daniel
Height: 69.6 cm; Width: 44.7 cm
No. 035.011.004 [67]

RIMMONIM/TORAH FINIALS
Kurdistan,1924
Silver
Artist: Hatan Ben Levi
Hebrew inscription on finial 1: "Dedicated to the Lord forever/initials of the first and last three words of Psalms 145:16/ initials of the first and last three words of Psalms 91:11/Sassoon Ben Yissachar, may the Lord sustain and protect him." On finial 2: "The 4th of Sivan, 724 of the year five thousand (i.e. 1924)/initials of the first words of Deut. 33:4/the work of my hand Hatan Ben Levi ..."
Height: 28 cm; Diameter: 7.3 cm
No. 050.001.054 [68]

TORAH-PLAQUE
Amadiya/Kurdistan, c. 1925
Silver
Hebrew inscription on back: "This plaque was dedicated by Nazee Bat Baton to the holy community of Amadiya, the year 685 according to the minor reckoning (i.e. 1925)." In front: engravings of the abbreviations for the Ten Commandments.
Height: 13.5 cm; Width: 9.1 cm
No. 045.001.001 [69]

* Carsten Niebuhr, Entdeckungen im Orient. Reise nach Arabien und anderen Ländern 1761–1767, p. 166–167

66 The manuscript contains religious poetry in Hebrew and Persian (written in Hebrew characters) by various payitanim (poets of religious texts and songs) such as Menahem Ben Sassoon, Rafael Bar Eliyahu Kazin, Israel Najara, Sassoon Ben Moshe, Abdulla Ben Zir, Shmuel Bar Nissim, et al. Illustration of a similar manuscript in: The Jews of Kurdistan, p. 11.

67 For this ketubah, see Index, Gross Family Collection, no. 84. For comparable marriage contracts: The Jews of Kurdistan, p. 24–27. For another ketubah from Sena: Mazal Tov, no. 48; for a contract fragment from Sena: Ketubbah, no. 222. The above manuscript is a gift from the Israeli artist Litvnovsky to the Gross Family Collection.

68 Based on their style, it can be assumed that these rimmonim here originate from the Iraqi part of Kurdistan. Comparable rimmonim in: The Jews of Kurdistan, p. 24. For Kurdish-Jewish art of silversmithing, see Ora Schwartz-Be'eri, in: The Israel Museum Journal, Kurdish Jewis Silvercraft, p. 75– 95.

69 In Kurdish communities it was custom for the gabbai to present the participant of the service who was called up to the Torah with such a Torah plaque. After the reading the plaque was returned. Today, this custom is only rarely observed in Israel. For comparable Torah plaques, see The Jews of Kurdistan, p. 31ff.

LEUCHTERPAAR

Wilna/Litauen, 1857
Silber
Künstler: Movsh As
H: 32,7 cm; B: 12,1 cm
Inv.Nr. 012.001.008 [70]

BSAMIM/GEWÜRZ-TURM

Wilna/Litauen, 1819
Silber
Künstler: JP, nicht identifiziert
H: 15,3 cm; B: 4,6 cm
Inv.Nr. 015.001.057 [71]

KIDDUSCHBECHER

Wilna/Litauen, 1888
Silber
Künstler: Chaim Katz
H: 17,4 cm; Dm: 7,3 cm
Inv.Nr. 017.001.077 [72]

MISRACH-SCHERENSCHNITT

Vilkavishkis/Litauen, 1897
Papier, Tusche, farbiges Gewebe
Hebräische Inschrift in der letzten Zeile: „Dieses Kunstwerk wurde heute, Dienstag den 21ten des Monats Adar I 5657 (i.e. 1897) von mir, Mosche Sofer beendet." In kyrillischen Buchstaben: „Movsha Oberschmidt".
H: 45,5 cm; B: 36,5 cm
Inv.Nr. 036.011.012 [73]

---

* Dr. Emil Schaeffer (ed.), Ein Ghetto im Osten. Wilna, Zürich/Leipzig 1931, S. 4

70 Zu diesem Paar s. Jüdische Lebenswelten, Nr. 3/15. Zu ähnlichen Stücken vgl. Sotheby's New York, June 1985, lot 333; Sotheby's New York, May 1986, lot 386; Collector's Guide, Abb. Nr. 30. Zur Stadtpunze s. Postnikova-Losseva, Nr. 169.

71 Zu weiteren litauischen Gewürz-Türmen s. Anglo-Jewish Historical Exhibition, nach S. 100; Jewish Museum London, S. 428, Abb. CXXI; Towers of Spice, Nr. 59.

72 Der vorliegende Typus des litauischen Kidduschbechers für den Segen über den Wein wurde in der 2. Hälfte des 19. Jhs. entwickelt. Zu ähnlichen Bechern vgl. Sotheby's London, February 1986, lot 481; Sotheby's New York, December 1988, lot 196; Parke Bernet New York, October 1974, lot 183. Zur Silberschmiedpunze von Chaim Katz (1859–97) s. Postnikova-Losseva, Nr. 210.

73 Zu dem vorliegenden Scherenschnitt s. Sotheby's Tel Aviv, Jewellery and Judaica, April 1989, lot 432. Andere bekannte Arbeiten von demselben Künstler finden sich im Spertus Museum Chicago (eine Jahrzeittafel), sowie im Lübecker Volkskundemuseum (ein Misrach).

Wilna. „… Wilna, meine große Ahne, Stadt und Mutter in Israel, Jerusalem des Galuth, Trost des Ostvolkes im Norden."

Salmen Schneur, 1929*

Wilna, die frühere Hauptstadt des Großfürstentums Litauen, zählte zu den bedeutendsten Zentren des jüdischen kulturellen und religiösen Lebens in Osteuropa. Die ersten Juden ließen sich im 15., nach anderen Quellen schon im 14., Jahrhundert in Wilna nieder. Politisch war die Stadt abwechselnd unter litauischer, polnischer oder russischer Herrschaft. Unter den zahlreichen jüdischen Rabbinern ragte besonders der Gaon von Wilna hervor, der als Vertreter der klassischen jüdischen Gelehrsamkeit in Gegnerschaft zum Chassidismus stand. Im 19. und zu Beginn des 20. Jahrhunderts war Wilna Sitz bedeutender hebräischer und jiddischer Druckereien. 1925 wurde das Jiddische Wissenschaftliche Institut (YIVO) in Wilna gegründet, das vor dem Zweiten Weltkrieg nach New York übersiedeln konnte. Aus Wilna stammt auch die berühmte Wilnaer Truppe, die dem Jiddischen Theater zu Weltruhm verhalf. Mit dem Einmarsch der Deutschen im Jahr 1941 begann in Wilna ein unvorstellbares Martyrium für die jüdische Bevölkerung. 100.000 Juden wurden im Wilnaer Getto umgebracht. Die übrigen wurden in Konzentrationslager nach Estland und Lettland deportiert und dort ermordet. Nur wenige konnten mit Hilfe der Jüdischen Widerstandsbewegung zu den Partisanen flüchten. Heute leben nur noch einige wenige Juden, zumeist ältere Menschen, in Wilna.

S/W Foto S. 84: Statue des Gaon von Wilna, Litauen, 1997; Jüdische Gemeinde Wilna

VILNIAUS
GAONUI
ELIJAHU

לזכר
הגאון
ר׳אליהו
מווילנא

PAIR OF CANDLESTICKS
Vilna/Lithuania, 1857
Silver
Artist: Movsh AS
Height: 32.7 cm; Width: 12.1 cm
No. 012.001.008 [70]

B'SAMIM/SPICE TOWER
Vilna/Lithuania,1819
Silver
Artist: JP, unidentified
Height: 15.3 cm; Width: 4.6 cm
No. 015.001.057 [71]

WINECUP
Wilna/Lithuania, 1888
Silver
Artist: Haim Katz
Height: 17.4 cm; Diameter: 7.3 cm
No. 017.001.077 [72]

MIZRAH-PAPERCUT
Vilkavishkis/Lithuania, 1897
Paper, ink, colored cloth
Hebrew inscription on last line: "This work of art was made and finished today, Tuesday, the 21st
of the month of Adar I, (5)657 (i.e. 1897)by me, Moshe Sofer. (In cyrillic characters) "Movsha
Oberschmidt."
Height: 45.5 cm; Width: 36.6 cm
No. 036.011.012 [73]

Vilna. "… Vilna, my great ancestor, city, and mother in Israel, Jerusalem of the Diaspora, comfort of the Eastern people in the north."

85

Salmen Schneur, 1929*

Vilna, former capital of the Principality of Lithuania, was one of the most important centers of Jewish cultural and religious life in Eastern Europe. The first Jews settled in the 15th, according to other sources already in the 14th century in Vilna. Politically, the city alternated between Lithuanian, Polish, or Russian rule. The Gaon of Vilna stood out among the city's numerous rabbis. As a representative of classic Jewish scholarship he strongly opposed Hassidism. In the 19th and at the beginning of the 20th century, Vilna was the seat of significant Hebrew and Yiddish presses. The Yiddish Scientific Institute (YIVO), which was established in Vilna in 1925, was able to relocate to New York before World War II. Also from Vilna is the famous Vilna Troupe, which brought Yiddish theater to world renown. German invasion in 1941 was the beginning of an unimaginable martyrdom for the Jewish population in Vilna. In the ghetto of Vilna 100,000 Jews were annihilated. The rest were deported to concentration camps in Estonia and Latvia and were murdered there. Only few were able to escape to the partisans with the help of the Jewish resistance movement. Today only a few Jews, mostly elderly persons, live in Vilna.

B/W Photo p. 84: Statue of the Vilna Gaon, Vilnius, Lithuania, 1997; Jewish community Vilnius

* Dr. Emil Schaeffer (ed.), Ein Ghetto im Osten. Wilna, Zürich/Leipzig 1931, p. 4
70 For this pair, see Jüdische Lebenswelten, no. 3/15. For similar items, cf. Sotheby's New York, June 1985, lot 333; Sotheby's New
    York, May 1986, lot 386; Collector's Guide, fig. no. 30. For city mark, see Postnikova-Losseva, no. 169.
71 For more Lithuanian spice towers, see Anglo-Jewish Historical Exhibition, after p. 100; Jewish Museum London, p. 428, fig.
    CXXI; Towers of Spice, no. 59.
72 This type of Lithuanian kiddush cup for the blessing over the wine was developed in the 2nd half of the 19th c. For similar cups,
    cf. Sotheby's London, February 1986, lot 481; Sotheby's New York, December 1988, lot 196; Parke Bernet New York, October
    1974, lot 183. For Haim Katz' silversmith mark (1859–97), see Postnikova-Losseva, no. 210.
73 For this paper cut, see Sotheby's Tel Aviv, Jewellery and Judaica, April 1989, lot 432. Other known works by the same artist are
    in the Spertus Museum Chicago (a yahrzeit plaque), as well as in the folklore museum of Lübeck (a Mizrah).

Interior of the Great City Synagogue, Vilna, Lithuania, 1916
Postcard, Beth Hatefutsoth Photo Archive, Tel Aviv

Innenansicht der Großen Stadtsynagoge, Wilna, Litauen, 1916
Postkarte, Beth Hatefutsoth Foto-Archiv, Tel Aviv

Isfahan. „Von Tabaristan sind es sieben Tagereisen bis zur Stadt Isfahan, einer sehr großen Stadt, der Residenzstadt des Königs. Ihre Ausdehnung beträgt zwölf Meilen. Dort leben etwa fünfzehntausend Juden."

Benjamin von Tudela, um 1170*

Die babylonisch-persisch-iranische Diaspora ist eine der ältesten, geht sie doch vermutlich auf die Zwangsumsiedlungen von Israeliten aus Samaria zurück, die Tiglath-Pileser im 8. Jh. v.d.Z. durchführen ließ. Nach der Zerstörung des Ersten Tempels durch Nebukadnezar wurde rund 250 Jahre später wieder eine erhebliche Anzahl der Oberschicht Israels nach Babylonien deportiert, die zum Teil hier blieb, auch nachdem Cyrus ihr 538 v.d.Z. die Rückkehr in die Heimat erlaubte. Im Laufe der Zeit verschoben sich die Siedlungszentren. Eine jüdische Ansiedlung in Isfahan ist seit dem Jahr 472 d.Z. bekannt. Sie war so groß, daß Isfahan zur Zeit des Kalifats auf arabisch „Die Stadt der Juden" genannt wurde. In der jüdischen Welt war sie berühmt für ihre hebräischen Grammatiker und Exegeten. Mit dem Aufkommen der abbassidischen Dynastie im 17. Jahrhundert wurde das politische System den Juden gegenüber intoleranter. Dazu wurden sie ab dem 19. Jahrhundert auch von Bahai-Aktivisten und christlichen Missionaren schwer bedrängt. Einerseits nach der Staatsgründung Israels, andererseits nach der Islamischen Revolution 1979 verließ ein Großteil der Juden den Iran, dessen jüdische Gesamtbevölkerung heute noch rund 25.000 ausmacht, wovon knapp 10% in Isfahan lebten.

S/W Foto S. 87: Judah Segal, Ein jüdischer Kupferschmied, Isfahan, Iran, 1978; Beth Hatefutsoth Foto-Archiv, Tel Aviv

KETUBBA/EHEVERTRAG
Isfahan/Iran, 1756
Papier, Tusche, Wasserfarben
Braut: Schifra Bat Schmuel
Bräutigam: Rachamin Ben Aaron
H: 83,5 cm; B: 60,3 cm
Inv.Nr. 035.011.032 [74]

BRAUT-AMULETT
Iran, um 1900
Silber, Handschrift auf Papier; Spiegel auf der Rückseite
Hebräische Beschriftung: Psalm 67 in Form einer Menora, sowie den 42 Buchstaben des Gottesnamens
Dm: 7 cm
Inv.Nr. 027.001.083 [75]

RIMMONIM/TORA-AUFSÄTZE
In Form von Händen
Iran, um 1920
Silber
Hebräische Stiftungsinschrift: „Gewidmet dem Herrn, nicht zu veräußern und nicht zu rauben. Stifter ist Rachamim Nisan. Die heilige Gemeinde wird gebeten, seinen Geist zu erhalten, indem seine Seele erhoben und ihrer gedacht wird, und das Kaddisch nach seinem Tod zu sprechen./ Krone/der Tora/."
H: 26,9 cm; Dm: 11 cm
Inv.Nr. 050.001.044 [76]

JAD/TORA-ZEIGER
Yazd/Iran, um 1890
Silber
Hebräische Widmungsinschrift: „Gewidmet dem Herrn im Andenken an die Seele des verstorbenen Mischla Ben Mosche Akai aus Yazd, möge er in Eden ruhen; am 27. Nissan 5650 (i.e. 1890)."
L: 25,5 cm; B: 4,5 cm
Inv.Nr. 052.001.088 [77]

* Benjamin von Tudela/Petachja von Regensburg, Jüdische Reisen im Mittelalter, Köln 1998, S. 89

74 Zu Ketubbot allgemein vgl. Feuchtwanger Collection, S. 37ff.; zu der vorliegenden: The Ketubah, Nr. 22.

75 Zu ähnlichen Amuletten vgl. Jewish Folk Art over the Ages, Abb. 79; Jewish Life in Art and Tradition, S. 46; Sotheby's Tel Aviv, Magnificent Judaica, April 2001, lot 327.

76 Die Hände, als die diese Rimmonim gestaltet sind, können sowohl die segnenden Hände der Kohanim symbolisieren als auch das amulettartig schützende orientalische Chamsa (die fünf-fingrige Hand) darstellen. Zu einem ähnlichen Stück, allerdings aus der Türkei stammend, vgl. Collector's Guide, Abb.Nr. 101–102.

77 Die als Chamsa gestaltete Zeigerhand findet sich auch in anderen orientalischen Ländern wie beispielsweise Marokko. Zu einer nach persischem Vorbild gestalteten Chamsa-Jad s. Crowning Glory, Nr. 841.

Esfahan. "From Tabaristan it is a seven days' journey to the city of Esfahan, a very large city, residence of the King. It spreads over twelve miles. About fifty thousand Jews live there."

Benjamin of Tudela, c. 1170*

The Babylonian-Persian-Iranian Diaspora is one of the oldest, presumably tracing back to the forced resettlement of Israelites from Samaria, which was carried out by Tiglath-Pileser in the 8th century B.C.E. After the destruction of the First Temple by Nebuchadnezzar, again a considerable number of Israel's upper class was deported to Babylon 250 years later. Part of them remained here even after Cyrus permitted them to return to their homeland in 538 B.C.E. In the course of time the centers of settlement shifted. A Jewish settlement in Esfahan is known since the year 472 C.E. Such was its size that Esfahan was called in Arabic "The City of the Jews" at the time of the caliphate. In the Jewish world it was known for its Hebrew grammarians and exegetes. With the rise of the Abbassid dynasty in the 17th century, the political system became less tolerant toward the Jews. From the 19th century onward they were also harassed by Bahai activists and Christian missionaries. After the founding of the State of Israel and after the Islamic Revolution in 1979, a majority of Jews left Iran. The Jewish population still totals 25,000, of which 10% live in Esfahan.

B/W Photo p. 87: Judah Segal, A jewish Coppersmith, Esfahan, Iran, 1978; Beth Hatefutsoth Photo Archive, Tel Aviv

Interior view of the synagogue in Esfahan, Iran, c. 1930. *From : Dvora and Menachem Hacohen, One People - The Story of Eastern Jews, New York 1986*

Innenansicht der Synagoge in Isfahan, Iran, um 1930. *Aus : Dvora and Menachem Hacohen, One People - The Story of Eastern Jews, New York 1986*

KETUBAH/MARRIAGE CONTRACT
Esfahan/Iran, 1756
Paper, ink, water colors
Bride: Shifra Bat Shemuel
Groom: Rachamim Ben Aharon
Height: 83.5 cm; Width: 60.3 cm
No. 035.011.032 [74]

BRIDAL AMULET
Iran, c. 1900
Silver, manuscript on paper; mirror on backside
Inscribed: Psalm 67 in form of a menorah-shape and the 42-letter name of God
Diameter: 7 cm
No. 027.001.083 [75]

RIMMONIM/TORAH FINIALS
Hand-shaped
Iran, c. 1920
Silver
Hebrew inscriptions: "Dedicated to the Lord neither to be sold and nor to be pledged. The donor is Rahamim Nisan. The Holy congregation is requested to sustain his spirit by elevating and commemorating his soul and to recite the Kaddish prayer after his death./Crown of the Torah."
Height: 26.9 cm; Diameter: 11 cm
No. 050.001.044 [76]

YAD/TORAH POINTER
Yazd/Iran, c. 1890
Silver
Hebrew inscription:"Dedicated to the Lord for the soul of the departed Mishla Ben Moshe Akai, from Yazd, may he rest in Eden, the date of 27 Nissan, 5650 (i.e. 1890)."
Width: 4.5 cm; Length: 25.5 cm
No. 052.001.088 [77]

* Benjamin von Tudela/Petachja von Regensburg, Jüdische Reisen im Mittelalter, Köln 1998, p. 89
74 For ketuboth in general, cf. Feuchtwanger Collection, p. 37ff.; for this one: The Ketubah, no. 22.
75 For similar amulets, cf. Jewish Folk Art over the Ages, fig. 79; Jewish Life in Art and Tradition, p. 46; Sotheby's Tel Aviv, Magnificent Judaica, April 2001, lot 327.
76 These hands may symbolize the blessing hands of the Cohanim as well as the amulet-like protective Oriental *hamsah* (the five-fingered hand). For a similar item, but from Turkey, cf. A Collector's Guide, fig. 101–102.
77 The pointer hand in the shape of a hamsah can also be found in other Oriental countries such as Morocco. For a hamsah pointer after a Persian model, see Crowning Glory, no. 841.

JAD/TORA-ZEIGER
Emden/Deutschland, um 1790
Silber, vergoldet, Brillanten
L: 29 cm
Inv.Nr. 052.001.042 [78]

TAS/TORA-SCHILD
Emden/Deutschland, 1639/um 1790
Silber, teilweise vergoldet; teilweise restauriert; neuer Rahmen Ende 18. Jh. hinzugefügt
Hebräische Stiftungsinschrift: „Der Lebensbaum ist für jene, die danach greifen, und die ihn hoch-
halten sind glücklich. Es ist unser hochgeschätzter, aufrechter und ehrenwerter Lehrer und Rabbiner
Jakob, Sohn des Josef, möge sein Andenken gesegnet sein, der mit seinem Vermögen das Buch
des Lebensbaumes für die Synagoge erhält; und seine Gattin, die Dame Goitlen (Gütlein?), Tochter
von Rabbiner Reb Abraham, möge sein Andenken gesegnet sein, für ihren Schöpfer und zu Ehren
der Tora. Von ihrem Reichtum wurde das Tas gemacht. Es wurde zur Synagoge gebracht am
Donnerstag, dem Gedenktag, um den Herrn zu bitten, ihrer zum Guten zu gedenken. Rosch
haSchana, im Jahr ,und du setzt das Zeichen des Lebens' (Chronogramm für 400) nach der kleinen
Zeitrechnung (i.e. 1639)."
Künstler: Claes Hoppenbrouer
H: 27 cm; B: 23 cm
Inv.Nr. 051.001.019 [79]

RIMMONIM/TORA-AUFSÄTZE
Emden/Deutschland, 1801
Silber
Künstler: Johannes Beekmann Hayens
H: 51 cm; Dm: 11 cm
Inv.Nr. 050.001.026 [80]

Emden. „Das war in das Jahr 364 (1604), da haben begonnen die Anusim von Spanien und Portugal zu entlafen, un' sein gekommen nach Holland. Denn in das Jahr sin zehn Anusim mit ihr Weiber un' Kinder gekommen un' sie haben beladen gehabt zwei holländischen Schiffen. Un' durch Sturm un' Unwetter seinen sie angekommen in der heiligen Gemeinde Emden, das da is in Friesland. Es leucht wohl ein, dass Gott es hat aso gewellt haben, dass sie sollen ankommen."

Menachem Man ben Salomo, um 1750*

Seit dem 16. Jahrhundert gab es eine jüdische Gemeinde in Emden, die sich in aschkenasische und sefardische Juden unterteilte. Die 1613 aufgenommene sefardische Gemeinde – bestehend aus portugiesischen Marranen, die re-konvertiert waren – war ökonomisch und damit auch sozial wesentlich besser gestellt als die aschkenasische, die die Stadt mehrmals versuchte auszuweisen. Die großzügig privilegierten Sefarden konnten bereits um 1700 das Bürgerrecht erwerben. Demgegenüber erhielten die aschkenasischen Emder, mit Ausnahme der napoleonischen Besatzungszeit, erst 1842 das Bürgerrecht. Mitte des 18. Jahrhunderts verließen die meisten Sefarden Emden wieder, um sich in ande-ren Städten Norddeutschlands oder auch in Amsterdam niederzulassen. 1930 umfaßte die jüdische Gemeinde Emdens 1.000 Personen, von denen die meisten ab 1933 flüchteten. 110 Emder Juden wurden 1941 ins Getto Lodz deportiert. 1967 lebten sechs Juden in Emden.

S/W Foto S. 90: Naomi Tereza Salmon, Leerer Himmel, 2001

---

* Zitiert nach: Max Grunwald, Portugiesengräber auf deutscher Erde, Hamburg 1902, S. 10

78 Der Zeiger ist vermutlich gemeinsam mit der Restaurierung des Schildes gewidmet worden. S. zur Jad: Zeugnisse einer zerstör-
    ten Vergangenheit, Nr. 3, Abb. 10–12. Zu vergleichbaren Zeigern: Synagoga, Recklinghausen, C76; Von der Bibel bis Chagall,
    Abb.Nr. 83; Collection juive du musée de Cluny, Nr. 150.

79 Zu weiteren so frühen und formal ähnlichen Schildern vgl. Synagoga, Frankfurt, S. 222f., Abb. 94; Jewish Art, Abb. 7; Monumenta
    Iudaica, E 375, Abb. 98; Parke Bernet New York, October 1950, lot 107. Zum Emdener Tas s. Zeugnisse einer zerstörten Vergangenheit,
    Nr. 2, Abb. 7, 18–20. Zum Silberschmied s. Scheffler, Niedersachsen, Nr. 89.

80 Die Emdener Aufsätze gehören einem Berliner Rimmonim-Typus an, der Ende des 18. Jhs. entwickelt wurde, vgl. dazu: 50
    Rimmonim, Nr. 37; Crowning Glory, Nr. 276, 277; Danzig 1939, Nr. 80. Zu dem vorliegenden Paar s. Zeugnisse einer zerstörten
    Vergangenheit, Nr. 1, Abb. 4, 17, 21. Zum Silberschmied s. Scheffler, Niedersachsen, Nr. 686. Zur Stadtmarke ebd., Nr. 685.

YAD/TORAH POINTER

Emden, Germany, c. 1790
Silver, gilt, diamonds
Length: 29 cm
No. 052.001.042 [78]

TAS/TORAH SHIELD

Emden/Germany, 1639/c. 1790
Silver, parcel gilt; partly restored; frame newly added in late 18th century
Hebrew inscription: "The tree of Life is for those who reach for it and its upholders are content. He is our esteemed, upright and honorable teacher and rabby, Jacob son of Joseph, may his memory be blessed, who upholds with his wealth the Book of the Tree of Life for the synagogue; and his wife, the Lady Goitlen (Gütlein?), daughter of the Rabbi, Reb Abraham, may the memory of the saints be blessed, in honor of her Creator, and in honor of the Torah. Her wealth brought forth this tas. It was taken to the synagogue on Thursday, the memorial day, to request the Lord's mercy, Rosh Hashana, the year 'and you put the mark of life' (chronogram for 400), according to the minor reckoning (i.e. 1639)."
Artist: Claes Hoppenbrouer
Height: 27 cm; Width: 23 cm
No. 051.001.019 [79]

RIMMONIM/TORAH FINIALS

Emden/Germany, 1801
Silver
Artist: Johannes Beekmann Hayens
Height: 51 cm; Diameter: 11 cm
No. 050.001.026 [80]

Emden. "It was in the year 364 (1604), when the Anusim (Marranos) of Portugal and Spain began to run away and they came to Holland. For in that year, ten Anusim with their wives and children came and they had loaded up two Dutch ships. And through stormy tempests they arrived in the holy community of Emden, which is in Friesland. It is quite apparent that God has wanted them to arrive here."

Menachem Man ben Salomo, c. 1750*

91

A Jewish community in Emden was in existence since the 16th century consisting of Ashkenazic and Sephardic Jews. The Sephardic Jews who were received in 1613, Portuguese Marranos who had reconverted, were economically and thus socially better off than the Ashkenazim, whom the city had attempted to evict several times. The generously privileged Sephardim were able to obtain the rights to full citizenship around 1700. Emden's Ashkenazic Jews, on the other hand, — except for the period of Napoleonic occupation — gained citizenship only in 1842. In mid-18th century most Sephardim left Emden to settle in other cities in northern Germany or else in Amsterdam. The Jewish community of Emden numbered 1,000 persons in 1930. Most of them fled starting in 1933 and 110 Emden Jews were deported to the ghetto in Lodz. In 1967, six Jews were living in Emden.

B/W Photo p. 90: Naomi Tereza Salmon, Empty Sky, 2001

* Zitiert nach: Max Grunwald, Portugiesengräber auf deutscher Erde, Hamburg 1902, p. 10

78 The pointer was probably donated together with the restauration of the shield. For yad, see: Zeugnisse einer zerstörten Vergangenheit, no. 3, fig. 10–12. For comparable pointers: Synagoga, Recklinghausen, C76; Von der Bibel bis Chagall, fig. 83; Collection juive du musée de Cluny, no. 150.

79 For further early and formally similar shields, cf. Synagoga, Frankfurt, p. 222f., fig. 94; Jewish Art, fig. 7; Monumenta Judaica, E 375, fig. 98; Parke Bernet New York, October 1950, lot 107. For the Emden Tas, see Zeugnisse einer zerstörten Vergangenheit no. 2, fig. 7, 18–20. For silversmith, see Scheffler, Niedersachsen, no. 89.

80 The Emden finials belong to a rimmonim type from Berlin that was developed toward the end of the 18th c. Cf. 50 Rimmonim, no. 37; Crowning Glory, no. 276, 277; Danzig 1939, no. 80. For this pair, see Zeugnisse einer zerstörten Vergangenheit, no. 1, fig. 4, 17, 21. For silversmith, see Scheffler, Niedersachsen, no. 686. For city mark id., no. 685.

The synagogue of Emden, built 1836, enlarged 1910, destroyed 9th Nov. 1938. *Ostfriesisches Landesmuseum, Emder Rüstkammer, Germany*

Die Synagoge von Emden, erbaut 1836, erweitert 1910, zerstört 9. Nov. 1938. *Ostfriesisches Landesmuseum, Emder Rüstkammer, Deutschland*

**Djerba. „Auf der Insel gibt es etwa fünf-
tausend Juden. Die Kohanim von Djerba
teilen sich in zwei Familien auf. Eine Familie,
die im Mittelalter aus Tangier kam, trägt den
Namen Tanuji. Die andere Familie behauptet
von einer Aaroniden Familie vom Geschlecht
des Zadok abzustammen, welche anscheinend
zur Zeit der Zerstörung der Heiligen Stadt
durch Nebuchadnezzar direkt von Jerusalem
nach Afrika gezogen ist."**

Nachum Slouschz, 1906*

Das antike Karthago war ungefähr seit dem Jahr 200 v.d.Z. von Juden besiedelt.
Eine Blütezeit erlebte die tunesische Judenheit unter islamischer Herrschaft
zwischen dem 9. und 11. Jahrhundert. 1881 kam Tunesien unter französische
Oberhoheit, die den Juden 1910 die französische Staatsbürgerschaft zuge-
stand. Durch die deutsche Besetzung Tunesiens 1942/43 kam es zu Deportationen nicht nur vom Festland, sondern auch von der Insel Djerba, deren jüdische Ansiedlung gar auf die Zeit Salomos zurückgehen soll. Im 12. Jh. hatten
die Juden Djerbas unter der Verfolgung der Almohaden zu leiden, im 16. Jahrhundert unter der der Spanier. Bis zur deutschen Besatzung waren sie ansonsten völlig toleriert. Im 19. Jahrhundert wurden sie für ihre Rabbiner-Ausbildung
bekannt, im 20. Jahrhundert für ihre Druckerei. Nach 1945 emigrierten viele
tunesische Juden nach Frankreich oder Israel. Von den 5.000 Juden, die 1946
auf Djerba lebten, hatten 1960 3.000 die Insel verlassen.

S/W Foto S. 93: Micha Bar-Am, In der El-Ghriba-Synagoge, Djerba, Tunesien, 1995; Beth Hatefutsoth
Foto-Archiv, Tel Aviv

RIMMONIM/TORA-AUFSÄTZE
Djerba/Tunesien, um 1880
Silber, Leder
H: 44,5 cm; Dm: 6,4 cm
Inv.Nr. 050.001.001 [81]

CHANUKKA-LEUCHTER
Djerba/Tunesien, um 1925
Zinn, Glas
H: 24 cm; B: 27,5 cm; T: 10 cm
Inv.Nr. 010.020.003 [82]

JAD/TORA-ZEIGER
Djerba/Tunesien, um 1900
Silber
Hebräische Inschrift: „Für die Ruhe des Barchani Katzentini";
auf der Hand: „Schalom Hadad"
L: 26,2 cm; B: 3,2 cm
Inv.Nr. 052.001.054 [83]

* Nahum Slouschz, Travels in North Africa, Philadelphia 1927, S. 252–258

81 Zu diesem für Djerba typischen Aufsatz-Paar s. auch: Index, Gross Family Collection, Nr. 6. Zu ähnlichen Stücken vgl. Christie's
    New York, October 1980, lot 187; Furman Collection, S. 49; Ingathering of the Nations, S. 36.

82 Zu diesem einfachen in Djerba gängigen Leuchter s. Sotheby's Tel Aviv, April 1998, lot 299.

83 Dieser Typus des tunesischen Tora-Zeigers wurde im 20. Jh. zu dem in Israel am häufigsten verwendeten. „Schalom Hadad" ist
    möglicherweise der Name des Silberschmieds.

Djerba. "There are about five thousand Jews on the island. The Cohanim of Jerba are divided into two families. One family, which came from Tangiers in the Middle Ages, bears the name of Tanuji. The other family claims to be descended from a family of Aaronides of the race of Zadoc which seems to have migrated to Africa direct from Jerusalem at the time of the destruction of the Holy City by Nebuchadnezzar."

Nahum Slouschz, 1906*

Jews have lived in antique Carthage approximately since the year 200 B.C.E. Tunisian Jewry peaked under Islamic rule between the 9th and 11th century. In 1881 Tunisia came under the rule of France, which granted the Jews French citizenship in 1910. Deportations in the wake of German occupation of Tunisia in 1942/43 took place not only on the mainland, but also on the island of Djerba whose Jewish settlement is presumed to trace back to Solomon's time. In the 12th century the Jews of Djerba had to suffer from persecutions by the Almohads, in the 16th century by the Spanish. Up to the German occupation they were then completely tolerated. In the 19th century they became known for their rabbinical training, in the 20th century for their presses. Many Tunisian Jews emigrated to France or Israel after 1945. Of the 5,000 Jews living on Djerba in 1946, 3,000 had left the island by 1960.

B/W Photo p. 93: Micha Bar-Am, In the El Ghriba Synagogue, Djerba, Tunesia 1995; Beth Hatefutsoth Photo Archive, Tel Aviv

Interior of the El Ghriba synagogue, Tunesia, c. 1920
From: Dvora and Menachem Hacohen, One People – The Story of Eastern Jews, New York 1986, p. 78

Innenansicht der El-Ghriba-Synagoge, Tunesien, c. 1920.
Aus: Dvora and Menachem Hacohen, One People – The Story of Eastern Jews, New York 1986, S. 78

RIMMONIM/TORAH FINIALS
Djerba/Tunisia, c. 1880
Silver, leather
Height: 44.5 cm; Diameter: 6.4 cm
No. 050.001.001 [81]

HANUKKAH LAMP
Djerba/Tunisia, c. 1925
Tin, glass
Height: 24 cm; Width: 27.5 cm; Depth: 10 cm
No. 010.020.003 [82]

YAD/TORAH POINTER
Djerba/Tunisia, c. 1900
Silver
Inscribed: "For the repose of Barhani Katzentini"; on the hand: "Shalom Hadad"
Width: 3.2 cm; Length: 26.2 cm
No. 052.001.054 [83]

* Nahum Slouschz, Travels in North Africa, Philadelphia 1927, p. 252–258
81 For this finial pair typical for Djerba, see also: Index, Gross Family Collection, no. 6. For similar items, cf.: Christie's New York, October 1980, lot 187; Furman Collection, p. 49; Ingathering of the Nations, p. 36.
82 For this simple lamp, popular in Djerba, see Sotheby's Tel Aviv, April 1998, lot 299.
83 This Tunesian type Torah pointer became the most widely used in Israel in the 20th c. "Shalom Hadad" is possibly the name of the silversmith.

TORA-WIMPEL

Mit den segnenden Priesterhänden und Davidsternen

Italien, um 1590

Leinen, Seidengarn

Hebräische Inschrift: „Mosche Bar Schabtai haCohen und seine Gattin Chana Bat Rabbi David Frend, möge er viele gute Tage erleben. Mögen sie Nachkommen sehen und leben und gedeihen und sich über die Erde ergießen./Dies ist das Gebot, das Mose den Kindern Israel gegeben hat (Deuteronomium 4,44)./Sie (die Tora) ist ein Lebensbaum allen, die nach ihr leben, und glücklich ist Jedermann, der sich an sie hält (Sprüche 3,18)./Die Tora ist der Baum des Lebens, sie ist Leben für jeden Menschen."

H: 15,4 cm; L: 375 cm

Inv.Nr. 019.014.005 [84]

ESTHER-ROLLE

Im Renaissance-Stil

Rom (?)/Italien, um 1750

Pergament, Tusche, Farben

H: 29,5 cm; L: 613 cm

Inv.Nr. 081.012.043 [85]

KETUBBA/EHEVERTRAG

Rom/Italien, 1638

Pergament, Tusche, Wasserfarben

Mikrographie, bestehend aus den Texten Hoheslied, Prediger, Ruth und Hochzeitsgedichten

Braut: Angelica Bat Mosche Da Pagliano

Bräutigam: Menachem Ben Schmuel Da Pagliano

H: 50,5 cm; B: 36 cm

Inv.Nr. 035.012.005 [86]

CHANUKKA-LEUCHTER

Rom (?)/Italien, um 1700

Messing

H: 11,6 cm; B: 22,7 cm

Inv.Nr. 010.002.041 [87]

---

* Abraham Berliner, Geschichte der Juden in Rom, Frankfurt am Main 1893, Bd. I, S. V

84 Zu vergleichbaren Wimpeln s. Fabric of Life, Nr. 16; Gardens and Ghettos, S. 124, Abb. 109; I TAL YA', Nr. 105; Jewish Ceremonial Art and Religious Objects, Nr. 334; Womanly Arts, Abb.Nr. 6.10-12. Zum vorliegenden Wimpel: Chotam Shelomo, Abb.Nr. 43.

85 Bereits im Spätmittelalter scheinen Esther-Rollen zumindest im italienischen und deutschen Raum illuminiert worden zu sein. Ab dem 17. Jh. gehörte dann die Illustrierung der Megillot für wohlhabendere Schichten bereits einfach dazu. Mit besonders elaborierten Illustrationen machte sich Schalom Italia einen Namen, dessen Renaissance-Megillot lange Zeit als Vorbilder für andere Illustratoren in Aschkenas dienten.

86 Zum Wappen der römischen Familie Pagliano, das auf der Ketubba zu sehen ist, s. Arte Ebraica a Roma, S. 163. Zu vergleichbaren Verträgen s. Cultura Ebraica in Emilia-Romagna, Nr. 6.1:1; Ketubbot Italiane, Nr. 3. Zu einer ebenfalls aus der 1. H. des 17. Jhs. stammenden Ketubba aus Rom vgl. Mazal Tov, Nr. 9. Zu weiteren römischen Ketubbot vgl. Ketubbah, Nr. 74–81 (jedoch alle später).

87 Zu ähnlichen Stücken s. Architecture in the Hanukkah Lamp, Nr. 9, 10; Cultura Ebraica in Emilia-Romagna, Nr. 5.7:4; Ticho Collection, Nr. 10; Joodse Feestdagen, Chanoeka, Nr. 10; Stieglitz Collection, Nr. 128; Furman Collection, S. 28; Hanukkah Lamp, Nr. 41, Pl. XV.

Rom. „Die Geschichte der Juden in Rom ist zugleich die Geschichte der ältesten jüdischen Gemeinde Europas, welche die Zeiten der Römerherrschaft, der Völkerwanderung, des Mittelalters, der Inquisition und des Pontificats überdauert und, im eigentlichen wie im figürlichen Sinne des Wortes, sich in ihrer Existenz behauptet hat."

Abraham Berliner, 1893*

Die italienische Geschichte Italiens reicht zurück bis in die Antike. Ab dem 2. Jahrhundert v.d.Z. wurden häufig diplomatische Delegationen, aber auch Abordnungen von Gelehrten aus Erez Israel nach Rom geschickt. Der daraus entstandene Grundstock einer Gemeinde wurde erheblich vergrößert, als nach der römischen Invasion Judäas im Jahr 63 v.d.Z. und nach der Zerstörung Jerusalems im Jahr 70 d.Z. viele Juden als Sklaven nach Rom verbracht wurden. Die jüdischen Zentren lagen allerdings bis zum Mittelalter in Süditalien und auf Sizilien. Die mittel- und norditalienischen Gemeinden wurden erst im 13. und 14. Jahrhundert durch Immigranten aus Deutschland und Frankreich, sowie im 15. Jahrhundert aus Spanien gegründet. Diese Gemeinden erlebten in der Zeit der Renaissance und des Humanismus eine ungeheure kulturelle Blütezeit. Die italienischen hebräischen Wiegendrucke waren die berühmtesten in Europa, die illustrierten Handschriften die ästhetischsten, die jüdisch-italienischen Ärzte waren die bestausgebildeten, und die hebräische Poesie erlebte in Italien ihren Höhepunkt. Umso schlimmer traf die Juden die absolute Gettoisierung im Zuge der Gegenreformation, die folgenden Restriktionen und teilweise Ausweisungen. Emanzipiert wurde die italienische Judenheit im 19. Jahrhundert je nach Herrschaftsgebiet in unterschiedlichen Jahrzehnten. Im ersten Viertel des 20. Jahrhunderts lebten 37.000 Juden in Italien, eine Zahl, die auch der heutigen jüdischen Bevölkerung ungefähr entspricht. Nach Mussolinis Einführung der Rassengesetze emigrierten 6.000. Nach der Besetzung Norditaliens durch Deutschland fielen 8.000 Juden den Massakern und Deportationen zum Opfer.

S/W Foto S. 96: Adriano Mordenti, Lello Perugia auf dem Dach der Synagogue in Rom, Italien, 1995

TORAH BINDER
With the hands of the Cohanim and the Star of David
Italy, c. 1590
Linen, silk thread
Hebrew inscription: "Moshe Bar Shabtai Hacohen and his wife Mrs. Hanah Bat Rabbi David Frent, may he live many good days. May they see progeny and will live and thrive and people the earth./And this is the law which Moses set before the children of Israel (Deut. 4:44)./She (the Torah) is a tree of life to those that embrace her; those who lay hold of her will be blessed. (Prov. 3:18)./The Torah is the tree of life and life for everyone."
Height: 15.4 cm; Length: 375 cm
No. 019.014.005 [84]

ESTHER SCROLL
In Renaissance style
Rome (?)/Italy, c. 1750
Parchment, ink, paint
Height: 29.5 cm; Length: 613 cm
No. 081.012.043 [85]

KETUBAH/MARRIAGE CONTRACT
Rome/Italy, 1638
Parchment, ink, watercolors
Micrography, with the texts of the Songs of Songs, Ecclesiastes, Ruth and wedding poems
Bride: Angelica Bat Moshe Da Pagliano
Groom: Menachem Ben Shemuel Da Pagliano
Height: 50.5 cm; Width: 36 cm
No. 035.012.005 [86]

HANUKKAH LAMP
Rome (?)/Italy, c. 1700
Brass
Height: 11.6 cm, Width: 22.7 cm
No. 010.002.041 [87]

Rome. "The history of the Jews of Rome is also the history of Europe's oldest Jewish community, which has survived the rule of the Romans, the migration of peoples, the middle-ages, the Inquisition, and the pontificate; they have stood their ground in the true and in the figurative sense of the word."

Abraham Berliner, 1893*

97

Italy's Jewish history traces back to antiquity. From the 2nd century B.C.E., diplomatic delegations, but also delegations of scholars, were frequently sent from Eretz Israel to Rome. The resulting foundation for a community broadened significantly when after the Roman invasion of Judea in 63 B.C.E. and after the destruction of Jerusalem in 70 C.E. many Jews were brought to Rome into slavery. However, the Jewish centers until the Middle Ages were located in southern Italy and Sicily. Immigrants from Germany and France in the 13th and 14th century and from Spain in the 15th century founded communities in central and northern Italy. These communities thrived tremendously in the age of the Renaissance and Humanism. The Italian-Hebrew incunabula were the most famed in Europe, the illustrated manuscripts the most esthetic, the Jewish-Italian physicians the best educated, and Hebrew poetry was at its peak in Italy. All the harder was the blow to the Jews when they got completely ghettoized in the wake of the Counter-Reformation as well as subjected to restrictions and partial expulsions. Emancipation reached Italian Jews in various decades of the 19th century, according to area of sovereignty. In the first quarter of the 20th century 37,000 Jews lived in Italy, a similar number as today. After the introduction of racial laws by Mussolini, 6,000 Jews emigrated. After German occupation of northern Italy, 8,000 Jews fell victim to massacres and deportations.

B/W Photo p. 96: Adriano Mordenti, Lello Perugia on the roof of the synagogue in Rome, Italy, 1995

* Abraham Berliner, Geschichte der Juden in Rom, Frankfurt am Main 1893, Bd. I, p. V
84 For comparable wimpel, see Fabric of Life, no. 16; Gardens and Ghettos, p. 124, fig. 109; I TAL YA', no. 105; Jewish Ceremonial Art and Religious Objects, no. 334; Womanly Arts, fig. 6.10–12. For this wimpel: Chotam Shelomo, fig. 43.
85 Esther scrolls were apparently illuminated already in the Late Middle Ages, at least in the Italian and German region. From the 17th c. onward, the illustration of megilloth became simply a matter of course for the wealthy. Shalom Italia became renowned with his particularly elaborated illustrations. For a long time, his Renaissance megilloth served as models for other illustrators in Ashkenaz.
86 For the coat of arms of the Roman family Pagliano, which can be seen on the ketubah, see Arte Ebraica a Roma, p. 163. For comparable contracts, see Cultura Ebraica in Emilia-Romagna, no. 6.1:1; Ketubbot Italiane, no. 3. For a ketubah, also from the 1st half of the 17th c., from Rome, cf. Mazal Tov, no. 9. For more Roman ketuboth, cf. Ketubbah, no. 74–81 (however, all of them later).
87 For similar items, see Architecture in the Hanukkah Lamp, no. 9, 10; Cultura Ebraica in Emilia Romagna, no. 5.7:4; Ticho Collection, no. 10; Joodse Feestdagen, Chanoeka, no. 10; Stieglitz Collection, no. 128; Furman Collection, p. 28; Hanukkah Lamp, no. 41, Pl. XV.

Synagogue in Rome, Italy, c. 1900
Jewish Museum Vienna, Inv.No. 1767

Die Synagoge in Rom, Italien, um 1900
Jüdisches Museum Wien, Inv.Nr. 1767

Buchara. „Die 4- oder 5000 Juden in Buchara bewohnen ein besonderes Viertel und tragen ein besonderes Zeichen an ihrer Kleidung. Viele waren weitgereiste Leute. Mindestens einige Hundert waren ‚Hadschis', die die Pilgerfahrt nach Jerusalem gemacht hatten. Die meisten derer, die größere Reisen machen, waren in Moskau, viele auch in Paris und einige in London gewesen."

E.N. Adler, um 1890*

Erste verlässliche Nachrichten über eine jüdische Gemeinde im zentralasiatischen Khanat Buchara, dem nachmaligen Usbekistan, stammen aus dem 13. Jahrhundert. Die Gemeinde in der Stadt Buchara dürfte sich im 14. Jahrhundert herausgebildet haben. Die Sprache der jüdischen Bucharen ist ein Tadschikisch-jüdischer Dialekt, bis 1935 in hebräischen Lettern geschrieben. Ursprünglich an der persischen Liturgie orientiert, übernahmen sie später die sefardische. Sowohl unter mongolischer als auch unter islamischer Herrschaft waren die bucharischen Juden mit zahlreichen Restriktionen und Diskriminierungen konfrontiert. Ab der 2. Hälfte des 19. Jahrhunderts setzten größere Auswanderungswellen nach Palästina ein. Nach der russischen Eroberung der Region wurden Teile Bucharas Turkestan zugeschlagen und es kam zu einer permanenten Migrationsbewegung zwischen dem Emirat Buchara und Turkmenien. Nach der Februar-Revolution 1917 wurde die bürgerliche Gleichstellung für alle Einwohner Russlands proklamiert, dem sich der bucharische Emir anschloß. Darauf kam es in der Stadt Buchara zu schweren antijüdischen Ausschreitungen und belastenden finanziellen Maßnahmen. 1920 eroberte die Rote Armee das Emirat und wandelte es in eine Sowjetrepublik um. Nach dem Zensus des Jahres 1959 lebten 23.000 bucharische Juden in Usbekistan, davon 20% in der Stadt Buchara und weitere 5.000 in Tadschikistan. Mit den Emigrationen der siebziger Jahre nach Israel hat sich diese Zahl erheblich verringert.

S/W Foto S. 99: Joan Roth, Legendäre Volks-Sängerin Yafa Pinkhasova (Mitte), Buchara, Usbekistan, 1998

KIDDUSCHBECHER

Mit Unterteller

Buchara/Usbekistan, um 1925

Silber

Hebräische Inschrift auf dem Unterteller: „Dies ist der Teller, der von Hefzi, der Tochter von Nathan, gewidmet wurde."

H: 7,1 cm; Dm: 6,3 cm

Inv.Nr. 017.001.033 [88]

RIMMONIM/TORA-AUFSÄTZE

Buchara/vermutlich aus dem Grenzgebiet zu Afghanistan, 1894/95

Silber

Hebräische Widmungsinschrift: „Dieses Paar Rimmonim wurde von Kalmak, der Gattin unseres Lehrers Mosche Tama im Jahr 655 der kleinen Zeitrechnung (i.e. 1894/95) gewidmet."

H: 33 cm; Dm: 10 cm

Inv.Nr. 050.001.035 [89]

SCHIWITI-TAFEL

Aus dem Text Menorot gebildet, die segnenden Priesterhände und die Gesetzestafeln

Buchara, 1904/05

Handschrift auf Papier, Tusche, Goldfarbe

Schreiber: Nissim Sejera

H: 63,4 cm; B: 46,3 cm

Inv.Nr. 058.011.011 [90]

DIE FÜNF BÜCHER MOSE

Buchara/Usbekistan, 1769

Handschrift auf Papier, Tusche, Farben

Geschrieben für Jizchak Ben Josef

Kolophon: „Ich, Oz Badal, der Sohn des Bo Fizi, Sohn des Bo Oz, Sohn unseres Lehrers Josef, Sohn unseres Lehrers Azim, habe dies geschrieben und beendet im Land Buchara am Fluß Kohach am 29. Marcheschwan 5530 (i.e. 1769)."

103 Seiten

H: 18,1 cm; B: 12 cm; T: 1,3 cm

Inv.Nr. BU.011.001 [91]

* Elkan Nathan Adler, Von Ghetto zu Ghetto. Reisen und Beobachtungen von Elkan Nathan Adler, Stuttgart 1909, S. 157–158

88 Ähnliche Stücke in: Bokhara, Nr. 2 u. 3; Jewish Folk Art over the Ages, Abb. XI. Zum vorliegenden Set s. Siddur Klal Jisrael, S.335; Shabbat Shalom, S. 38; Jüdische Lebenswelten, Nr. 3/40.

89 Vgl. auch: Afghanistan, Nr. 13.

90 Obwohl die Schiwiti-Tafel in Buchara hergestellt worden ist, entspricht sie dem Jerusalemer Typus des Schiwiti, ist also vermutlich eine Kopie eines Jerusalemer Stückes.

91 Zur vorliegenden Handschrift s. Judaica Jerusalem. Rare Books, Manuscripts, Documents, and Jewish Arts, January 1995, lot 147.

Bukhara. "The 4- or 5000 Jews in Bukhara inhabit a special quarter and wear a special sign on their garments. Many of them were widely traveled people. At least a few hundreds were 'Hajjis' who had made the pilgrimage to Jerusalem. Most of those who travel long distances, have been to Moscow, many also to Paris, and some to London."

E.N. Adler, c. 1890*

100

First reliable information about a Jewish community in the central Asian Khanat Bukhara, the later Uzbekistan, originates from the 13th century. The community in the city of Bukhara developed probably in the 14th century. The language of the Jewish Bukhars is a Tajik-Jewish dialect, written in Hebrew letters until 1935. Originally using the Persian liturgy, they later adopted the Sephardic. Bukharian Jews were faced with numerous restrictions and discriminations under Mongolian as well as Islamic rule. The second half of the 19th century saw the onset of large waves of emigration to Palestine. After the Russian conquest of the region, parts of Bukhara were attached to Turkistan, which was followed by a permanent migratory movement between the emirate Bukhara and Turkmenia. After the February Revolution in 1917, civil equality for all inhabitants of Russia was proclaimed and the Bukharian emir followed suit. As a result, severe anti-Jewish excesses occurred in the city of Bukhara and drastic financial measures were taken. The Red Army conquered the emirate in 1920 and it was turned into a Soviet republic. According to the 1959 census, 23,000 Bukharian Jews lived in Uzbekistan, 20% of them in the city of Bukhara and further 5,000 in Tajikistan. Emigration waves to Israel in the 1970s considerably decreased these numbers.

B/W Photo p. 99: Joan Roth, Legendary folksinger and dancer Yafa Pinkhasova (center), Bukhara, Uzbekistan, 1998

WINECUP FOR KIDDUSH

With saucer
Bukhara/Uzbekistan, c. 1925
Silver
Hebrew inscription: "This is the plate which was dedicated by Hefzi, the daughter of Nathan."
Height: 7.1 cm; Diameter: 6.3 cm
No. 017.001.033 [88]

RIMMONIM/TORAH FINIALS

Bukhara/probably from the region of the border with Afghanistan, 1895
Silver
Hebrew inscription: "This pair of rimmonim was dedicated by Kalmak the wife of our teacher Moshe Tamah in the year 655 according to the minor reckoning (i.e. 1894/95)."
Height: 33 cm; Diameter: 10 cm
No. 050.001.035 [89]

SHIVITI-TABLET

Decorated with Menorot text, the hands of the priestly blessing and the Tablets of the Law
Bukhara, 1904/05
Manuscript on paper, ink, gold paint
Scribe: Nissim Sejera
Height; 63.4 cm; Width: 46.3 cm
No. 058.011.011 [90]

THE FIVE BOOKS OF MOSES

Bukhara/Uzbekistan, 1769
Manuscript on paper, ink, paint
Written for Yitzhak Ben Yosef
Colophon: "I have written and I have finished, I, Oz Badal, Son of Bo Fizi, the son of Bo Oz, the son of our teacher Yosef, son of our teacher Azim, in the country of Bukhara which is on the river Kohakh, in the year 5530 on the 29th day of the moon of Marcheshvan (i.e. 1769)."
Pages: 103
Height: 18.1 cm; Width: 12 cm; Depth: 1.3 cm
No. BU.011.001 [91]

Interior view of synagogue in Bukhara, Uzbekistan, 1890
Russian Museum of Ethnography, St. Petersburg

Innenansicht der Synagoge in Buchara, Usbekistan, 1890
Staatliches Ethnographisches Museum, St. Petersburg

* Elkan Nathan Adler, Von Ghetto zu Ghetto. Reisen und Beobachtungen von Elkan Nathan Adler, Stuttgart 1909, p. 157–158
88 Similar items in: Bokhara, no. 2 and 3; Jewish Folk Art over the Ages, fig. XI. For this set, see Siddur Klal Jisrael, p. 335; Shabbat Shalom, p. 38; Jüdische Lebenswelten, no. 3/40.
89 Cf. also: Afghanistan, no. 13.
90 Although the shiviti tablet was manufactured in Bukhara, it matches the Jerusalem type of shiviti, i.e., presumably, it is a copy of a Jerusalem object.
91 For this manuscript, see Judaica Jerusalem, Rare Books, Manuscripts, Documents, and Jewish Arts, January 1995, lot 147.

DRASCHOT LE-PARSCHIOT HA-SCHAWUA

Exegetisches zur Bibel

Prag/Böhmen/Tschechien, 1702/03

Handschrift auf Papier, Tusche, Farben; illuminiert

Autor: Abraham Ben Schaul Broda [92]

Kolophon auf S. 1: „Auslegungen und Erklärungen zu Kommentaren und der Gemara, die sich auf das erste Buch Mose beziehen, und die ich aus dem Mund unseres hochgelehrten Lehrers vernommen habe, möge der Gnädige ihn beschützen und segnen, dem Haupt des Hofes in der heiligen Gemeinde Prag, und von anderen Hochgelehrten, als ich in der Jeschiwa der heiligen Gemeinde Prag studiert habe."

257 Seiten

H: 15,5 cm; B: 10 cm; T: 2,5 cm

Inv.Nr. CZ.011.001

TAS/TORA-SCHILD

Prag/Böhmen/Tschechien, 1817

Silber

Künstler: Karl Skremenec

H: 21 cm, B; 16 cm

Inv.Nr. 051.001.028 [93]

ESTHER-ROLLE

Prag/Böhmen/Tschechien, um 1700

Handschrift auf Pergament, Tusche, Kupferstiche

Kupferstecher: Jean-Paul Franck

H: 38,5 cm: L; 258 cm

Inv.Nr. 081.012.044 [94]

Prag. „Der Prager Jude ist ein Unicum unter den Juden, wie Prag unter den Städten. Seht den alten jüdischen Friedhof an und lest es seinen verwitterten Steinen ab!"

Hermann Bahr, um 1900*

Seit dem 10. Jh. bereits gab es eine jüdische Ansiedlung in Prag, wo heute die älteste noch genutzte Synagoge Europas aus dem Mittelalter steht, die Altneuschul. Obwohl das Schicksal der Prager jüdischen Gemeinde im Mittelalter und in der Neuzeit ähnlich tragisch wechselhaft war wie das der anderen aschkenasischen Gemeinden und es zur vollen bürgerlichen Gleichstellung unter den Habsburgern erst 1867 kam, gehörte Prag immer zu den jüdisch-kulturellen und intellektuellen Zentren Europas. Hier wirkten die größten rabbinischen Autoritäten, hier wurde der Golem „erfunden" und hier wurde die erste hebräische Buchdruckerei nördlich der Alpen gegründet. 1938 lebten in Prag 45.000 Juden, nach Kriegsende 11.000, eine Zahl, die sich durch die Emigrationswelle 1948/49 nach Israel und durch die Repressalien, die die kommunistische Ära ausübte, noch erheblich verringerte.

S/W Foto S. 102: Ben Eden, Ein Chabad Lubavitcher zündet die Menora, Prag, Tschechische Republik, 1998

---

* Max Brod (ed.), Das Jüdische Prag. Eine Sammelschrift mit Texten von Max Brod, Franz Kafka, Else Lasker-Schüler, Isidor Pollak, Robert Weltsch, Franz Werfel u. a., Frankfurt am Main 1978, S. 4

92 Abraham Ben Schaul Broda (gest. 1717), in Böhmen gebürtig, war als religionsgesetzliche Autorität weithin anerkannt. In seinen Hauptwirkungsstätten Metz und Frankfurt richtete er Jeschiwot ein, die zahlreiche Studenten anzogen.

93 Zu Tora-Schildern desselben Meisters s. Ars Judaica Bohemiae, Nr. 64 u. 80; Das jüdische Museum in Prag, S. 159; Gems of the Prague Ghetto, Abb. XIV; Furman Collection, S. 4; Precious Legacy, S. 46, Abb. 106; Toraschilder aus den Werkstätten der Prager Silberschmiede, Abb. 1, Tafel I, II, III. Zur Silberschmied-Punze s. Hrasky, Nr. 422, Abb. 3.4; zur Stadtmarke: Reitzner, S. 290, P 231, zur Taxmarke: Reitzner, S. 206, P 135.

94 Zu anderen Kopien dieser Esther-Rolle s. Génie du Judaisme, Abb.Nr. 257; Papier ist doch weiss?, S. 72; Jewish Life in Art and Tradition, S. 167; Israël à travers les ages, Nr. 361; Sotheby's Tel Aviv, Fine Judaica, May 1988, lot 260.

DRASHOT LE-PARSHIOT HA-SHAVUA

Exegeses to the Pentateuch

Prague/Bohemia/Czech Republic, 1702/03

Manuscript on paper, ink, paint; illuminated

Author: Avraham Ben Shaul Broda[92]

Colophon on page 1: "Arguments and Explanations on commentaries and the Gemara which are related to the Book of Genesis, which I heard from the mouth of our highly learned teacher, may the Merciful one protect him and bless him, the head of the religious court in the holy community of Prague and from other scholars when I studied in the Yeshiva in the holy community of Prague."

Pages: 257

Height: 15.5 cm; Width: 10 cm; Depth: 2.5 cm

No. CZ.011.001

TAS/TORAH SHIELD

Prague/Bohemia/Czech Republic, 1817

Silver

Artist: Karl Skremenec

Height: 21 cm; Width: 16 cm

No. 051.001.028[93]

ESTHER SCROLL

Prague/Bohemia/Czech Republic, c. 1700

Manuscript on parchment, ink, copper plate engravings

Artist: Jean-Paul Franck

Height: 38.5 cm, Length: 258 cm

No. 081.012.044[94]

Prague. "The Prague Jew is as unique among the Jews as is Prague among the cities. See the old Jewish cemetery and read it off its weathered stones!"

Hermann Bahr, c. 1900*

In Prague a Jewish settlement is in existence since the 10th century. It is also the site of the Altneuschul, Europe's oldest medieval synagogue still in use. The fate of the Prague Jewish community in the Middle Ages and in the Modern era was similarly tragic and volatile as that of the other Ashkenazic communities, and Jews obtained equal civil rights under the Habsburgs only in 1867. Still, Prague was always part of Europe's Jewish cultural and intellectual centers. Here, the most eminent rabbinical authorities were active and here, the Golem was "invented," and here, the first Hebrew press was established north of the Alps. In 1938, 45,000 Jews lived in Prague, after the end of the war 11,000. This number further declined considerably through a wave of emigration to Israel in 1948/49 and in the wake of the repressions of the Communist era.

B/W Photo p. 102: Ben Eden, A Chabad Lubavitch lights the menorah in Prague at the beginning of Hanukka, Prague, Czech Republic, 1998

* Max Brod (ed.), Das Jüdische Prag. Eine Sammelschrift mit Texten von Max Brod, Franz Kafka, Else Lasker-Schüler, Isidor Pollak, Robert Weltsch, Franz Werfel u. a., Frankfurt am Main 1978, p. 4

92 Abraham Ben Shaul Broda (d. 1717), native of Bohemia, was a widely recognized authority on religious law. In his main places of activity, Metz and Frankfurt, he established yeshivas that attracted numerous students.

93 For Torah shields by the same maker, see Ars Judaica Bohemiae, no. 64 and 80; Das jüdische Museum in Prag, p. 159; Gems of the Prague Ghetto, fig. XIV; Furman Collection, p. 4; Precious Legacy, p. 46, fig. 106; Toraschilder aus den Werkstätten der Prager Silberschmiede, fig. 1, table I, II, III. For silversmith mark, see Hrasky, no. 422, fig. 3.4; for city mark: Reitzner, p. 290, P 231, for tax mark: Reitzner, p. 206, P 135.

94 For other copies of this Esther scroll, see Génie du Judaisme, fig. 257; Papier ist doch weiss?, p. 72; Jewish Life in Art and Tradition, p. 167; Israël à travers les ages, no. 361; Sotheby's Tel Aviv, Fine Judaica, May 1988, lot 260.

The Jewish Banner (1648) and the Gothic vault in the Altneuschul, Prague, Czech Republic, c. 1900. *Jindrich Eckert, Beth Hatefutsoth Photo Archive, Tel Aviv*

Das Jüdische Banner (1648) und die gotischen Gewölbe der Altneuschul, Prag, Tschechische Republik, um 1900. *Jindrich Eckert, Beth Hatefutsoth Foto-Archiv, Tel Aviv*

Gibraltar. „Erst seit der Eroberung Gibraltars durch die Engländer im Jahre 1701, konnten sich Juden in jener merkwürdigen Festung, welche den Eingang zum Mittelmeer beherrscht wieder niederlassen. Gegenwärtig besteht die Gemeinde aus 1583 Seelen."

Anonym, 1878*

Die ersten Juden kamen aus Spanien nach Gibraltar, dem Felsklotz gegenüber dem Djebel Musa. Im Zusammenhang mit der Inquisition Ende des 15. Jhs. in Spanien und im 16. Jh. in Portugal verstärkte sich der Zuzug. Nach der Eroberung Gibraltars durch England wurde die jüdische Gemeinde ausgewiesen. Erst 1749 erhielten Juden hier wieder Siedlungsrecht. Die Gemeinde begann aufzublühen, als Gibraltar zu einer wichtigen britischen Hafen- und Militärbasis wurde, und erreichte mit der Einwanderung auch aus Nordafrika eine Zahl von rund 2000 Mitgliedern. Während des 2. Weltkriegs wurde die gesamte Bevölkerung evakuiert, und nur ein Teil kehrte zurück. Heute leben rund 600 Juden auf Gibraltar, die in vier Synagogen beten können.

S/W Foto S. 105: Yosef Almaliach, Feierliches Gebet während der 20-Jahrfeier der Sha'ar Hashamayim Synagoge, Gibraltar, 1969; Beth Hatefutsoth Foto-Archiv, Tel Aviv

MESUSA
Zum Gebrauch im Innenraum
Gibraltar, um 1825
Silber
Beschriftet: „Schadai"
H: 14 cm; B: 11,5 cm; T: 4 cm
Inv.Nr. 040.001.005

KETUBBA/EHEVERTRAG
Gibraltar, 1833
Pergament, Tusche, Farben
Braut: Chimol Bat Mosche Rafael Tauril
Bräutigam: Masoud Ben Abraham Benbonan
H: 54,8 cm; B: 78,2 cm
Inv.Nr. 035.012.011 [95]

RIMMONIM/TORA-AUFSÄTZE
Gibraltar, um 1775
Silber
Hebräische Stiftungsinschrift: „Dies Paar Rimmonim gehört der hiesigen heiligen Gemeinde Etz Chajim und wurde gestiftet von Raw Jehuda Zarfati und Raw Chaim Hassan."
H: 28,7 cm; Dm: 9 cm
Inv.Nr. 050.001.036 [96]

* Allgemeine Zeitung des Judentums, Sept. 10, 1878

95 Obwohl die Familien der Brautleute sefardisch waren, ist der europäische Charakter der Ketubba eindeutig. Zu einer weiteren außergewöhnlichen und frühen Ketubba aus Gibraltar s. Sotheby's Tel Aviv, October 1993, lot 229; zu einer weiteren, ungefähr zeitgleichen: Ketubbah, Nr. 162.

96 Die Etz Chajim-Synagoge war die erste, die in Gibraltar errichtet wurde. Zu einem anderen dieser Synagoge gestifteten Paar Tora-Aufsätze s. Crowning Glory, Nr. 364.

Gibraltar. "Only since the English have conquered Gibraltar in 1701, have the Jews been able to settle again in this peculiar fortress that controls the entrance to the Mediterranean Sea. At present, the community consists of 1583 souls."

Anonymous, 1878*

The first Jews came from Spain to Gibraltar, the rock facing the Djebel Musa. Influx increased in the wake of the Inquisition in Spain at the end of the 15th century and in Portugal in the 16th century. After the English conquest of Gibraltar, the Jewish community was evicted. Only in 1749 the Jews again obtained the right to settle here. The community started to blossom when Gibraltar became an important British naval and military basis. With immigration also from North Africa, it eventually numbered 2,000 members. During World War II the entire population was evacuated and only part of them returned. Today, around 600 Jews live on Gibraltar and they are able to choose between four synagogues to pray in.

B/W Photo p. 105: Yosef Almaliach, Festive Prayer commemorating, the bicentennial of the Sha'ar Hashamayim Synagogue, Gibraltar, 1969; Beth Hatefutsoth Photo Archive, Tel Aviv

MEZUZAH
For interior use
Gibraltar, c. 1825
Silver
Hebrew inscription: "Shadai"
Height: 14 cm; Width: 11.5 cm; Depth: 4 cm
No. 040.001.005

KETUBAH/MARRIAGE CONTRACT
Gibraltar, 1833
Parchment, ink, paint
Bride: Chimol Bat Moshe Raphael Tauril
Groom: Masoud Ben Avraham Benbonan
Height: 54.8 cm; Width: 78.2 cm
No. 035.012.011 [95]

RIMMONIM/TORAH FINIALS
Gibraltar, c. 1775
Silver
Hebrew inscription: "This pair of Rimmonim belongs to the local Holy congregation of Etz Hayim and was donated by the Rav Yehudah Tzarfati and the Rav Haim Hassan."
Height: 28.7 cm; Diameter: 9 cm
No. 050.001.036 [96]

Interior of the Nefutsoth Yehuda Synagogue, also known as "Esnoga Flomenga", Gibraltar, c. 1940. *Gladis Pimienta, Beth Hatefutsoth Photo Archive*

Innenansicht der Nefutsoth Yehuda-Synagoge, auch bekannt als „Esnoga Flomenga", Gibraltar, um 1940. *Gladis Pimienta, Beth Hatefutsoth Foto-Archiv*

* Allgemeine Zeitung des Judentums, Sept. 10, 1878
95 Although the couple's families were Sephardic, the ketubah's European character is unmistakable. For another extraordinary and early ketubah from Gibraltar, see Sotheby's Tel Aviv, October 1993, lot 229; for another, almost contemporaneous one: Ketubbah, no. 162.
96 The Etz Haim Synagogue was the first one to be built in Gibraltar. For another pair of Torah finials donated to this synagogue, see Crowning Glory, no. 364.

JAD/TORA-ZEIGER

London/England, 1813

Silber, vergoldet, Brillianten

Künstler: Bateman (keine Punze)

Spätere hebräische Inschrift: „Dies ist ein Geschenk von Rabbi Josef Rafael, dem Sohn des Rabbi
Nathan, zu dessen 80. Geburtstag am heiligen Schabbat … des Jahres 504 (i.e. 1844/45) nach
der kleinen Zeitrechnung."

L: 33 cm; Dm: 1,5 cm

Inv.Nr. 052.001.076 [97]

HÜLLE FÜR ESTHER-ROLLE

Chester/England, 1853

Silber

Künstler: John Hilsby

L: 27 cm; Dm: 8,5 cm

Inv.Nr. 080.001.029 [98]

KIDDUSCHBECHER

Frankreich, um 1810

Mit späterer Inschrift, England, 1823

Silber

Künstler: nicht identifizierbar

Hebräische Inschrift: „Nathaniel, dem Sohn von David Abarbanel Lindo zu seiner Bar Mizwa im
Elul 1823". Im Wappen: „Be just and fear not".

H: 7,1 cm; Dm: 7,4 cm

Inv.Nr. 017.001.029 [99]

SEDER TIKKUN LE-MOHEL

Beschneidungs-Buch

London/England, 1827/28

Handschrift auf Papier, Tusche, Farben; illustriert und illuminiert; Mikrographie

Künstler: Aaron Levy

44 Seiten

H: 18,8 cm; B: 11,9 cm; T: 0,7 cm

Inv.Nr. EN.011.001 [100]

London. „Von der Viertel Million englischer Juden wohnen etwa 175.000, also 75% in London. Das Wesen der englischen Juden ist weitgehend bestimmt durch den Charakter der englischen Gesellschaft. Denn der englische Jude hat, wie der Engländer überhaupt, ein starkes Gemeinschafts- und Staatsbürgerbewußtsein. Dieses ist aristokratisch und religiös."

Rudolf Stahl, um 1925*

Im 11. Jahrhundert folgten Juden Wilhelm dem Eroberer nach England. Ging es ihnen unter normannischer Herrschaft relativ gut, so verschärfte sich ihre Lage unter dem Haus Anjou-Plantagenet vom ersten Ritualmordvorwurf in Europa bis hin zur Vertreibung im Jahr 1290. Erst Mitte des 17. Jahrhunderts wurden Juden aufgrund von Verhandlungen zwischen Manasse ben Israel und Oliver Cromwell wieder zugelassen. Als Lionel de Rothschild 1858 als liberaler Abgeordneter ins Unterhaus gewählt wurde, war das Ringen um die Emanzipation abgeschlossen. Ab den achtziger Jahren des 19. Jahrhunderts veränderten die zahlreichen, vielfach proletarischen Neueinwanderer aus Osteuropa die Sozialstruktur der eingesessenen aschkenasischen und sefardischen englischen Judenheit erheblich. Ab 1933 kam es zu einer neuerlichen Immigrationswelle, als die Juden vom europäischen Kontinent Zuflucht vor Nazi-Deutschland suchten. Die jüdische Gemeinde Englands umfaßt heute um die 330.000 Menschen, von denen allein zwei Drittel in London leben. Je nach Zugehörigkeitsgefühl und Religiosität gehören sie der sefardischen oder der orthodoxen, der konservativen, der liberalen oder der Reform-Gemeinde an.

S/W Foto S. 108: Judy Goldhill, „Sag' nein zur PLO"-Demonstration, Trafalgar Square, London, Großbritannien, 1981

* Rudolf Stahl, Englisches Judentum. Reiseeindrücke, in: Der Morgen, III. Jahrgang, Berlin 1927, S. 227–228

97 Zu Arbeiten von demselben Meister s. Sotheby's New York, May 1981, lot 274; Christie's East New York, June 1998, The A.L. Shane Collection, lot 46, 47. Zur Familie der Bateman-Silberschmiede s. Women Silversmiths 1685–1845; zur Stadt- und Jahresmarke: Jackson, S. 60.

98 Die Hülle für die Esther-Rolle stammt aus dem Besitz der Familie Montegue, von deren Judaica ausgewählte Stücke bereits in der Anglo-Jewish Exhibition des Jahres 1887 gezeigt wurden. Zur Punzierung des Stückes s. Jackson, S. 394.

99 David Abarbanel Lindo, der aktiv in der sefardisch-britischen Gemeinde wirkte, war der Mohel, der Benjamin Disraeli, den späteren englischen Premierminister beschnitten hat. Zum Wappen auf dem Becher s. Anglo-Jewish Notabilities, Plate XV, Nr. 110 [Wappen des Nathaneel Lindo (1810–1889)]; zur Verleihung des Wappens an die Familie s. S. 105.

100 Die Handschrift bietet zum Teil jiddisch-sprachige Erklärungen und Erläuterungen zu den hebräischen Segenssprüchen und Vorschriften, sowie auch die englische Version etlicher religionsgesetzlicher Teile. Zum Objekt vgl. Sign and a Wittness, Nr. 77; Sotheby's New York, December 1989, lot 42; Mikrografia ivrit, Nr. 32, S. 4 u. S. 11.

YAD/TORAH POINTER
London/England, 1813
Silver, gilt, diamonds
Artist: Bateman (no mark)
Later inscribed: "This was donated by Rabbi Yosef Rafael, son of rabbi Nathan, on the day of his 80th birthday on the holy Sabbath … in the year 504 (i.e. 1844/45) according to the minor reckoning."
Length: 33 cm; Diameter: 1.5 cm
No. 052.001.076 [97]

CASE FOR ESTHER SCROLL
Chester/England, 1853
Silver
Artist: John Hilsby
Length: 27 cm; Diameter: 8.5 cm
No. 080.001.029 [98]

WINECUP
France, c. 1810
With later inscription, England, 1823
Silver
Artist: unidentified
Hebrew inscription: "Nathaniel, son of David Abarbanel Lindo, for his Bar Mitzvah in Elul, 1823"; in family crest: "Be just and fear not"
Height: 7.1 cm; Diameter: 7.4 cm
No. 017.001.029 [99]

SEDER TIKKUN LE-MOHEL
Circumcision book
London/England, 1827/28
Manuscript on paper, ink, paint; illustrated and illuminated; Micrography
Artist: Aaron Levy
Pages: 44
Height: 18.8 cm; Width: 11.9 cm; Depth: 0.7 cm
No. EN.011.001 [100]

* Rudolf Stahl, Englisches Judentum. Reiseeindrücke, in: Der Morgen, III. Jahrgang, Berlin 1927, p. 227 - 228

97 For works by the same maker, see Sotheby's New York, May 1981, lot 274; Christie's East New York, June 1998, The A.L. Shane Collection, lot 46, 47. For the Bateman silversmith family, see Women Silversmiths 1685–1845; for city- and year mark: Jackson p. 60.

98 The case for the Esther scroll originates from the property of the Montegue family. Selected items from their Judaica were presented already in 1887 at the Anglo-Jewish Exhibition. For this item's mark, see Jackson, p. 394.

99 David Abarbanel Lindo, who was active in the Sephardic-British community, was the mohel who circumcised Benjamin Disraeli, the later English prime minister. For the coat-of-arms on the cup, see Anglo-Jewish Notabilities, Plate XV, Nr. 110 [coat-of-arms of Nathaneel Lindo (1810–1889)]; for the conferment of the coat-of-arms onto the family, see p. 105.

100 The manuscript partially offers explanations and comments in Yiddish to the Hebrew blessings and commandments as well as the English version of several sections on religious law. For object, cf. Sign and a Witness, no. 77; Sotheby's New York, December 1989, lot 42; Mikrografia ivrit, no. 32, p. 4 and p. 11.

London. "Of the quarter million English Jews, roughly 175,000, that is 75%, live in London. Their manner is largely determined by the character of English society. The English Jew, as the Englishman in general, has a strong sense of community and citizenship. It is aristocratic and religious."
Rudolf Stahl, c. 1925*

In the 11th century Jews followed William the Conqueror to England. Under Norman rule they were relatively well off, but under the house of Anjou-Plantagenet their situation deteriorated beginning with the first accusation of ritual murder in Europe to their expulsion in 1290. Only in the 17th century, Jews were allowed back as a result of negotiations between Manasseh ben Israel and Oliver Cromwell. Lionel de Rothschild's election to the House of Commons as liberal Member of Parliament in 1858 concluded the battle for emancipation. From the 1880s onward, the numerous, oftentimes proletarian, new immigrants from Eastern Europe changed the social structure of established Ashkenazic and Sephardic English Jewry considerably. Another wave of immigration began in 1933 when Jews from the European continent looked for refuge from Nazi-Germany. Nowadays, England's Jewish community numbers around 330,000 people, of whom two thirds reside in London. They belong to the Sephardic, Orthodox, Conservative, Liberal, or Reform community, depending on sense of belonging and religiosity.

B/W Photo p. 108: Judy Goldhill, "say no to the PLO"-demonstration, Trafalgar Square, London, Great Britain, 1981

The Great Synagogue in Duke's Place, opened by Ashkenazi Jews in 1722, London, England. *Tony Travis, Beth Hatefutsoth Photo Archive*

Die Große Synagoge in Duke's Place, 1722 eröffnet von Aschkenasischen Juden, London, England. *Tony Travis, Beth Hatefutsoth Foto-Archiv*

Algerien. „In Algerien haben die Franzosen genaue Zählungen vorgenommen, und diesen zufolge enthält das grosse Land unter einer Gesamtbevölkerung von 5 Millionen nur 53000 Juden in 12000 Haushaltungen.“

Ernst von Hesse-Wartegg, 1910*

Die Gründung einer jüdischen Gemeinde in Algerien erfolgte mit der Exilierung der Juden nach der Zerstörung des Zweiten Tempels. Zuzug erhielt sie durch Flüchtende aus dem Spanien der Goten, später aus dem Spanien der katholischen Inquisition. Als Frankreich Algerien 1830 besetzte, erhielten die Juden die französische Staatsbürgerschaft. Während des 2. Weltkrieges waren die algerischen Juden sowohl einem starken moslemischen Antisemitismus ausgesetzt als auch dem des Vichy-Regimes. Ende der fünfziger Jahre lebten 130.000 Juden in Algerien, die es nach dem Bürgerkrieg und der 1962 erfolgten Unabhängigkeit von Frankreich vorzogen, nach Frankreich, in geringerem Maße auch nach Israel, auszuwandern. Die jüdische Gemeinde, die heute nur noch in Algier existiert, hat zwar eine Synagoge, aber keinen Rabbiner.

S/W Foto S. 111: Donna Wosk, Hr. und Fr. Cohen Adda, die beiden letzten Juden in Constantin, Algerien, 1985; Beth Hatefutsoth Foto-Archiv, Tel Aviv

RIMMONIM/TORA-AUFSÄTZE
Algerien, um 1900
Silber
Hebräische Widmungsinschrift: „Eine Widmung der großzügigen und ehrenwerten Rabbiner Jakob und Zabah Partusch.“
H: 30,5 cm; Dm: 7 cm
Inv.Nr. 050.001.062 [101]

KETER/TORA-KRONE
Bou Saada/Algerien, um 1875
Silber
Hebräische Inschrift auf Paneel 1: „Dies ist die Tora-Krone, die von Herzen gewidmet wurde von Efraim Sulam, sein Licht leuchte. Sie war beschädigt … und mußte erneuert werden und ist dem Herrn gewidmet. Das war die Arbeit meiner Hände, des älteren Schalom, des Sohnes meines Vaters, dem ehrenwerten Rabbi Jakob Monsonego, sein Licht leuchte.“ Darunter: „Faite à Bou Saada le 30 Octobre 1910.“ Auf Paneel 2: Segenssprüche; Auf Paneel 3: die Anfänge der Zehn Gebote; auf Paneel 4: Psalm 67, 1–8 in Form einer Menora und die 42 Buchstaben des Gottesnamens; auf Paneel 5: Numeri 6, 24–26; auf Paneel 6: Mischna, Awot IV, 13; auf Paneel 7: Deuteronomium 6, 5–9.
H: 13,5 cm; Dm: 21,5 cm
Inv.Nr. 053.001.006 [102]

SCHIWITI-SCHERENSCHNITT
Algerien, 1843/44
Papier, Metall, Folie, Tusche
Künstler: Jakob Jaj
Stifter: Mosche de Elijahu Ada
Hebräische Inschrift: „Dies ist die Arbeit des Dieners des Herrn Jakob Jaj, möge sein Ende gut sein, fertiggestellt im Jahr 5604 (i.e. 1843/44)./ Mosche de Elijahu Ada.“
H: 88 cm; B: 69 cm
Inv.Nr. 036.011.013 [103]

* Ernst von Hesse-Wartegg, Die Juden von Nordafrika, ihre Verbreitung und Abstammung, in: Ost und West, Jahrgang X, 1910, S. 285
101 Zu ähnlichen Stücken s. Crowning Glory, Nr. 15; Sephardic Journey, S. 328, Nr. 328.
102 Zu dieser Krone s. Torah and Magic, Abb. 10; Sephardic Journey, S. 340, Abb. 340.
103 Zum selben Scherenschnitt s. Jewish Papercuts, Pl. 31; Sephardic Journey, Nr. 391.

Algeria. "The French have conducted precise counts according to which in this large country with a total population of 5 million there are only 53,000 Jews in 12,000 households."

Ernst von Hesse-Wartegg, 1910*

After the destruction of the Second Temple, exiled Jews founded a Jewish community in Algeria. It received influx from Jews escaping Gothic Spain, later Catholic-Inquisition Spain. When France occupied Algeria in 1830, the Jews received French citizenship. During World War II the Algerian Jews were subjected to anti-Semitism from Islamic side as well as from the Vichy-regime. At the end of the 1950s, 130,000 Jews lived in Algeria. After the civil war and independence from France, they preferred to move to France and, to a lesser extent, to Israel. The Jewish community, which today only exists in Algiers, still has a synagogue, but no rabbi.

B/W Photo p. 111: Donna Wosk, Mr. and Mrs. Cohen Adda, the two last jews of Constantine, Algeria 1985; Beth Hatefutsoth Photo Archive, Tel Aviv

RIMMONIM/TORAH FINIALS

Algeria, c. 1900

Silver

Inscribed: "Given by the generous and honorable Rabbis Yaakov and Tzabah Partush."

Height: 30.5 cm; Diameter: 7 cm

No. 050.001.062 [101]

KETER/CROWN

Bou Sa'ada/Algeria, c. 1875

Silver

Hebrew inscription on panel 1: "This is the Torah crown, the heartfelt donation of Ephraim Sulam, may his light shine, which was damaged … to repair it anew and it is dedicated to the Lord, the work of my hands, the elderly Shalom, the son of my father, the honorable Rabbi Yaakov Monsonego, may his light shine." Followed by the French inscription: "Finished in Bou Sa'ada, the 30th of October, 1910." On panel 2: blessings; on panel 3: the beginning words of the Ten Commandments; on panel 4: Psalm 67: 1–8 in form of a Menorah and the 42-letter name of God; on panel 5: Numeri 6: 24–26; on panel 6: Mischna Awot, IV, 13; on panel 7: Deuteronomium 6: 5–9.

Height: 13.5 cm; Diameter: 21.5 cm

No. 053.001.006 [102]

SHIVITI-PAPERCUT

Algeria, 1843/44

Paper, metal, foil, ink

Artist: Ya'akov Jaj

Donor: Moshe De Eliyahu Ada

Inscription: "The workmanship of the servant of the Lord Ya'akov Jaj, may his end be good. Finished in the year 5604 (i.e. 1843/44)./Moshe de Eliyahu Ada."

Height: 88 cm; Width: 69 cm

No. 036.011.013 [103]

Interior of the synagogue at Bou Sa'ada, Algeria
Jacques Assouline, Beth Hatefutsoth Photo Archive

Innenansicht der Synagoge in Bou Sa'ada, Algerien
Jacques Assouline, Beth Hatefutsoth Foto-Archiv

* Ernst von Hesse-Wartegg, Die Juden von Nordafrika, ihre Verbreitung und Abstammung, in: Ost und West, Jahrgang X, 1910, p. 285

100 For similar items, see Crowning Glory, no. 15; Sephardic Journey, p. 328, no. 328.

102 For this crown, see Torah and Magic, fig. 10; Sephardic Journey, p. 340, fig. 340.

103 For the same paper cut, see Jewish Papercuts, Pl. 31; Sephardic Journey, no. 391.

TAS/TORA-SCHILD
Rumänien, 1850/51
Silber, teilweise vergoldet
Hebräische Inschrift: „Die Gesetzestafeln (Anfänge der zehn Gebote)/ Das heilige Tora-Schild/Dies heilige Objekt gehört dem Herrn; [von] dem großzügigen Herrn, unserem Lehrer, dem Rabbiner Reb Leib, dem Sohn des Abraham, im Jahr 611 der kleinen Zeitrechnung (i.e. 1850/51)."
H: 34,6 cm; B: 28 cm
Inv.Nr. 051.001.017 [104]

TEFILLIN-TASCHE
Bessarabien/Rumänien, 1907
Samt, Seide, Wolle
Hergestellt von Rachel Millman
Hebräische Inschrift: „Leib Millman"
H: 25 cm; B: 20 cm
Inv.Nr. 018.015.002 [105]

PINKAS CHEWRAT MISCHNAJOT
Der karitativen Bruderschaft Jassi
Jassi/Moldau/Rumänien, 1860–1944
Handschrift auf Papier, Tusche, Farben
Hebräische Inschrift auf dem Einband: „Dies ist der Pinkas, der nur der Gemeinschaft der Mischnajot gehört, bekannt als Balter hier in der Stadt Jassi."
290 Seiten
H: 31,2 cm; B: 19,2 cm; T: 3,3 cm
Inv.Nr. EE.011.117

Moldau. „Erst um die Mitte des XIX. Jahrhunderts sollte die Bukowina und die benachbarte Moldau einer eigenen Zaddikim-Dynastie teilhaftig werden, der Sadagorer, deren Begründer R. Israel von Rushin genötigt gewesen war, aus seiner russischen Heimat nach Jassy zu fliehen, um sich dann in dem unweit Czernowitz gelegenen Flecken Sadagora niederzulassen."
Simon Dubnow, 1931*

Vermutlich kamen die ersten Juden mit den römischen Legionen ins nachmalige Rumänien. Im 14. Jahrhundert flüchteten sich die aus Ungarn vertriebenen Juden in die Walachei. Ebenfalls im späten Mittelalter ließen sich Juden wegen seiner günstigen Verkehrslage zwischen Polen und Bessarabien im Gebiet Moldau nieder. Die jüdische Gemeinde der Stadt Jassy ist die älteste Moldaus. Viele polnische Juden flohen zur Zeit der Chmielnicki-Massaker (1648/49) hierher. 1650 und 1652 wurde jedoch auch Jassy von den Kosaken heimgesucht.

Die lokalen Machthaber förderten die Niederlassung polnischer Juden. Handwerk und Handel waren in hohem Maße jüdisch geprägt. Zu weiteren Einwanderungen in die Provinz Moldau kam es nach der Annexion der Bukowina durch Österreich 1775 und Bessarabiens durch Russland 1812, da viele Juden es vorzogen, in das rumänische Moldau zu übersiedeln. Im 19. Jahrhundert wendete sich das Blatt. Prinz Michael Sturdza setzte die Juden unter Druck, damit sie seine Schulden annullierten. 1867 kam es ungeachtet internationaler Proteste zu Massenausweisungen. In den achtziger Jahren wurde Jassy zu einem Zentrum des rumänischen Antisemitismus, was es bis zur Schoa blieb. 1940 wurde Rumänien Satellitenstaat Deutschlands. 1941 wurde damit begonnen, jüdische Bevölkerungsteile hauptsächlich nach Transnistrien zu deportieren, andere zur Zwangsarbeit zusammenzufassen. Im August 1944 brach Rumänien mit Deutschland und schlug sich auf die Seite der Alliierten. Bis dahin waren von den 607.000 rumänischen Juden 265.000 ermordet worden.

S/W Foto S. 114: Edward Serotta, Kinder vor ihrem Auftritt in der Synagogue in Bacau, Rumänien, 1986

---

* Simon Dubnow, Geschichte des Chassidismus, Bd. 2, Berlin 1931, S. 323
104 Zu diesem Tas s. Sotheby's Tel Aviv, Jewellery and Judaica, April 1989, lot 625, 630. Zu ähnlichen Tasim s. Sotheby's New York, Fine Judaica, June 1982, lot 524; Sotheby's Tel Aviv, June 1983, lot 407; Sotheby's Tel Aviv, April 1990, lot 250.
105 Die Tefillin-Tasche wurde von der Großmutter des Besitzers in jungen Jahren nach altem Brauch für ihren Verlobten, den späteren Großvater gemacht.

TAS/TORAH SHIELD

Romania, 1850/51

Silver, parcel gilt

Hebrew inscription: "The tablets of the Law (The beginning words of the Ten Commandments) The holy Torah shield / This, the holy object belongs to the Lord, it was given by the affluent gentleman, our teacher the honorable Rav Reb Leib son of Avraham, the year 611 according to the minor reckoning (i.e. 1850/51)."

Height: 34.6 cm; Width: 28 cm

No. 051.001.017 [104]

TEFILIN BAG

Bessarabia/Romania, 1907

Velvet, silk, wool

Maker: Rachel Millman

Inscribed: "Leib Millman"

Height: 25 cm; Width: 20 cm

No. 018.015.002 [105]

PINKAS HEVRAT MISHNAYOT

Of the charitable Society of Jassi

Iassi/Moldava/Romania, 1860–1944

Manuscript on paper, ink, paint

Hebrew inscription on binding: "This is the Pinkas which belongs only to the society of Mishnayot in the synagogue that is known as Balter here in the capital Iassi."

Pages: 290

Height: 31.2 cm; Width: 19.2 cm; Depth: 3.3 cm

No. EE.011.017

* Simon Dubnow, Geschichte des Chassidismus, Bd. 2, Berlin 1931, p. 323

104 For this tas, see Sotheby's Tel Aviv, Jewellery and Judaica, April 1989, lot 625, 630. For similar tasim, see Sotheby's New York, Fine Judaica, June 1982, lot 524; Sotheby's Tel Aviv, June 1983, lot 407; Sotheby's Tel Aviv, April 1990, lot 250.

105 The tefillin bag was made by the owner's grandmother in her youth for her fiancee, the later grandfather, according to custom.

Moldava. "Only around the middle of the nineteenth century did the Bukovina and the neighboring Moldava obtain a dynasty of zaddikim of their own, the Sadgor Hassidim, whose founder, R.Israel of Ruzhin, had been compelled to flee from his Russian homeland to Jassy and then settled in the townlet of Sadgora, not far from Chernovtsy."

Simon Dubnow, 1931*

Presumably, the first Jews came with the Roman legions to the later Romania. In the 14th century, Jews expelled from Hungary escaped into Walachia. Again in the late Middle Ages, Jews settled in the Moldova region because of its advantageous location between Poland and Bessarabia. The Jewish community of Jassy is the oldest in Moldova. Many Jews fled here at the time of the Chmielnitzki-massacres (1648/49), but in 1650 and 1652 the Cossacks reached Jassy as well.

The local rulers promoted the settlement of Polish Jews. To a large extent Jews were the carriers of trade and commerce. Further immigration to the province of Moldova came with the annexation of the Bukovina by Austria in 1775 and of Bessarabia by Russia in 1812. Many Jews then preferred to move to Romanian Moldova. Things changed in the 19th century when Prince Michael Sturdza pressured the Jews to cancel his debts. In 1867 mass expulsions were undertaken, international protests notwithstanding. In the 1880s Jassy became and remained a center of Romanian anti-Semitism until the Shoah. Romania turned into a German satellite in 1940. In 1941 deportations began of parts of the Jewish population mainly to Transnistria, others were taken into forced labor. In August of 1944 Romania broke away from Germany and shifted to the Allies' side. By that time, 265,000 of the 607,000 Jews had been murdered.

B/W Photo p. 114: Edward Serotta, Children before their performance at the synagogue in Bacau, Romania, 1986

The Great Synagogue in Jassy, Romania, c. 1900. *From: Pierre Guiral/Gérard Nahou et al. (ed.), Les juifs en Roumanie (1919–1938), Paris 1996, p. 403*

Die große Synagoge in Jassy, Rumänien, um 1900. *Aus: Pierre Guiral/Gérard Nahou et al. (ed.), Les juifs en Roumanie (1919–1938), Paris 1996, S. 403*

Griechenland. „Sie haben so viele Gemeinden in Griechenland, daß das Land Israel sie nicht alle aufnehmen könnte, wenn sie alle in ihm sein wollten."

Petachja von Regensburg, 1187*

Die ersten sicheren Nachweise jüdischer Präsenz in Griechenland stammen aus dem 3. Jahrhundert v.d.Z. Im 2. vorchristlichen Jahrhundert kamen im Zuge des Makkabäer-Aufstandes Juden nach Griechenland in die Sklaverei. Während der Hasmonäer-Herrschaft selbst entwickelten sich schließlich die ältesten jüdischen Zentren, die in den folgenden Jahrhunderten beständigen Zuwachs aus dem römischen, byzantinischen und osmanischen Reich, aus Ungarn, Italien, Spanien und Polen erhielten. Neben den beiden Gruppen der Aschkenasen und der Sefarden gibt es die Gruppe der griechischsprachigen Romanioten, der Nachfahren des antiken hellenistischen Judentums, die ihr eigenes Brauchtum haben. Romaniotische Gemeinschaften bestanden u.a. auf Kreta, Chalki und in Ioannina, wo die Gemeinde heute aus nur mehr 51 Personen besteht. Die in Griechenland erschienene hebräische Religionsliteratur legt beredtes Zeugnis von der Gelehrsamkeit der griechischen Rabbinen ab, die nicht nur im größten jüdischen Zentrum, Saloniki, sondern auch in anderen Gemeinden wirkten. Im Zusammenhang mit dem griechischen Befreiungskampf kam es teils zu schweren antijüdischen Ausschreitungen, da die jüdische Bevölkerung die Türken unterstützte. Am Vorabend des Zweiten Weltkrieges zählte die jüdische Gemeinde Griechenlands fast 80.000 Menschen. Von ihnen wurden 85% in den Konzentrationslagern ermordet. Zahlreiche der Überlebenden wanderten nach der Staatsgründung nach Israel aus.

S/W Foto S. 117: Freunde des Jüdischen Museums Ioannina, Befestigung der Mesusa am Haupteingang des geplanten Museums, Ioannina, Griechenland, Oktober 2000

PAROCHET-PLAKETTE/PLAKETTE FÜR DEN TORA-VORHANG
Ioannina/Griechenland, 1690
Silber, Niello
Hebräische Inschrift: „Allmächtiger Herr. Diese Zier, die Gewandung und die Tora-Rolle wurden gewidmet von unserem ehrenwerten Lehrer, R. Schmu(el) Jehuda zur Buße der Seele seines Sohnes R. Jehuda Schmu(el), möge er in Eden ruhen, und für die Buße der Seele seiner Schwiegertochter, Frau Kalomira, genannt Milia, möge sie in Eden ruhen. Ihre Seelen mögen eingebunden sein im Bündel des Lebens, in heiterer Ruhe, voller Glück, gemeinsam mit allen Heiligen im Garten Eden. Amen. Und der sich dem heiligen Dienst hingibt, mögen seine ihm verbliebenen Söhne leben und mögen sie wertvolle, ehrliche Söhne und Sohnessöhne haben. Amen. Am Tag von Schmini Azeret im Jahr ‚Und ich schickte einen Boten nach Jerusalem' (Chronogramm; Jesaja 41,27) 451 nach der kleinen Zeitrechnung (i.e. Montag, 25. September 1690)."
H: 14,9 cm; B: 8,6 cm
Inv.Nr. 049.001.006 [106]

TORA-BEDECKUNG
Ioannina/Griechenland, um 1900
Leinen, Seidenfäden
Hebräische Inschrift: „Malka Bat Chawa Battinou/die heilige Gemeinde der Juden in Ioannina"
L: 92 cm; B: 41 cm
Inv.Nr. 046.013.002 [107]

RIMMONIM/TORA-AUFSÄTZE
Ioannina/Griechenland, um 1890
Silber, teilweise vergoldet
L: 34 cm; B: 9 cm
Inv.Nr. 050.001.048 [108]

HÜLLE FÜR EINE ESTHER-ROLLE
Ioannina/Griechenland, um 1875
Silber, Filigran
L: 24,5 cm; Dm: 4 cm
Inv.Nr. 080.001.016 [109]

* Benjamin von Tudela/Petachja von Regensburg, Jüdische Reisen im Mittelalter, Köln 1998, S. 164
106 Der Brauch, aus verschiedenen Anlässen eine Parochet-Plakette zu stiften, ist nur von den romaniotischen Juden bekannt und wurde insbesondere in Ioannina gepflegt. Die Bezeichung für diese Art Votiv-Plakette ist „Schaddaja".
107 Das Textil war ursprünglich ein gürtelähnliches Kleidungsstück, das geheiligt wurde, indem es für den rituellen Zweck der Bedeckung einer Tora-Rolle, bzw. eines Tik umfunktioniert wurde. Abb. in: Jüdische Lebenswelten, Nr. 13/14.
108 Zu Vergleichsstücken s. Collector's Guide, Nr. 104; Ohel Moshe, S. 82.
109 Zu weiteren Filigran-Hüllen für Esther-Rollen aus Ioannina s. z.B. The Maurice Spertus Museum of Judaica, S. 54f.; Christie's Amsterdam, December 1986, lot 225; Sotheby's New York, December 1988, lot 162. Sotheby's Tel Aviv, October 2000, lot 197.

Greece. "So numerous are their communities in Greece that the Land of Israel could not take in all of them if they all wished to be in it."

Petachja of Regensburg, 1187*

The first positive evidence of Jewish presence in Greece originates from the 3rd century B.C.E. In the wake of the Maccabees' uprising, Jews came to Greece into slavery in the 2nd century B.C.E. The oldest Jewish centers developed, in fact, during Hasmonean rule and eventually received constant influx from the Roman, Byzantine, and Ottoman empires as well as from Hungary, Italy, Spain, and Poland. Besides Ashkenazim and Sephardim, there is the group of Greek-speaking Romaniotes, the descendants of antique Hellenic Jewry who have their own customs. Romaniote communities were, among others, on Crete, Chalki, and in Ioannina, where today's community consists of only fifty-one persons. The Hebrew religious literature from Greece is eloquent proof of Greek rabbinical scholarship not only in the largest Jewish center, Salonika, but also in other communities. In connection with the Greek War of Independence, heavy anti-Jewish excesses ensued at times since the Jewish population supported the Turks. On the eve of World War II, the Jewish community of Greece numbered almost 80,000 people of whom 85% were murdered in concentration camps. Numerous survivors immigrated to Israel after the establishment of the State.

B/W Photo p. 117: The Friends of the Jewish Museum Ioannina, Installation of the mezuzah on the main entrance of the planned museum, Ioannina, Greece, Oct. 2000

Holocaust survivors in the Synagogue of Ioannina, Greece, winter 1945. *Archive of the Jewish Museum of Greece*

Holocaust-Überlebende in der Synagoge in Ioannina, Griechenland, im Winter 1945. *Archiv des Jüdischen Museums Griechenland*

PAROKHET PLAQUE/PLAQUE FOR TORAH CURTAIN

Ioannina/Greece, 1690

Silver, Niello

Inscribed: "Almighty God. The ornament and cloth and Torah scroll were dedicated by the honorable, our teacher, R. Shemu(el) Yehudah, for the expiation of the soul of his son, R. Yehuda Shemu(el), may he rest in Eden, and for the expiation of the soul of his daughter-in-law, Mrs. Calomira, may she rest in Eden, called Milia, may their souls be bound up in the bond of life, in serene rest, in abundance of happiness, together with all the saints in the garden of Eden. Amen. And for the one who strives in sacred worship, may his remaining sons live and be awarded with worthy and honest sons and sons of sons. Amen. This occurred on the day of Shemini Atzeret, the year 'And I sent a herald to Jerusalem', according to the minor reckoning (Chronogram, Isaiah 41:27) (5)451 (i.e. Monday, September 25, 1690)."

Height: 14.9 cm; Width: 8.6 cm

No. 049.001.006 [106]

TORAH COVERING

Ioannina/Greece, c. 1900

Linen, silk thread

Hebrew inscription: "Malcah Bat Chavah Battinou/The holy congregation of the Jews of Ioannina"

Length: 92 cm; Width: 41 cm

No. 046.013.002 [107]

RIMMONIM/TORAH FINIALS

Ioannina/Greece, c. 1890

Silver, parcel gilt

Length: 34 cm; Width: 9 cm

No. 050.001.048 [108]

CASE FOR ESTHER SCROLL

Ioannina/Greece, c. 1875

Silver filigree

Length: 24.5 cm; Diameter: 4 cm

No. 080.001.016 [109]

---

* Benjamin von Tudela/Petachja von Regensburg, Jüdische Reisen im Mittelalter, Köln 1998, p. 164

106 The custom to donate parokhet plaques on various occasions, is only known to be cultivated by the Romaniote Jews and especially in Ioannina. This kind of votive plaque is called "shaddaya".

107 This textile was originally a beltlike garment, which was sanctified by giving it a ritual purpose as a cover for a Torah scroll or tik. Illustration in: Jüdische Lebenswelten, no. 13/14.

108 For comparable items, see Collector's Guide, no. 104; Ohel Moshe, p. 82.

109 For more filigree cases for Esther scrolls from Ioannina, see, e.g., The Maurice Spertus Museum of Judaica, p. 54f.; Christie's Amsterdam, December 1986, lot 225; Sotheby's New York, December 1988, lot 162. Sotheby's Tel Aviv, October 2000, lot 197.

SCHABBAT-LAMPE

Achtzackiger sogenannter „Judenstern"

Nürnberg/Bayern/Deutschland, um 1800

Messing

H: 61 cm; Dm: 32 cm; Säge: 56 cm

Inv.Nr. 013.002.010 [110]

BSAMIM-/GEWÜRZTURM

Nürnberg/Bayern/Deutschland, um 1780

Silber

Künstler: JR – nicht positiv identifiziert (möglicherweise Johann Jacob Rosch)

H: 25,5 cm; Dm: 6,3 cm

Inv.Nr. 015.001.036 [111]

TAS/TORA-SCHILD

Nürnberg/Bayern/Deutschland, um 1760

Silber, teilweise vergoldet

Künstler: CA – nicht identifiziert

H: 42,2 cm; B: 32,5 cm

Inv.Nr. 051.001.049 [112]

Nürnberg. „Hier fun ein Stund is die Hoiptstadt Nirinburg, ein scheine starke und woilbemannte Handelsstadt. In diese Stadt mussin die Jehudim allei Tag ein Guldn Zahl gebin, un mussin oich ein Christin Froi bai sich habin, wan si in die Stadt gihn, sunder die selbe is sie nit erloibt die Stadt zu betretin."

Abraham Levi, 1764*

Seit dem Ende des 12. Jhs. lebten Juden in Nürnberg, wo 1296 die erste Synagoge eingeweiht wurde. Das Schicksal der mittelalterlichen bayrischen Gemeinde war geprägt von den Rindfleisch-Verfolgungen des Jahres 1298, den Pest-Massakern 1349, Ritualmordbeschuldigungen 1467, zahlreichen Enteignungen und der endgültigen Ausweisung im Jahr 1499. Erst Ende des 17. Jhs. konnten sich einzelne Juden wieder in Nürnberg ansiedeln, die dem Fürther Rabbinat unterstanden. Es dauerte bis zur Mitte des 18. Jhs., dass sich eine Gemeinde konstituieren konnte. Diese wuchs bis 1933 auf 9.000 Personen an, womit sie die größte Gemeinde in Bayern darstellte. Von ihnen flüchteten 1938 zwischen 2.000 und 3.000 aus der Stadt Julius Streichers, 1.600 wurden in die Vernichtungslager deportiert. 65 Juden kehrten nach dem Krieg nach Nürnberg zurück, wo sie den Kern einer neuen Gemeinde bildeten, die heute rund 700 Personen umfasst.

S/W Foto S. 120: Jim G. Tobias, Lisa mit Restitutions-Akte vor dem Gebäude der Oberfinanzdirektion Nürnberg, Deutschland, 2000

* Reisebeschreibung fun Abraham Levi durch Teitschland un Behmin Mehrin Ungarin Steiarmark Istraich Tirohl in Italia als in Friaul Lombardia Marke Rumania Tuskania Boloniensis, Amsterdam 1764, S. 2

110 Zu vorliegender Lampe s. Geschichten von Gegenständen, Nr. 36; Shabbat Shalom, S. 7.

111 Zum vorliegenden Turm s. Geschichten von Gegenständen, Nr. 34. Zu ähnlichen Stücken s. beispielsweise Collector's Guide, Pl. IV; Sotheby's Tel Aviv, May 1987, lot 130; Sotheby's Tel Aviv, May 1988, lot 138; Das Jüdische Museum in Budapest, Nr. 76. Zur Stadtmarke s. Rosenberg III, Nr. 3799, zum möglichen Silberschmied ebenda, Nr. 4301.

112 Zu formal vergleichbaren Nürnberger Schildern s. Crowning Glory, Nr. 22; Furman Collection, S. 51.

SABBATH LAMP

Eight-branched socalled "Judenstern"

Nuremberg/Bavaria/Germany, c. 1800

Brass

Height: 61 cm; Diameter: 32 cm; Ratchet: 56 cm

No. 013.002.010 [110]

B'SAMIM/TOWER OF SPICE

Nuremberg/Bavaria/Germany, c. 1780

Silver

Artist: JR – not positively identified (possibly Johann Jacob Rosch)

Height: 25.5 cm; Diameter: 6.3 cm

No. 015.001.036 [111]

TAS/TORAH SHIELD

Nuremberg/Bavaria/Germany, c. 1760

Silver, parcel gilt

Artist: CA – unidentified

Height: 42.2 cm; Width: 32.5 cm

No. 051.001.049 [112]

Nuremberg. "An hour from here there is the capital city of Nirinburg, a beautiful, strong, and well-manned market place. For each day of their stay, the Jews must pay one guilder, and must be accompanied by a Christian woman if they wish to enter this town; for without such they are not permitted to enter."

Abraham Levi, 1764*

Jews lived in Nuremberg since the end of the 12th century, and the first synagogue was consecrated in 1296. The fate of the Bavarian community during the Middle Ages was marked by the beef-persecutions of 1298, the Black Death massacres in 1349, the accusations of ritual murder in 1467, numerous confiscations, and the final expulsion in 1499. Only at the end of the 17th century was it possible for individual Jews to settle again in Nuremberg. They belonged to the Fürth rabbinate and it would be only in the mid-18th century when a community was established again. It grew to 9,000 persons in 1933, which made it the largest community in Bavaria. Between 2,000 and 3,000 of them fled in 1938 from the city of Julius Streicher, 1,600 were deported to concentration camps. After the war, 65 Jews returned to Nuremberg where they formed the core of a new community, which today numbers 700 persons.

B/W Photo p. 120: Jim G. Tobias, Lisa with her restutution file in front of the Headfinance Department, Nuremberg, Germany, 2000

*   Reisbeschreibung fun Abraham Levi durch Teitschland un Behmin Mehrin Ungarin Steiarmark Istraich Tirohl in Italia als in Friaul Lombardia Marke Rumania Tuskania Boloniensis, Amsterdam 1764, p. 2
110 For this lamp, see Geschichten von Gegenständen, no. 36; Shabbat Shalom, p. 7.
111 For this tower, see Geschichten von Gegenständen, no. 34. For similar items, see, for instance, Collector's Guide, Pl. IV; Sotheby's Tel Aviv, May 1987, lot 130; Sotheby's Tel Aviv, May 1988, lot 138; Das Jüdische Museum in Budapest, no. 76. For city mark, see Rosenberg III, Nr. 3799, for possible silversmith ibid., no. 4301.
112 For formally comparable items, see Crowning Glory, no. 22; Furman Collection, p. 51.

The synagogue of Nuremberg, Germany. *Lithography, Beth Hatefutsoth Photo Archive*

Die Synagoge in Nürnberg, Deutschland. *Lithographie, Beth Hatefutsoth Foto-Archiv*

Krim. „Im Lande Qedar gibt es keine (rabbanitischen) Juden, sondern nur Minim, Karaiten nämlich. Als Rabbi Petachja ihnen unser Hauptgebet und das Tischgebet vortrug, fanden sie Gefallen daran und sagten ‚Noch nie haben wir gehört, was der Talmud ist'."

Petachja von Regensburg, um 1175*

Gegründet von Anan Ben David in Bagdad, entstand um die Mitte des 8. Jhs. die Sekte der Karäer. Im Gegensatz zum rabbinischen Judentum lehnen die Karäer die mündliche Tradition, also den Talmud, ab und akzeptieren nur die Bibel als religionsgesetzlich verbindlich. Von Anfang an lagen die großen karäischen Gemeinden in Jerusalem, Syrien, Ägypten und Persien, ab dem 12. Jh. auch in der Türkei. Einige dieser Gemeinden, wie beispielsweise die kairinische wiesen eine Kontinuität von einem Jahrtausend auf. Erst um 1960 verließen die meisten Karäer Kairo, um sich in Israel oder den USA niederzulassen. Schon im 12. Jh., verstärkt dann aber unter tartarischer Herrschaft im 13. Jh., siedelten sich viele Karäer auf der Krim an, ein Jahrhundert später auch in Litauen, von wo aus sich die Gemeinden weiter bis nach Wolhynien und Galizien ausbreiteten. Ihre zahlenmäßige und intellektuelle Blüte erlebten die Krim-Gemeinden im 18. und 19. Jh. Zu dieser Zeit wurden in Chufat-Kalé (Kirkeir) und Yevpatoriya hebräische Druckereien gegründet. Während um 1900 Chufat-Kalé zugunsten Odessas aufgegeben wurde, blieb Yevpatoriya für lange Zeit das spirituelle karäische Zentrum auf der Krim. 1932 wurde die Zahl der Karäer in Russland, fast alle auf der Krim beheimatet, noch mit 10.000 angegeben. Heute lebt nur noch ein Bruchteil von ihnen auf der Halbinsel am Schwarzen Meer.

S/W Foto S. 123: Frédéric Brenner, David Abramovitch Gabay und seine Frau, Sara Yosifovna, zwei Krymchaks unter wenigen, welche die deutsche Besetzung der Krim im Zweiten Weltkrieg überlebten, Simferopol, Krim, 1990

KARÄISCHE KETUBBA/EHEVERTRAG
Kirkeir/Krim, 1796 [113]
Papier, Gouache
Braut: Biknasch Bat Azaria
Bräutigam: Mordechai Ben Josef Sinan Kalpa
H: 79,2 cm; B: 55 cm
Inv.Nr. 035.011.019 [114]

DECKE FÜR DAS VORLESER-PULT – SPIEGELTEIL
Aus einer karäischen Synagoge
Yevpatoriya/Krim, 1823
Seide, Goldfaden
Hebräische Widmungsinschrift: „Dies ist der Vorhang für das Vorbeter-Pult, gewidmet von dem ehrenwerten, gebildeten und weisen Rabbi Mordechai, möge sein Fels ihn schützen und erhalten, der Sohn des ehrbaren Lehrers, dem ehrwürdigen und gebildeten Elijahu seligen Angedenken, für die heilige Gemeinde von Goslow (i.e. Yevpatoriya), zum Ablaß der Seele seiner Gattin, der ehrenwerten und bescheidenen Frau Rachel …, und zum Ablaß der Seele seiner Tochter Altin, der angenehmen, jungen, unverheirateten Frau …, und zum Ablaß der Seele seines einzigen Sohnes, … dem angenehmen Elijahu, möge er in Eden ruhen, … Im Jahr 5584 zu Rosch Chodesch (zum Monatsanfang) Kislew (i.e. 1823)."
H: 41 cm; B: 50 cm
Inv.Nr. 049.13.004 [115]

ADDERET ELIJAHU
Karäischer Gesetzeskodex
Yevpatoriya/Krim, 1835
Autor: Elija Ben Mosche Baschyazi
Druckerei: David Ben Mordechai
H: 31,5 cm; B: 21,5 cm; T: 2,5 cm
Inv.Nr. B.515 [116]

* Benjamin von Tudela/Petachja von Regensburg, Jüdische Reisen im Mittelalter, Köln 1998, S. 125

113 Der Ortsname Kirkeir ist der tatarische Name für Chufut-Kalé, türkisch für „Festung der Juden".

114 Weitere karäische Eheverträge in: Scripture and Schism, Nr. 50; Parke Bernet New York, March 1967, lot 174; Ketubbah, Nr. 199. Zu einer karäischen Ketubba ebenfalls aus Kirkeir s. Mazal Tov, Nr. 53.

115 In der Widmungsinschrift ist die hebräische Ortsbezeichnung „Goslow" gewählt, eine Bezeichnung, die auf den früheren tatarischen Namen für Yevpatoriya zurückgeht, nämlich „Gezelew".

116 Die Erstausgabe dieses von den karäischen Gemeinden Europas und Asiens (nicht Nordafrikas) als grundlegend akzeptierten Kodex erschien 1530–31 bei Gerschom Soncino in Konstantinopel; vgl. Scripture and Schism, Nr. 47.

Crimea. "In the land of Qedar there are no (rabbanite) Jews, only heretics, that is Karaites. When Rabbi Petachja recited our main prayer and said the grace, they took pleasure in it and said 'Never have we heard of the Talmud'."

Petachja of Regensburg, c. 1175*

Anan Ben David founded the Karaite sect in Baghdad around the mid-8th century. In contrast to rabbinical Judaism, the Karaites reject oral tradition, that is, the Talmud and solely accept the Bible as the binding religious law. From the start, the large Karaite communities were in Jerusalem, Syria, Egypt, and Persia and from the 12th century in Turkey as well. Some communities, such as, for instance, the Cairene were in continuous existence for a millennium. Only around 1960 did most Karaites leave Cairo to settle in Israel or the USA. In the 12th century many Karaites settled on the Crimea as well, but increasingly so under Tatar rule in the 13th century. A century later they also came to Lithuania and from there communities spread as far as Wolhynia and Galicia. The Crimean communities peaked in population size and intellectual achievements in the 18th and 19th century. During that time, Hebrew presses were founded in Chufut-Kalé (Kirkeir) and Yevpatoriya. While around 1900 Chufut-Kalé was abandoned in favor of Odessa, Yevpatoriya remained for a long time the Karaites' spiritual center on the Crimea. The number of Karaites in Russia – almost all of them living on the Crimea – was indicated to be 10,000 in 1932. Today, only a small part is still living on the Black Sea peninsula.

B/W Photo p. 123: Frédéric Brenner, David Abramovitch Gabay and his wife, Sara Yosifovna, two krymchaks among very few who escaped extermination during the German occupation of Crimea in World War II, Simferopol, Crimea, 1990

Interior view of the Karaite Synagogue in Yevpatoriya, Crimea, c. 1905. *The Library of The Jewish Theological Seminary of America*

Innenansicht der karäitischen Synagoge in Yevpatoriya, Krim, um 1905. *The Library of The Jewish Theological Seminary of America*

KARAITE KETUBAH/MARRIAGE CONTRACT
Kirkeir/Crimea, 1796 [113]
Paper, gouache
Bride: Biknash Bat Azariah
Groom: Mordechai Ben Yosef Sinan Kalpa
Height: 79.2 cm; Width: 55 cm
No. 035.011.019 [114]

COVER FOR THE READER'S DESK – CENTRAL MIRROR
From a Karaite synagogue
Yevpatoriya/Crimea, 1823
Silk, gold thread
Hebrew inscription: "This is the parochet which is on the reader's stand, dedicated by the honorable teacher, the cultured and understanding Rabbi Mordechai, may his rock protect and sustain him, Kapli, the son of the honorable teacher, the elderly and cultured Eliyahu, of blessed memory, to the synagogue of the holy community of Goslov, for indulgence of the soul of his wife, the honorable, modest woman Rachel ... and for indulgence of the soul of his daughter Altin, the pleasant young unmarried woman, ..., and for indulgence of the soul of his only son, the ... and pleasant Eliyahu, may he rest in Eden, ..., in the year 5584 on Rosh Chodesh Kislev (i.e. 1823)."
Height: 41 cm; Width: 50 cm
No. 049.013.004 [115]

ADDERET ELIYAHU
Caraite code of law
Yevpatoriya/Crimea, 1835
Author: Elija Ben Moshe Bashyazi
Publisher: David Ben Mordechai
Height: 31.5 cm; Width: 21.5 cm; Depth: 2.5 cm
No. B.515 [116]

* Benjamin von Tudela/Petachja von Regensburg, Jüdische Reisen im Mittelalter, Köln 1998, p. 125
113 Kirkeir is the Tatar place name for Chufut-Kalé, Turkish for "Fortress of the Jews."
114 More Karaite marriage contracts in: Scripture and Schism, no. 50; Parke Bernet New York, March 1967, lot 174; Ketubbah, no. 199. For a Karaite ketubah also from Kirkeir, see Mazal Tov, no. 53.
115 In the dedication inscription the Hebrew name of place "Goslov" was chosen, which goes back to "Gezelev," the former Tatar name for Yevpatoriya.
116 The first edition of this code, which was accepted as fundamental by the Karaite communities of Europe and Asia (not North Africa), appeared in 1530–31 at Gershom Soncino in Constantinople; cf. Scripture and Schism, no. 47.

LEUCHTERPAAR FÜR SCHABBAT
New York/USA, um 1960
Silber
Künstler: Ludwig Yehuda Wolpert
Beschriftet: „Erwache! Erwache!/Es kommt dein Licht, steh auf und leuchte!" (aus der Hymne der Schabbat-Liturgie „Lecha dodi")
H: 42 cm; B: 13,3 cm
Inv.Nr. 012.001.004 [117]

BSAMIM-/GEWÜRZBÜCHSE
New York/USA, 1965
Silber
Künstler: Moshe Zabari
Bewegliche hebräische Inschrift: „Gewürze"
H: 8,7 cm; B: 5 cm
Inv.Nr. 015.001.012 [118]

New York. „Die Lower East Side in New York, und in sich selbst eine der größten jüdischen Siedlungen der Welt, beherbergt Zehntausende von Gelegenheitsbesuchern, die auch nach Generationen noch Gelegenheitsbesucher blieben. Wo und wann sie oder ihre Voreltern die Gelegenheit beim Schopfe gepackt haben, ist durchaus verschieden."

Egon Erwin Kisch, um 1940*

125

Die erste jüdische Ansiedlung in Amerika begann 1654 in Neu-Amsterdam mit einigen wenigen aus Holland stammenden sefardischen, aber auch aschkenasischen Juden. Unter den Engländern kam es zu weiteren jüdischen Ansiedlungen hauptsächlich deutschstämmiger Juden. Die Pogrome in Osteuropa sowie der Erste Weltkrieg brachten Flüchtlingsströme jiddischsprachiger Immigranten in die USA, vor allem nach New York, wodurch sich die soziale Struktur der jüdischen Gemeinde radikal änderte, die bis dahin hauptsächlich aus Händlern, Freiberuflern, Bankiers und Ladenbesitzern bestanden hatte. Nun entstand ein jüdisches Proletariat, das teils sozialistischen, teils zionistischen Ideen anhing. Auch die religiöse Struktur veränderte sich. Waren die Alteingesessenen zumeist Anhänger eines liberalen oder reformierten Judentums, so ließen viele der Neueinwanderer die Orthodoxie zu einer neuen Größe werden. Und schließlich veränderten sie auch die Kulturlandschaft. Ob ihrer zahlenmäßigen Größe konnten die Zuwanderer ihre eigenen jüdischen Kulturbereiche in einem Maße schaffen, das vorher unbekannt war, dies insbesondere auf den Gebieten des Unterhaltungs- und Publikationswesens. Im Laufe der Zeit wurden diese Kulturen zum integralen Bestandteil der amerikanischen. Zwei Drittel der jüdischen Gesamtbevölkerung leben heute in den Vereinigten Staaten, davon fast zwei Millionen in New York.

S/W Foto S. 126: Frédéric Brenner, Minjan der Sterne/Sukka des Himmels, New York, USA, 1994

* Egon Erwin Kisch, Auf der unteren Ostseite New Yorks oder die Rolle der Gelegenheit, in: Gesammelte Werke in Einzelausgaben, Berlin und Weimar 1985, Bd. VI, S. 379

117 Zu dem in Deutschland gebürtigen, nach seiner Emigration 1935 in Jerusalem und ab 1956 in USA lebenden Ludwig Wolpert (1900–1981), einem der „Väter" moderner Judaica s. Anm. 27, sowie Wolpert. A Retrospective. Beispiele von Wolperts Arbeit sind in in nahezu allen öffentlichen Judaica-Sammlungen zu finden, sowie auch in verschiedenen US-amerikanischen Synagogen.

118 Moshe Zabari (geb. 1935) war Wolperts Schüler an der Bezalel-Schule in Jerusalem und folgte ihm 1967 an den dem Jewish Museum New York angeschlossenen Tobe Pascher Workshop, dessen Leitung er nach Wolperts Tod auch übernahm. Seine funktionalen, minimalistischen Judaica finden sich heute in allen bedeutenden Judaica-Sammlungen. Zu seinen Arbeiten und zu seinem Werdegang vgl. Torah Ornaments by Moshe Zabari; sowie Moshe Zabari: A Twenty-Five Year Retrospective.

New York. "The Lower East Side in New York, one of the world's largest Jewish settlements by itself, hosts tens of thousands of chance visitors who even after generations have still remained chance visitors. Where and when they or their forebears have jumped at the chance varies greatly."

Egon Erwin Kisch, c. 1940*

SHABBAT CANDLESTICKS
New York/USA, c.1960
Silver
Artist: Ludwig Yehuda Wolpert
Hebrew inscription: "Wake up! Wake up!/For your light has come, rise up and shine!" (from the Kabbalat Shabbat Hymn "Lecha Dodi")
Height: 42 cm; Width: 13.3 cm
No. 012.001.004 [117]

B'SAMIM/SPICE BOX
New York/USA, 1965
Silver
Artist: Moshe Zabari
Movable Inscription: "Spices"
Height: 8.7 cm; Width: 5 cm
No. 015.001.012 [118]

The first Jewish settlement in America was established in 1654 in New Amsterdam by a few Sephardic as well as Ashkenazic Jews from Holland. Under English rule, Jews, mainly of German origin, established further settlements. Eastern European pogroms as well as World War I brought throngs of Yiddish-speaking refugees to the USA, especially to New York. That changed the social structure of the Jewish community considerably, which up to then had consisted mainly of merchants, professionals, bankers, and store owners. Now a Jewish proletariat developed that pursued in part Socialist, in part Zionist ideas. The religious structure changed as well. While the locals mostly adhered to a liberal or reformed Judaism, many of the new-immigrants caused Orthodox Judaism to become a significant factor. Finally, they also changed the cultural scene. Thanks to their large numbers, the Jewish immigrants were able to create their own culture in a scope previously unknown, especially in the areas of entertainment and publishing, which in the course of time became an integral part of American culture. Today, two thirds of the entire Jewish population live in the United States, almost two millions of them in New York.

B/W Photo p. 126: Frédéric Brenner, Minyan of the stars/sukkah in the sky, New York, USA, 1994

* Egon Erwin Kisch, Auf der unteren Ostseite New Yorks oder die Rolle der Gelegenheit, in: Gesammelte Werke in Einzelausgaben, Berlin und Weimar 1985, Bd. VI, p. 379

117 For Ludwig Wolpert (1900–1981), born in Germany, living after his emigration in 1935 in Jerusalem and from 1956 in the USA, one of the "fathers" of modern Judaica, see note 27, as well as Wolpert. A Retrospective. Examples of Wolpert's work can be found in almost all public Judaica collections as well as in United States synagogues.

118 Moshe Zabari (b. 1935) was Wolpert's student at the Bezalel Academy in Jerusalem and followed him in 1967 to the Tobe Pascher Workshop, which is connected to the Jewish Museum New York. After Wolpert's death he succeeded him as the workshop's director. Today, his functional, minimalistic Judaica can be found in all major Judaica collections. For his works and career, cf. Torah Ornaments by Moshe Zabari; as well as Moshe Zabari: A Twenty-Five Year Retrospective.

Temple Beth-El, 5th Ave. & 76th St.; New York, USA, c. 1909. *Jewish Museum Vienna, Stern Collection*

Temple Beth-El, 5th Ave. & 76th St.; New York, USA, um 1909. *Jüdisches Museum Wien, Sammlung Stern*

Eine virtuelle Gemeinde? „Erst wenn die jüdische Diaspora wirklich von einem Ende der Welt bis zum anderen reicht, können die Juden von dort in das Land der Verheißung zurückgeführt werden."

Menasse ben Israel, 1656*

Eine der weitreichendsten Revolutionen der jüngsten Vergangenheit stellt das Internet dar, die Möglichkeit, auf eine neue Art und Weise zu kommunizieren, und die Möglichkeit, Informationen in nie gekanntem Ausmaß auf Knopfdruck abzurufen. Die Welt ist noch kleiner geworden, als sie durch die modernen Transportmittel und die Angebote der Tourismus-Industrie ohnehin schon war. Global village ist Wirklichkeit geworden. Sogenannte virtual communities sind entstanden, die man als Zaungast besuchen, in die man eintreten und austreten kann, in denen man sich einen anderen Kontext schaffen kann als den räumlich gebundenen. Die jüdischen Gemeinschaften haben sich, wie alle anderen Gemeinschaften weltweit auch, dem Trend angeschlossen, virtuelle Gemeinden zu schaffen, via die sie Informationen über ihre Vergangenheit und Gegenwart, ihre jeweiligen Aktivitäten, Ziele und Probleme im Netz für Jedermann zugänglich machen und zur Stellungnahme in kleineren Kreisen auffordern, chat-rooms einrichten, in denen sich treffen kann, wer will. Ist die Judenheit mit diesem Eintritt in die Virtualität an einem Ende der Welt angekommen? Die Frage scheint zu sein, inwieweit diese Virtualität nichts anderes ist als die Verschiebung der Realität auf eine andere Ebene, inwieweit also die Virtualität nichts anderes als eine neue Realität ist, die genauso begrenzt ist wie all unsere anderen Realitäten auch.

S/W Foto S. 129: David Peters, Ohne Titel, 2001

SKULPTUR: MOTHER OF BOARDS
Azur-Cholon, 2000
Metall/Computer-Abfall, Kunststoff
Künstlerin: Lisa Gross
H: 94,5 cm; B: 36 cm
Sammlung Steven Meyer, Genf

* Menasseh ben Israel, Mikwe Israel. Esperanca de Israel, Amsterdam 1650; zitiert nach: M. Dorman, Menasseh ben Israel, Hakibbuz Hameuchad Israel, 1989, S. 158

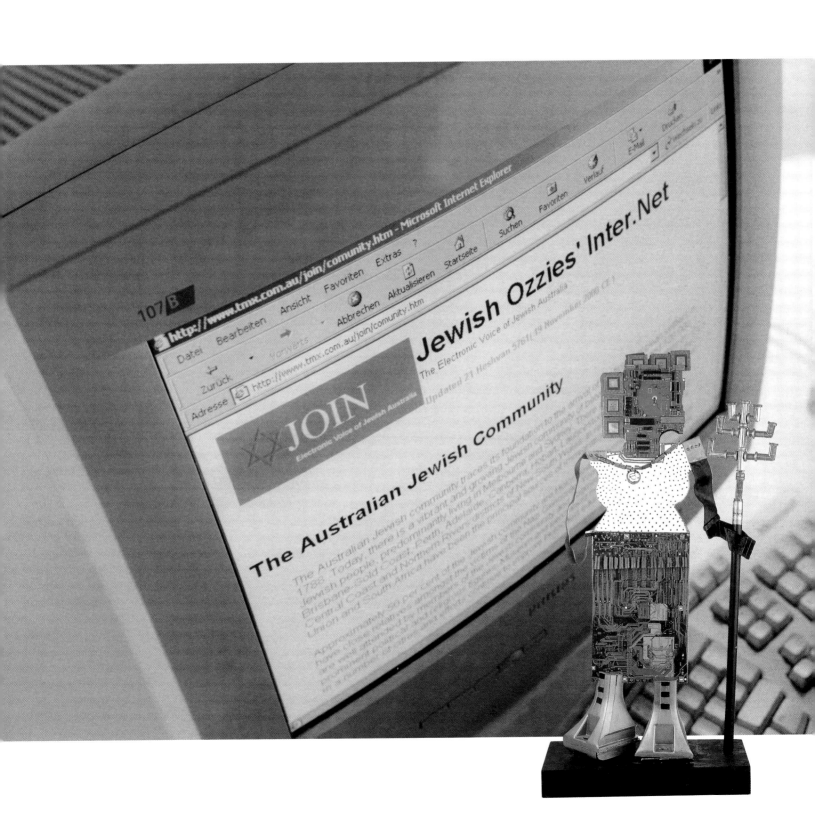

A virtual community? "It will be only when the Jewish Diaspora reaches from one end of the world to the other that the Jews can be led back from there to the Promised Land."

Menasseh ben Israel, 1656*

One of the most far-reaching revolutions of the recent past is the Internet, the possibility to communicate in new ways, and the possibility to receive information on a scale never known before at the click of a button. The world has become even smaller than it had already been as a result of modern transportation and the offers of modern tourism. The global village has become reality. So-called virtual communities have developed, which one can visit as an onlooker, enter and exit, where one can create a new context for oneself other than the limited physical space. Jewish communities, like all other communities, have joined the trend to create virtual communities. Through the net they are able to provide access for everybody to information on their past and present, their activities, goals, and problems, and to ask for comments in smaller circles, set up chat rooms, where anybody who wishes can meet. Have the Jews reached the end of the world with this entry into virtuality? The question seems to be rather whether virtuality is nothing else than a shift of reality to another level, whether virtuality, therefore, is nothing else than a new reality that is as limited as all our other realities.

B/W Photo p. 129: David Peters, untiteled, 2001

SCULPTURE: MOTHER OF BOARDS
Azur-Holon, 2000
Metal/computer trash, plastic
Artist: Lisa Gross
Height: 94.5 cm; Width: 36 cm
Steven Meyer Collection, Geneva

* Menasseh ben Israel, Mikwe Israel. Esperanca de Israel, Amsterdam 1650; zitiert nach: M. Dorman, Menasseh ben Israel, Hakibbuz Hameuchad, Israel 1989, p. 158

Bibliographie Bibliography

50 Rimmonim = Rafi Grafman (ed.), 50 Rimmonim. A Selection of Torah Finials from a European Family Collection, Tel Aviv 1998.

Afghanistan = Zohar Hanegbi/Bracha Yaniv (ed.), Afghanistan. The Synagogue and the Jewish Home, Jerusalem 1991.

Anglo-Jewish Historical Exhibition = Joseph Jacobs/Lucien Wolf (ed.), Catalogue of the Anglo-Jewish Historical Exhibition, Royal Albert Hall, London, 1887, London 1888.

Anglo-Jewish Notabilities = The Jewish Historical Society of England, Anglo-Jewish Notabilities. Their Arms and Testamentary Dispositions, London 1949.

Architecture in the Hanukkah Lamp = Architecture in the Hanukkah Lamp. Architectural Forms in the Design of Hanukkah Lamps at the Israel Museum, Exhibition Catalogue, Jerusalem 1978.

Ars Judaica Bohemiae = Ars Judaica Bohemiae, Bratislava 1968.

Art and Tradition = Dorian Liebgott, Art and Tradition. Treasures of Jewish Life, Toronto 2000.

Art in the Jewish Tradition = Silvio G. Cusin, Art in the Jewish Tradition, Milano 1963.

Arte Ebraica a Roma = Daniela di Castro (ed.), Arte Ebraica a Rome e nel Lazio, Roma 1994.

Bibliotheca Rosenthaliana, Treasures = Adri K. Offenberg et al. (ed.), Bibliotheca Rosenthaliana, Treasures of Jewish Booklore, Amsterdam 1994.

Bokhara = Bokhara, Exhibition Catalogue, The Israel Museum, Jerusalem 1967.

Chanukah Menorah = Idit Pinchas (ed.), The Chanukah Menorah from Baghdad. A Mirror of the Relations between Jews and Moslems, Jerusalem 1995.

Chotam Shelomo = Rachel Milstein, Chotam Shelomo, Tower of David, Jerusalem, exh. 1352, 1975.

Citroen = K.A. Citroen, Amsterdamse Zilversmeden En Hun Merken, Amsterdam 1975.

Collection juive du musée de Cluny = Victor Klagsbald (ed.), Catalogue raisonné de la collection juive du musée de Cluny, Paris 1981.

Collector's Guide = Jay Weinstein (ed.), A Collector's Guide to Judaica, New York 1985.

Collector's Room = Cissy Grossman (ed.), The Collector's Room. Selections from the Michael and Judy Steinhardt Collection, New York 1993.

Continuity and Change = Muli Ben Sasson (ed.), Continuity and Change. 92 years of Judaica at Bezalel, Jerusalem 1999.

Crowning Glory = Vivian B. Mann/Rafi Grafman (ed.), Crowning Glory. Silver Torah Ornaments of The Jewish Museum New York, New York 1996.

Cultura Ebraica in Emilia-Romagna = Simonetta M. Bondoni (ed.), Cultura Ebraica in Emilia-Romagna, Rimini 1987.

Danzig 1939 = Vivian B. Mann (ed.), Danzig 1939. Treasures of a Destroyed Community, New York 1980.

Das jüdische Jahr = Naftali Rosenan, Das jüdische Jahr, Basel 1976.

Das Jüdische Museum in Budapest = Ilona Benoschofsky/Alexander Scheiber (ed.), Das Jüdische Museum in Budapest, Budapest 1987.

Das jüdische Museum in Prag = Das jüdische Museum in Prag. Von schönen Gegenständen und ihren Besitzern, Ausstellungskatalog, Alte Synagoge Essen, Bonn 1991.

Der Bildhauer Leo Horovitz = Der Bildhauer Leo Horovitz (Zu seinem 50. Geburtstage), in: Aus alter und neuer Zeit. Illustrierte Beilage zum Israelitischen Familienblatt, HH, Nr. 52, Juli 1926, Beilage zu Nr. 26.

Dort und Jetzt = Bernhard Purin (ed.), Dort und jetzt. Zeitgenössische Judaica in Israel, Fürth/Schnaittach 1997.

Fabric of Life = Barbara Kirshenblatt-Gimblett/Grace Cohen Grossman, Fabric of Jewish Life. Textiles from the Jewish Museum Collection, New York 1997.

Feast of Freedom = Anita Plous, Passover Haggadah: The Feast of Freedom, Detroit 1994.

Feuchtwanger Collection = Isaiah Shachar (ed.), Jewish Tradition in Art. The Feuchtwanger Collection of Judaica, Jerusalem 1971, 1981.

Flat Torah Finials = Bracha Yaniv, The Mystery of the Flat Torah Finials from East Persia, in: Padyavand, Vol. 1, Costa Mesa 1996.

For Every Thing a Season = Claudia Fechter/John Hunter (ed.), For Every Thing a Season. Jewish Ritual Art in Cleveland, Cleveland 2000.

Furman Collection = Jacobo Furman (ed.), Treasures of Jewish Art. From the Jacobo and Asea Furman Collection of Judaica, Hong Kong 1997.

Gardens and Ghettos = Vivian B. Mann (ed.), Gardens and Ghettos. The Art of Jewish Life in Italy, New York 1989.

Gems of the Prague Ghetto = Dolezelová/Kuntos, Gems of the Prague Ghetto, Prague 1993.

Génie du Judaisme = Françoise Beer-Poitevin (ed.), Génie du Judaisme, Paris 1975.

German Jewish Heritage = Gertrude Hirschler (ed.), Ashkenaz. The German Jewish Heritage, New York 1992.

Geschichten von Gegenständen = Eva Grabherr (ed.), Geschichten von Gegenständen. Judaika aus dem Beziehungsraum der Hohenemser Juden. The Gross Family Collection, Tel Aviv, Hohenems 1994.

Gestalten und Symbole der jüdischen Kunst = Rachel Wischnitzer Bernstein, Gestalten und Symbole der jüdischen Kunst, Berlin 1935.

Golden Age = Vivian B. Mann, The Golden Age of Jewish Ceremonial Art in Frankfurt. Metalwork of the Eighteenth Century, in: Leo Baeck Institute Yearbook 31/1986, S. 389–403.

Hanukkah Lamp = M. Narkiss (ed.), The Hanukkah Lamp, Jerusalem 1939.

Heilige Gemeinde Wien = Felicitas Heimann-Jelinek/Karl Albrecht-Weinberger (ed.), „Heilige Gemeinde Wien". Judentum in Wien. Sammlung Max Berger, Wien 1988.

Hrasky = Josef Hrasky, Vyrobni Znacky Zlatnickych, Stribrnickych A Ozdobnickych Mistru V Cechach V Letech 1806–1860, Prague 1981.

134 Illustrations of the Amsterdam Haggadah = Bezalel Narkiss (ed.), The Illustrations of the Amsterdam Haggadah and its Place in the History of Hebrew Printing, Jerusalem 1972.

Imagerie juive d'Alsace = Robert Weyl, L'imagerie juive d'Alsace, Strasbourg 1979.

In the Light of the Menorah = Daisy Racca-Djivre et al. (ed.), In the Light of the Menorah. Story of a Symbol, The Israel Museum, Jerusalem 1998.

In the Paths = Jacob Pinkerfeld (ed.), Be-shvilei Omanut Yehudit (In the Paths of Jewish Art), Tel Aviv 1957.

Index, Gross Family Collection = Bezalel Narkiss/Bracha Yaniv (ed.), Index of Jewish Art. Gross Family Collection, 2 vols., Jerusalem 1985.

Ingathering of the Nations = Ariella Amar/Ruth Jacoby, Ingathering of the Nations. Treasures of Jewish Art: Documenting an Endangered Legacy, Jerusalem 1998.

Israël à travers les ages = Israël à travers les ages, Ausstellungskatalog, Petit Palais, Paris 1968.

I TAL YA' = Vivian B. Mann (ed.), I TAL YA', Duemila anni di arte e vita ebraica in Italia, Milano 1990.

Jackson = Charles J. Jackson, English Goldsmiths and their Marks, London 1921 (reprint New York 1964).

Jewish Art = Franz Landsberger, A History of Jewish Art, Cincinnati 1946.

Jewish Ceremonial Art = Stephen S. Kayser/G. Schoenberger (ed.), Jewish Ceremonial Art, Philadelphia 1959.

Jewish Ceremonial Art and Religious Objects = Jewish Ceremonial Art and Religious Objects, B'nai B'rith/Klutznick Exhibit Hall, Washington 1964.

Jewish Ceremonial Art and Religious Observance = Abram Kanof (ed.), Jewish Ceremonial Art and Religious Observance, New York 1969.

Jewish Folk Art = Joy Ungerleider-Mayerson (ed.), Jewish Folk Art. From Biblical Days to Modern Times, New York 1986.

Jewish Folk Art Over the Ages = Eli and Elise Davis (ed.), Jewish Folk Art Over the Ages. A Collector's Choice, Jerusalem 1977.

Jewish Home = Leo Gross, Jewish Art in the Jewish Home, in: Identity, Vol. 4, No. 1.

Jewish Life in Art and Tradition = Yehuda L. Bialer et al. (ed.), Jewish Life in Art and Tradition.

Based on the Collection of the Sir Isaac and Lady Edith Wolfson Museum, Hechal Shlomo Jerusalem, London 1976.

Jewish Museum London = R.D. Barnett (ed.), Catalogue of the Permanent and Loan Collection of the Jewish Museum London, London 1974.

Jewish Papercuts = Joseph and Yehudit Shadur (ed.), Jewish Papercuts. A History and Guide, Berkeley/Jerusalem 1994.

Jews in The Ottoman Empire = Esther Juhasz (ed.), Sephardi Jews in The Ottoman Empire. Aspects of Material Culture, Jerusalem 1990.

Jews under Islam = Julie-Marthe Cohen (ed.), Jews under Islam. A Culture in Historical Perspective, Amsterdam 1993.

Joods Historisch Museum = Judith C.E. Belinfante (ed.), Joods Historisch Museum – Jewish Historical Museum, Haarlem 1978.

Joodse Feestdagen. Chanoeka = Joods Historisch Museum, Joodse Feestdagen. Chanoeka, Amsterdam 1963.

Juden im Elsaß = Katia Guth-Dreyfus/Eve-M. Hoffmann (ed.), Juden im Elsaß, Basel 1992.

Judenfragen = Felicitas Heimann-Jelinek (ed.), Judenfragen. Jüdische Positionen von Assimilation bis Zionismus, Wien 1997.

Jüdische Buchkunst II = Ursula und Kurt Schubert, Jüdische Buchkunst, 2 Bände, Bd. 2, Graz 1992.

Jüdische Kunst = Hannelore Künzl, Jüdische Kunst. Von der biblischen Zeit bis in die Gegenwart, München 1992.

Jüdische Lebenswelten = Andreas Nachama/Gereon Sievernich (ed.), Jüdische Lebenswelten. Katalog, Berlin 1991.

Jüdische Lehre = Jüdische Lehre, jüdisches Jahr, jüdisches Leben. Aus Anlaß des 50. Jahrestages der Zerstörung der Synagoge in Ulm. Kulturgegenstände aus dem Jüdischen Museum der Schweiz, Basel, Ulm 1988.

Juifs d'Algérie = Jean Laloum/Jean-Luc Allouche et al. (ed.), Les Juifs d'Algérie. Images et Textes, Paris 1987.

Ketubbah = Shalom Sabar, Ketubbah. Jewish Marriage Contracts of the Hebrew Union College, Skirball Museum and Klau Library, Philadelphia/New York 1990.

Ketubbot Italiane = Ketubbot Italiane, Antichi Contratti Nuziali Ebraici Miniati, Ausstellungskatalog, Biblioteca Ambrosiana, Milano 1981.

Kleine Geschichte = Miriam Magall, Kleine Geschichte der jüdischen Kunst, Köln 1984.

Kurdish Jewish Silvercraft = Ora Schwartz-Be'eri, Kurdish Jewish Silvercraft, in: The Israel Museum Journal, VII/1988, S. 75–95.

Le'or ha-menora = Le'or ha-menora. Gilgulo schel semel, The Israel Museum, Jerusalem 1998 (hebr.).

Magic and Superstition = Marcia Reines Josephy, Magic and Superstition in the Jewish Tradition, Chicago 1975.

Mazal Tov = Shalom Sabar, Mazal Tov. Illuminated Jewish Marriage Contracts from the Israel Museum Collection, Jerusalem 1993.

Mikrografia ivrit = Mikrografia 'ivrit; elef shnot omanut ketav za'ir, Jerusalem 1981.

Mirror of Jewish Life = Rafi Grafman (ed.), A Mirror of Jewish Life. A Selection from the Moldovan Family Collection, Tel Aviv 1999.

Moderne israelitische Kunst = H.v.H., Moderne israelitische Kunst, in: Die Kirche, Bd. IX, Heft 3, 1912.

Möcht' ich ein Österreicher sein = Felicitas Heimann-Jelinek (ed.), möcht' ich ein Österreicher sein. Judaica aus der Sammlung Eisenberger, Wien 2000.

Monumenta Iudaica = Konrad Schilling (ed.), Monumenta Iudaica. 2000 Jahre Geschichte und Kultur der Juden am Rhein, Katalog, Köln 1963.

Moshe Zabari. A Twenty-Five Year Retrospective = Nancy M. Barman (ed.), Moshe Zabari: A Twenty-Five Year Retrospective, New York/Los Angeles 1986.

Ohel Moshe = Naomi Feuchtwanger (ed.), Ohel Moshe. Centennial of the Neighbourhood and its Synagogue (1828–1928), Jerusalem 1981.

Papier ist doch weiss? = Werner Hanak (ed.), Papier ist doch weiss? Eine Spurensuche im Archiv des Jüdischen Museums Wien, Wien 1998.

Postnikova-Losseva = Marina M. Postnikova-Losseva, Russian Jewellery, its Centres and Masters, XVIth-XIXth Centuries, Moskau 1974 (russisch).

Precious Legacy = David Altshuler (ed.), The Precious Legacy. Judaic Treasures from the Czechoslovak State Collections, Washington 1983.

Reise nach Jerusalem = Hendrik Budde/Andreas Nachama (ed.), Die Reise nach Jerusalem. Eine kulturhistorische Exkursion in die Stadt der Städte. 3000 Jahre Davidsstadt, Berlin 1995.

Reitzner = Viktor Reitzner, Edelmetalle und deren Punzen (in der Reihe Alt-Wien-Lexikon für österreichische und süddeutsche Kunst und Kunstgewerbe, Bd. 111), Wien 1952.

Rosenberg = Marc Rosenberg, Der Goldschmiede Merkzeichen, 4 Bände, Frankfurt a.M., 1922 – 1928.

Scheffler, Hessen = Wolfgang Scheffler, Goldschmiede Hessens. Daten, Werke, Zeichen, Berlin et al. 1976.

Scheffler, Niedersachsen = Wolfgang Scheffler, Goldschmiede Niedersachsens. Daten, Werke, Zeichen, 1. Halbband, Berlin 1965.

Scripture and Schism = Scripture and Schism. Samaritan and Karaite Treasures from the Library of the Jewish Theological Seminary of America, New York 2000.

Sephardic Journey = Sylvia Herskowitz (ed.), The Sephardic Journey 1492–1992, New York 1992.

Sermon in Metal = Günther Plaut, A Sermon in Metal: The Artwork at Temple Emanuel of Great Neck by Ludwig Wolpert, Great Neck New York o.J. (um 1980).

Shabbat Shalom = Bracha Yaniv (ed.), Shabbat Shalom, Bar-Ilan University 1998.

Siddur Klal Jisrael = Yoel Rappel (ed.), Siddur Klal Jisrae'el, Tel Aviv 1991 (hebr.).

Sign and a Wittness = Leonard S. Gold (ed.), A Sign and a Witness. 2000 Years of Hebrew Books and Illuminated Manuscripts, New York 1988.

Spirit and Matter = Nitza Behrouzi (ed.), Jerusalem – Spirit and Matter, Tel Aviv 1993.

Stieglitz Collection = Chaya Benjamin (ed.), The Stieglitz Collection. Masterpieces of Jewish Art, Jerusalem 1987.

Symbols = Ida Hubermann (ed.), Living Symbols. Symbols in Jewish Art and Tradition, Tel Aviv 1988.

Synagoga, Frankfurt = Synagoga. Jüdische Altertümer, Handschriften und Kultgeräte, Ausstellungskatalog, Historisches Museum Frankfurt am Main, Frankfurt a.M. 1961.

Synagoga, Recklinghausen = Synagoga. Kultgeräte und Kunstwerke von der Zeit der Patriarchen bis zur Gegenwart, Ausstellungskatalog, Städtische Kunsthalle Recklinghausen, Recklinghausen 1960.

Synagogale Kunst. Leo Horovitz = B. Samuel, Synagogale Kunst. Leo Horovitz, in: Ost und West, IV/1904, Heft 1, Sp. 49–52.

The Jews and Europe = Elena Romero Castello (ed.), The Jews and Europe. 2000 Years of History, New York 1994.

The Jews of India = Orpa Slapak (ed.), The Jews of India. A Story of Three Communities, Jerusalem 1995.

The Jews of Kurdistan = Schapira Epstein et al. (ed.), The Jews of Kurdistan, Exhibition Catalogue, The Israel Museum, Jerusalem 1981 (hebr.).

The Ketubah = Frederick Leach (ed.), The Ketubah. An Exhibition of Jewish Marriage Contracts, Hamline University 1975.

The Maurice Spertus Museum of Judaica = G.C. Grossman (ed.), The Maurice Spertus Museum of Judaica. An Illustrated Catalog of Selected Objects, Chicago 1974.

The Yemenites = Ester Muchawsky-Schnapper (ed.), The Yemenites. Two Thousand Years of Jewish Culture, Jerusalem 2000.

Ticho Collection = Hanukkah Lamps from the Ticho Collection, Bezalel National Museum, Jerusalem 1960.

Torah and Magic = Shalom Sabar, Torah and Magic. The Torah Scroll and Its Access in Jewish Culture in Europe and in Muslim Countries, in: Pe'amim No. 85, Jerusalem 2000.

Torah Ornaments by Moshe Zabari = Torah Ornaments by Moshe Zabari, The Jewish Museum New York, 1982.

Toraschilder aus den Werkstätten der Prager Silberschmiede = Toraschilder aus den Werkstätten der Prager Silberschmiede in den Sammlungen des Staatlichen jüdischen Museums, in: Judaica Bohemiae, XIX, Prague 1983.

Towers of Spice = Chaja Benjamin (ed.), Towers of Spice. The Tower-Shape-Tradition in Havdalah Spiceboxes, Jerusalem 1982.

Treasures of the Aleppo Community = Vivianne Barsky et al. (ed.) Treasures of the Aleppo Community, Jerusalem 1988.

Treasures of the Jewish Museum = Norman L. Kleeblatt/Vivian B. Mann (ed.), Treasures of the Jewish Museum, New York 1986.

Victoria & Albert Museum = Michael E. Keen (ed.), Jewish Ritual Art in the Victoria & Albert Museum, London 1991.

Vie juive au Maroc = Aviva Muller-Lancet/Dominique Champault (ed.), La vie juive au Maroc, Jerusalem 1986.

Von der Bibel bis Chagall = Ludwig Gutfeld (ed.), Von der Bibel bis Chagall. Judentum und Kunst, Frankfurt a.M. 1963.

Wolpert. A Retrospective = Abram Kanof, Ludwig Yehuda Wolpert. A Retrospective, New York 1976.

Womanly Arts = Cissy Grossman, Womanly Arts: A Study of Italian Torah Binders in the New York Jewish Museum Collection, in: Journal of Jewish Art, Vol. VII, 1980.

Women Silversmiths 1685-1845 = Philippa Glanville/Jennifer F. Goldsborough, Women Silversmiths 1685–1845. Works from the Collection of the National Museum of Women in the Arts, New York 1990.

Wooden Lecterns and Torah Pointers = Zussia Efron, Carved Wooden Lecterns and Torah Pointers, in: Treasures of Jewish Galicia, Tel Aviv 1994.

Yemenite Jewry = Jahadut Teman, The Ministry of Education and Culture, Jerusalem 1970 (hebr.).

Yiddishe Folks-Ornament = David Davidovitch, Yiddishe Folks-Ornament, Folklore and Ethnography Museum, Tel Aviv 1970 (hebr.).

Zauber der Volkskunst = Rachel Wischnitzer-Bernstein, Der Zauber der Volkskunst, in: Menorah, V/1927, Nr. 1, S. 58–64.

Zedaka = Georg Heuberger (ed.), Zedaka. Jüdische Sozialarbeit im Wandel der Zeit. 75 Jahre Zentralwohlfahrtsstelle der Juden in Deutschland 1917-1992, Frankfurt a.M. 1992.

Zeugnisse einer zerstörten Vergangenheit = Zeugnisse einer zerstörten Vergangenheit. Jüdisches Kultgerät aus Emden 1639-1806. Ausstellung des Ostfriesischen Landesmuseums Emden, Emden 1992.

Zwischen Ost und West = Gabriele Kohlbauer-Fritz (ed.), Zwischen Ost und West. Galizische Juden und Wien, Wien 2000.

Weiterführende Literatur Further Literature

Majer Balaban, Historia Zydow w Krakowie i na Kazimierzu, 2 Bde., Krakau 1931–1936.

Malgorzata Niezabitowska/Tomasz Tomaszewsi, Die letzten Juden in Polen, Schaffhausen/Zürich/Frankfurt a.M./Düsseldorf 1987.

Marian Fuks/Zygmunt Hoffman et al., Polnische Juden – Geschichte und Kultur, o.O., o.J.

Hana Volavková, A Story of the Jewish Museum in Prague, Prague 1968.

Milada Vilímková, Le Ghetto de Prague, Prag 1990.

Jirí Fiedler, Jewish Sights of Moravia and Bohemia, Prague 1991.

Salo Wittmayer Baron, The Jews in Roumania, New York 1930.

Naphtali Bar Giora, A note on the history of the synagogues in Cochin, in: Sefunot, Annual for Research on the Jewish Communities in the East, Vol. II, Publications of the Ben-Zvi Institute, The Hebrew University, Jerusalem 1958, S. 214–245 (hebr.).

Shemtob Gaguin, The Jews of Cochin, Brighton 1955 (hebr.).

Abraham Barak Salem, Cochin Jew Town Synagogue, 2. Aufl. Kiryat Motzkin 1972.

P.S. Velayudhan et al. (ed.), Commemoration Volume: The Cochin Synagogue, 400th Anniversary celebrations, Cochin 1971.

Reuben Kashani, The Jewish Communities in India, Jerusalem 1977 (hebr.).

Abraham Firkovich/Albert Harkavy, Altjüdische Denkmäler aus der Krim, St. Petersburg 1876.

Ruben Fahn, Aus dem Leben der Karaiten, in: Ost und West, 12. Jg., Heft I, S. 65–70; Heft II, S. 135–144.

Reuben Kashani, The Karaites. History – Traditions – Customs, Jerualem 1978 (hebr.).

Ben-Zion Luria, The Jews of Syria, Jerusalem 1957 (hebr.).

David Solomon Sassoon, A History of the Jews of Baghdad, Letchworth 1949.

Wolfgang Weisl, Die Juden Mesopotamiens. Ihre soziale und politische Gegenwart, in: Menorah, VI. Jg., 1928, Nr. 9, S. 537–543.

Reuben Kashani, The Jewish Communities in Persia-Iran, Jerusalem 1980 (hebr.).

Shaul Shaked/Amnon Netzer (ed.), Irano-Judaica IV. Studies Relating to Jewish Contacts with Persian Culture Throughout the Ages (The Ben-Zvi Institute for the Study of Jewish Communities in the East), Jerusalem 1999.

Reuben Ahroni, Yemenite Jewry. Origins, Culture and Literature, Bloomington 1986.

Joseph Kafih, Jewish Life in Sanà (Publication of the Ben-Zvi Institute), Jerusalem 1961 (hebr.).

Grace Cohen Grossman (ed.), The Jews of Yemen, Exhibition Catalogue, The Maurice Spertus Museum of Judaica, Chicago 1976.

Aviva Klein-Franke, The Jews of Yemen, in: Werner Daum (ed.), Yemen. 3000 Years of Art and Civilisation in Arabia Felix, Innsbruck/Frankfurt a.M. 1987, S. 265–299.

Paul Assall, Juden im Elsaß, Bühl/Moos 1984.

M. Ginsburger, Das Jüdische Museum für Elsaß-Lothringen, Gebweiler 1909.

Freddy Raphaël et al. (ed.), Le Judaïsme alsacien. Histoire, Patrimoine, Traditions, Strasbourg 1999.

Pinkas Hakehillot. Encyclopaedia of Jewish Communities from their Foundation till after the Holocaust: Bracha Rivlin (ed.), Greece, Jerusalem 1998 (hebr.).

Rae Dalven, The Jews of Joannina, Pennsylvania/Athens 1990.

Nicholas Stavroulakis, The Jews of Greece, Athens 1990.

Nicholas Stavroulakis/Timothy J. DeVinney, Jewish Sites and Synagogues of Greece, Athens 1992.

Albert M. Hymson, A History of the Jews in England, London 1928.

Elkan Nathan Adler, London (Jewish Communities Series), Philadelphia 1930.

Uri Ram (ed.), World of Yesterday, Jews in England 1870–1920, Exhibition Catalogue, Beth Hatefutsoth, Tel Aviv 1984.

Paul Lindsay, The Synagogues of London, London 1993.

Erich Brauer, The Jews of Kurdistan. An Ethnological Study (in der Reihe: Studies in Folklore and Ethnology, ed. by Raphael Patai and Joseph J. Rivlin, Vol. II), Jerusalem 1947 (hebr.). Englische Neuauflage: Detroit 1993.

Walter J. Fischel, The Jews of Kurdistan a Hundred Years ago. A Traveler's Record. Reprinted from Jewish Social Studies Vol. VI, No. 3, New York 1944.

Hans Tietze, Die Juden Wiens, Wien 1987 (Ndr. der Ausgabe Wien 1933).

Josef Fraenkel (ed.), The Jews of Austria. Essays on their Life, History and Destruction, London 1967.

Klaus Lohrmann, Judenrecht und Judenpolitik im mittelalterlichen Österreich, St. Pölten 1990.

Martha Keil (ed.), Jüdisches Städtebild Wien, Frankfurt a.M. 1995.

Gerhard Milchram (ed.), Museum Judenplatz zum mittelalterlichen Judentum, Wien o.J. (2000).

Abraham L. Udovitch/Lucette Valensi, The Last Arab Jews. The Communities of Jerba, Tunisia, Glasgow 1984.

Kamel Tmarzizet/Jacques Perez, Djerba, Synagogue El Ghriba, Tunis 1993.

Pinkas Hakehillot. Encyclopaedia of Jewish Communities from their Foundation till after the Holocaust: Irit Abramski-Bligh (ed.), Libya – Tunisia, Jerusalem 1997 (hebr.).

Reuben Kashani, The Jews of Afghanistan, Jerusalem 1975 (hebr.).

Michael A. Meyer/Michael Brenner (ed.), Deutsch-jüdische Geschichte in der Neuzeit, 4 Bde., München 1996–97.

Rachel Heuberger/Helga Krohn, Hinaus aus dem Ghetto … Juden in Frankfurt am Main 1800–1950, Frankfurt a.M. 1988.

Stefan Schwarz, Die Juden in Bayern im Wandel der Zeiten, München 1963.

Max Grunwald, Portugiesengräber auf deutscher Erde, Hamburg 1902.

Wolf Balk, Aus jüdischen Gassen 35: Emden, in: Aus alter und neuer Zeit. Illustrierte Beilage zum Israelitischen Familienblatt, HH, Nr. 40, 21. Januar 1926, Beilage zu Nr. 3.

Bernhard Brilling, Die Entstehung der jüdischen Gemeinde in Emden (1570–1613), in: Westfalen. Hefte für Geschichte, Kunst und Volkskunde, Bd. 51, 1973, H. 1–4, S. 210–224.

Michael Studemund-Halévy, Die portugiesisch-spanischen Grabinschriften in Norddeutschland: Glückstadt und Emden, in: Aschkenas, 7. Jg./Heft 2, 1997, S. 389–440.

Maurice Grosman, Jüdisches Wilna in Wort und Bild, Wilna 1925 (jidd.).

Israel Cohen, Vilna (Jewish Communities Series), Philadelphia 1943.

Masha Greenbaum, The Jews of Lithuania. A History of a Remarkable Community. 1316-1945, Jerusalem 1995.

Leyzer Ran, Jerusalem of Lithuania – Illustrated and Documented, 2 Bde., New York 1974.

Nechemias Zucker (ed.), Pinkos Galitzia (Libro de Galitzia), Buenos Aires 1945 (jidd.).

Josef Tennenbaum, Galizien – meine alte Heimat, Buenos Aires 1952 (Jidd.).

Israel Cohen, Israel in Italien, Berlin 1909.

Hermann Vogelstein, Rome (Jewish Communities Series), Philadelphia 1940.

Salvatore Fornari, La Roma del Ghetto, Roma 1984.

Ruth Liliana Geller/Henryk Geller, Roma Ebraica. Duemila anni di storia in innagini, Roma 1984.

Abraham Galanté, Histoire des Juifs d'Anatolie, Istanbul 1937-39, 2 Bde., Bd. 2 : Izmir.

Reuben Kashani, The Jewish Communities in Turkey, Jerusalem 1978 (hebr.).

Avigdor Levy (ed.), The Jews of the Ottoman Empire, Princeton 1994.

Jan Stoutenbeek/Paul Vigeveno, A Guide to Jewish Amsterdam, Amsterdam 1985.

Julie-Marthe Cohen (ed.), Guide – Jewish Historical Museum, Amsterdam 1995.

Salo Wittmayer Baron, The Russian Jew under Tsars and Soviets, New York 1964.

W.J. Fischel, Jews in the Economic and Political Life of Medieval Islam, New York 1937.

Albert Katz, Die Juden im Kaukasus, Berlin 1894.

Reuben Kashani, The Jews of Bukhara, Jerusalem 1973 (hebr.).

Rudolf Löwenthal, The Jews of Bukhara, in: Revue des Études Juives, Troisième série, Tome III (CXX), Juillet-Decembre 1961 S. 345–351.

138

"...are related to those "ancient" Jews whose emigration from the Land of Israel

Ben-Zion Yehoshua, 1973

שהגירתם מארץ-ישראל מאוחרת יותר.

בן-ציון יהושע, 1973